Inside the
Black Box of
Classroom Practice

Inside the Black Box of Classroom Practice

Change Without Reform in American Education

Larry Cuban

Harvard Education Press
Cambridge, Massachusetts

KH

Library of Congress Control Number 2013930676

Paperback ISBN 978-1-61250-556-5
Library Edition ISBN 978-1-61250-557-2

Published by Harvard Education Press,
an imprint of the Harvard Education Publishing Group

Harvard Education Press
8 Story Street
Cambridge, MA 02138

Cover Design: Patrick Ciano
Cover Photo: © Najlah Feanny/Corbis

The typefaces used in this book are Adobe Garamond and ITC Legacy Sans.

10/6/14

For Barbaraciela Cuban Goodwin

Contents

Preface

I have written a great deal over the past thirty years on teaching, curriculum, school organization, technology, and reform. The topics are all interconnected. After all, reform-driven policy makers, seeing schools as agents of societal change, have sought to alter classroom practices and what students learn for nearly two centuries in the United States. They have used structural reforms from the age-graded school to the nongraded school; from pushing new technologies into classrooms, from the nineteenth-century slate blackboard to the twenty-first-century "smart" whiteboard. The same holds for curricular reform; late-nineteenth-century reformers established one academic curriculum for all students and then dumped it a quarter-century later for a differentiated curriculum tailored to their estimates of whether high school students would go directly into industrial and commercial jobs, take up white-collar occupations, or attend college. Then, yet again, twenty-first-century policy makers returned to the Common Core standards for all U.S. schools. All of these and many more structural reforms in school governance, curriculum, organization, and technology aimed to change school practices and teacher lessons so that students would learn more, faster, and better. Then those students would complete college, get jobs, and make the nation a better place.

Over many years, I have developed these themes independently in books, articles, op-ed pieces, and now in my twice-weekly blog. What I do in this book is draw together these separate themes about structural reforms, societal changes, the role of public schools in a democracy, and teaching in what I call the black box of the classroom. In my career as a teacher, administrator, superintendent, and scholar, I have seen up close these connections between policy and practice; top policy makers making decisions and first-grade teachers implementing those decisions; and societal conditions of poverty, inequality, and race influencing school practices and classroom lessons again and again.

I lay out the tangled nature of these reforms, analyze successes and failures, and offer my thinking on why the black box of classroom instruction has been largely impervious to structural reforms aimed at moving teaching practices from teacher-centered to student-centered, moving students from absorbing subject matter to critical thinking and problem solving, and erasing the effects of race, poverty, and inequalities from daily lessons. Classroom lessons, however, have been, paradoxically, largely stable, seldom fulfilling reformers' ambitions.

In this book, I synthesize and connect my thinking about reform-driven policy making and classroom instruction; at the same time, I try to break new ground in understanding the contradiction of enormous structural change in U.S. public schools amid stability in teaching practices.

Larry Cuban
Professor Emeritus of Education
Stanford University

Introduction

For the past thirty years, national and state policy makers, backed by an influential coalition of business and civic leaders—groups I call policy elites—have initiated reform after reform with the express purpose of making U.S. schools competitive with other nations. Why?[1]

With U.S. schools falling in the middle to lower rungs of rankings based on international test scores—an ominous sign to top policy makers that the U.S. economy will fall short in recruiting skilled and knowledgeable employees—reform-minded civic and business leaders want American schools to graduate youth who could enter a labor market skewed toward an information-based economy that is no longer national but global. National economic growth, innovation, and productivity, these policy makers and CEOs have asserted for three decades, are closely tied to increasing the quality of high school and college graduates. Growing the all-important human capital in graduates depends on how schools are structured, what teachers teach, how they teach, and what students learn.[2]

A similar economic rationale for major school reforms also permeated policy makers' rhetoric and decision making at the end of the nineteenth century, when the United States, then in competition with the United Kingdom and Germany, sought global markets in Europe and Asia. Like the contemporary coalition of business and civic leaders lobbying policy makers, that earlier generation of reformers believed that U.S. schools needed to produce skilled graduates who could enter what was then a thriving industrial-based economy and make the nation competitive globally.

Between the 1890s and 1920s, vocational education lodged in a newly structured organization, called the *comprehensive high school*, became the educational solution to making the U.S. economy becoming more globally competitive. Few contemporary policy makers or ardent reformers, however, consider this earlier period as helpful in learning from the results—both positive and perverse—of the connections between the comprehensive high school, vocational curricula, and classroom practices.[3]

Although historical periods seldom duplicate contemporary ones, such inquiries into earlier school reforms can illuminate current policy-making assumptions and decisions as surely as studying previous wars informs contemporary military and foreign policy decisions and examining past presidential elections offers suggestions to present-day campaigns. There are, then, contemporary policy questions that can benefit from historical scrutiny to inform decisions in current nonstop efforts to draft public schools into making the United States economically competitive.

Because most contemporary school reforms (e.g., charter schools, pay-for-performance, Common Core standards, and schools that blend online and conventional instruction) aim at creating, modifying, or dissolving structures (i.e., funding, organization, governance, curriculum, instruction) for producing graduates equipped to enter a technology-driven economy, inquiring into past reforms offers a chance to examine key assumptions in the policy logic that drive present-day reformers. Specifically, reformers from both sides of the political spectrum have assumed that changing particular school structures will alter the composition of the teacher corps, which will in turn change classroom practices. Those changed practices will then yield desired student outcomes in graduates who will contribute to national economic growth, innovation, and productivity.[4]

My inquiry challenges this policy logic. The challenge comes down to questioning the causal linkages between structures, teaching practices, and outcomes, linkages that few, if any, policy makers have considered explicitly or carefully.[5]

Because I point to flaws in the assumptions driving contemporary reforms, I need to be sure that the terms I use are clear to readers and what I say is historically accurate by spelling out past structural changes that have transformed U.S. schools. In doing so, I explain the *black box* of the book title.

I distinguish between two kinds of planned changes, fundamental and incremental, that have occurred in U.S. schools over the past two centuries. By *fundamental* change, I mean altering the basic building blocks of U.S. schooling—for example, requiring taxpayers to fund public schools and give access to all students, establishing goals for schooling (e.g., all students will be literate, discharge their civic duties, and be vocationally prepared for the labor market), and organizing curricula and instructional practices in age-graded elementary and secondary schools. These building blocks are structures that have defined public schools for the past two centuries.

Changing them fundamentally means altering funding (e.g., vouchers, charter schools), governance (e.g., site-based management, mayoral control), organization (e.g., moving from an age-graded school to nongraded teams and entire schools), curriculum (e.g., *new* math, *hands-on* science), and instruction (e.g. moving from teacher-centered to student-centered pedagogy). When I initially wrote about planned school change, I called these fundamental shifts in structure *second-order changes*.[6]

Often, those who champion second-order changes in public schools talk about "real reform" or "transformation of schooling." What they refer to are fundamental changes in one or more structures of schooling, not incremental changes.[7] *Incremental* changes are amendments to current structures, not deep changes to or removal of these core components of schooling. I call these *first-order* changes.

Incremental changes—including creating new academic courses, extending the school day or year, reducing class size, raising teacher salaries, and introducing new reading or math programs—do not alter the basic structures of public schools. They correct deficiencies and improve existing structures. They are add-ons. Many promoters of change in schools call such changes "tinkering," usually in a dismissive way, because they want "real reform" or fundamental reordering of existing structures.[8]

Thus, in the subtitle of this book, when I use the phrase *change without reform*, I mean that first-order or incremental changes occur frequently, without fundamentally altering school funding, governance, organization, curriculum, and instruction. Schools do make planned changes. That is a fact. That such incremental changes contribute to organizational continuity—what some scholars call *dynamic conservatism*—helps to explain how so many changes end up sustaining the stability and longevity of formal schooling.[9]

I attach no positive or negative connotation to either first-order or second-order changes. Both are important in improving schools but they need to be distinguished, since they derive from different organizational assumptions and theories of change.[10]

Structural Changes in Public Schooling

Let's now consider the major structural changes over the past two centuries, many of which were fundamental in reconfiguring U.S. public schools.

Access to public schools has evolved from rural one-room schoolhouses enrolling largely white male children in the early nineteenth century to become a system of age-graded schools spanning pre-kindergarten to college and enrolling females, racial and ethnic minorities, and children with disabilities.

Any fair-minded observer familiar with the history of U.S. education would be hard-pressed to deny the fundamental changes in funding, organization, governance, and curriculum that have occurred in public schools over the past two centuries. Schooling in the United States has gone from a largely private, religious, and short-term schooling for a narrow slice of middle-class and affluent Americans in the eighteenth century to a public, tax-supported, secular system governed by state and local school boards that has provided, over time, equal access to knowledge and age-graded structures for children and youth from kindergarten through high school.

By the beginning of the twenty-first century, a national system of tax-supported public schooling—albeit decentralized in 50 states and 14,000 locally governed school districts—welcomed children and youth. Staffed by over 3 million teachers in over 100,000 age-graded schools, this massive decentralized system has made access to public schooling universal. And in the early decades of the twenty-first century, reformers have promoted policies aimed at ensuring that all students graduate high school (just over 70 percent do) and then enter college. Today, a K–16 system of schooling is emerging in the United States.

From a largely religion-infused curriculum in early nineteenth-century schools, public school curricula two centuries later have changed into largely secular, vocationally driven courses of study.

From "In Adam's Fall, we sinned all," a couplet taken from the eighteenth-century *New England Primer* and appearing again in lessons in the early-nineteenth-century *McGuffey Readers* (William McGuffey was a Protestant minister), school reformers insured that the public school curriculum included prayer and taught moral lessons steeped in Protestantism. As non-Protestant immigrants increasingly sent their children to public schools and different ethnic groups wanted their language and culture to be present in tax-supported schools, state and federal court decisions began to separate religious activities from public schools. Within decades of those immigrant waves of the late-nineteenth century, U.S. Supreme Court decisions had banned daily prayer and religious practices while public school was in session.[11]

By the early twentieth century, the school curriculum was becoming secular and aimed at preparing the young for jobs in an industrial economy. Public schools had come to include academic subjects and nonacademic activities (e.g., extracurricular sports, clubs, health care, nutritious breakfasts and lunches). A high school diploma opened doors for jobs.

By the end of the twentieth century, however, an ideology of everyone going to college had permeated K–12 schooling as the belief gripped parents and students, from wealthy to poor, that a college diploma was essential for entering the labor market and climbing the ladder of economic success. Going to school and earning credentials would lead to good jobs, a stronger economy, and market competitiveness for U.S. companies. In the early twenty-first century, academics in schools had become thoroughly vocationalized.

In the past century, U.S. cultural norms and behaviors have changed from formal to informal in social relations, dress, and language; and those new norms have transformed the social organization of public schools and classrooms.

In the early twentieth century, dress-clad women and tie-wearing men, facing rows of fifty or more bolted-down desks, controlled students' every move. They gave or withheld permission for students to leave their seat. They required students to stand when reciting from the textbook or answering a question. Teachers often scowled, reprimanded, and paddled students for misbehaving. They were guardians of civility.

Since World War II, social changes in the larger culture created new norms and social practices. As that happened, formality in teacher-student relations and classroom practices diminished. As in the larger American culture, where informal dress, manners, talk, and behavior became the norm, school and classroom daily life became more casual. By the 1980s, classrooms were furnished with moveable tables and desks, particularly in the early grades, so students faced one another and saw walls festooned with colorful posters and student work. Jeans-wearing teachers drinking coffee smiled at their classes, and students went to a pencil sharpener or elsewhere in the room without asking the teacher's permission. The atmosphere of dread of early twentieth-century class-rooms—often marked by the swish of a paddle and a teacher's sneer—slowly gave way, decade by decade, to classrooms where teachers were kinder, more informal in language and dress, and had a light touch in controlling unacceptable behavior. Classrooms became less fearful and more comfortable places for students, even in big-city schools equipped with security aides and scanners.[12]

Yet amid these fundamental changes in public school structures, there are apparent contradictions.

While the organizational, governance, curricula, and formal school cul-ture has changed dramatically in the past century, reformers have failed to alter substantially how teachers teach (e.g., textbook-driven lessons, more teacher talk than student talk, mostly whole group instruction with occa-sional small-group work, and periodic quizzes and tests).

For nearly a century and a half, U.S. reformers—from late-nineteenth-century progressive educators, to open classroom advocates in 1960s, to small-high-school champions in the 1980s and 1990s—have tried hard to turn teacher-centered classroom practices into more flexible student-centered pedagogies that include substantial intellectual content and a deeper understanding of ideas, learning through inquiry, collab-orative work, and ways of teaching that bridged in-school and out-of-school worlds. They have sought a second-order or fundamental change in pedagogy. More often than not, when policy-driven reformers talk about wanting to "improve teaching" they are using verbal shorthand to mean increased student-centered classrooms.[13]

Technological innovations have often been drafted into the task of altering teacher-centered practices. Since the mid-nineteenth cen-tury, slate blackboards, textbooks, stereopticon viewers, film, and over-head projectors were adopted in the classroom. Late-twentieth-century technological advances in work, commerce, and entertainment have penetrated schools, up to the contemporary push for cyberschools and online instruction. Yet today most K–12 students in age-graded schools abundantly supplied with laptops, desktop computers, and handheld devices still experience classroom lessons that unfold in the familiar progression of tasks and activities (e.g., homework, textbook assignments, worksheets, whole group discussions, small group activities, tests, etc.). For the most part, teachers have tailored the technological innovations meant to achieve fundamental reforms in pedagogy to fit the classroom practice that has prevailed since the early twentieth century.[14]

In short, generations of reformers have sought a student-centered pedagogy that would engage children and youth in learning basic academic content and lead to their accumulating sufficient social and intellectual skills to enter into and participate successfully in communities, jobs, and a democratic society. These reformers wanted to "improve" teaching. In some places, sea changes in pedagogy have occurred and been sustained, but these comprise hardly more than a tiny fraction of U.S. public schools. Efforts to create engaging, student-centered, even adventurous, teaching have led to some incremental changes that have slightly modified traditional classroom practices (e.g., small-group work, student projects, use of laptops to make Internet searches in daily lessons) by creating mixes of old and new practices—hybrids. Yet, overall, these first-order or incremental changes have largely left intact teaching routines that students' grandparents visiting these schools would find familiar.[15]

While many important instructional changes have occurred since the late nineteenth century in elementary and secondary school classrooms, no transformation in classroom authority or how teachers teach on the scale of the above fundamental structural, curricular, and cultural changes have altered classroom instruction. Certainly, over the years curricular change in content (e.g., new academic and vocational courses) have come and gone. Innovative textbooks in reading, math, science, social studies, and foreign language have entered and exited classrooms. The *what* of teaching has, indeed, changed, but when it comes to the *how*—the pedagogy—few major changes have occurred. The growth of hybrids— mixes of teacher-centered and student-centered classroom practices— have, indeed, emerged as part of classroom repertoires. Nonetheless, basic instructional practices such as lectures, whole-group activities, question/answer recitations, textbooks, homework, blackboards, work sheets, paper-and-pencil tests persist. In short, continuity in classroom practice has trumped fundamental reforms in teaching.

A Puzzling Question

Because this persistence in classroom instruction (including mixes of old and new practices and adoption of different classroom technologies) differs dramatically from the other fundamental structural changes in organization, governance, curricular changes, and shift in cultural norms in school behavior, I return to the puzzling question raised earlier: *With so many major structural changes in U.S. public schools over the past century, why have classroom practices been largely stable, with a modest blending of new and old teaching practices leaving contemporary classroom lessons familiar to earlier generations of school-goers?*

Is this puzzling question worth answering? For policy makers, novice and veteran reformers, parents, and practitioners, it is.

Using an economic rationale to spur school changes in the 1890s and since the 1980s, reform-driven coalitions of business and civic leaders wanted graduates to be fully prepared to enter the labor market. For the past three decades, they have lobbied district school boards and superintendents, state legislatures and governors, and the U.S. Congress and presidents to adopt policies to alter existing structures. And they were successful.

These policies are anchored in a number of key assumptions.[16] Reformers are certain that teachers using intellectually ambitious, inquiry-driven, skill-rich forms of teaching are superior to what has routinely occurred in classrooms. They assume that teachers who have integrated these better ways of teaching across the K–12 curriculum for all students will lead to richer and far more effective learning. And they have no doubt that the knowledge and skills accumulated from that richer and more effective learning will lead to college and careers that will create economic growth, increase productivity, and spur innovation in business and society. Those linked assumptions drive the current policy logic among contemporary reformers.

But which of these structures and strategies would change classroom teachers, and how they deliver lessons to boost student learning?

Changing teachers has been the dominant policy strategy to improve classroom instruction. Change the teacher, the logic goes, and you improve student learning. Over decades, reformers have established structures that raised standards in recruiting, preparing, selecting, and evaluating teachers. Where once a grammar school certificate and high school diploma were sufficient credentials to enter the classroom, now U.S. teachers need a bachelor's degree and, in many states, a master's degree to teach. Whereas in earlier decades, only college and university schools of education produced credentialed teachers, now alternative paths to classrooms (e.g., Teach for America, districts certifying midcareer changes for business and military personnel) have produced a steady stream of energetic, capable novice teachers with the personal traits that will energize teaching and motivate students to learn. Moreover, recently established testing and accountability structures include ways to evaluate and pay individual teachers on the basis of student performance on tests. Spurred by philanthropic and federal grants, state lawmakers and district policy makers have generated procedures aimed at distinguishing between effective and less-effective teachers based on test scores and other measures. This favored strategy aims at improving the caliber of teachers.

Although these strategies have been put into place in the past century and teachers have created hybrids of old and new approaches, classroom practices still remain eerily similar to earlier periods. These new structures and strategies, while important and worthwhile in upgrading the quality of instruction, have yet to alter substantially how teachers teach.[17]

Nor have popular market-driven structures that encourage competition, such as creating thousands of charter schools or issuing parental vouchers, transformed classroom teaching and learning. Altering funding patterns of public schools and expanding parental choice of schools, reformers believed, would prod district schools to compete with one another in attracting teachers and students by inventing new forms of schooling and innovative classroom practices. These newly created structures have yet to show results in either teaching practices or student learning that promoters of market-based schooling have promised time and again.[18]

The policy of importing electronic technologies into classrooms over the past century (e.g., film, instructional television, desktop computers, interactive whiteboards, laptops) also has not substantially altered teacher and student daily routines and relationships. The promise that high-tech solutions would magically transform old teacher-directed practices into ambitious new student-centered pedagogies has become a cliché. Yet evidence of transformed classroom practice remains sparse compared with the accumulated evidence that most teachers have "domesticated" innovative technologies by incorporating them into their existing repertoire of teacher-directed practices.[19]

In short, current and past structures and strategies aimed at school improvement have yet to substantially revise routine classroom practices teachers have used for decades—ones that reformers have continually criticized and tried to alter. The inescapable fact of stability amid modest changes in classroom practices after so much policy talk and action over decades make the question important to answer for policy makers, parents, and practitioners who demand improved schools and better teaching.

After all, incremental changes—tinkering—aim to improve the efficiency and effectiveness of existing structures without fundamentally overhauling those structures, what some would call *true reform*. Is this remarkable stability and lack of true reform due to inertia, stubborn resistance from teachers, or, perhaps, sensible adaptations to the complexity of multiple goals and school structures in the past century? The need, then, is to get inside the black box of the classroom and find out why teaching practices have been the target of change efforts for decades, yet have been durable in the face of extending public school attendance to all students for at least a dozen or more years, the dominance of age-graded organizational structures, new curricula repeatedly succeeding old curricula, and the considerable change in the social organization of the classroom.[20]

The Black Box of the Classroom

I use *black box* as a metaphor for what happens daily in classrooms. Even though it should be known to all, since every policy maker, researcher, parent, and taxpayer attended school, it remains out of public sight—what occurs in classrooms remains mysterious to nonteachers because memories fade and children's reports of what they do in school are, at best, laconic, hiding more than revealing. To paraphrase that well-advertised Las Vegas slogan: *What happens in the classroom, stays in the classroom.*

Teachers' memories also fade, and recollections of what happened on particular days, weeks, or months become hard to retrieve. While many teachers retain records of daily interactions or journal entries, lessons, and materials for a few years, most do not. As a colleague once said, teaching is like dry ice evaporating at room temperature. So historians, anthropologists, social linguists, educational researchers, and other social scientists have inspected teaching artifacts, described teacher-student interactions, and observed classroom dynamics to restore what has evaporated.

This black box, then, is the very opposite of the well-publicized in-flight recorder that documents cockpit communication. Instead, I use the term *black box* as it is used in systems engineering and economic production functions where inputs (e.g., money spent per pupil, facilities, teacher qualifications) go into a box called "schools" or "classrooms" and outputs emerge (e.g., test scores, skilled and knowledgeable high school graduates) with no clue as to how that transformation occurred.[21]

The lack of documentation and transparency about the complex mechanics and relationships that occur in classrooms make it tough to unpack, much less understand. There have naturally been efforts to see inside elementary and secondary classrooms, for example, through qualitative studies of teacher and student talk during classroom lessons (e.g., the work of Hugh Mehan and Courtney Cazden in the 1970s).[22] Most recently, the Bill and Melinda Gates Foundation funded the "Measures of Teacher Effectiveness" project for 2010–2011 where researchers worked with practitioners in six school districts to capture through on-site videos and observations what teachers and students do in their classrooms.[23]

Such real-time records of lessons and teacher-student interactions help considerably in making sense of what occurs after the teacher closes the classroom door. But far more data over time converted into knowledge about what happens in classrooms during short and long lessons need to be captured and analyzed by teachers, administrators, parents, policy makers, and researchers in order to open the black box and see the complex realities of teaching and learning.

Why Is This Knowledge Important?

School reformers and policy makers generally recognize—as parents have always done—that teachers are the single most important in-school factor to students' well-being and achievement. So the policy focus has been on recruiting, training, selecting, and supporting teachers with the requisite personal traits that get students to learn: their knowledge, caring, dedication, ability to engage others, and other features. This policy focus on the teacher's characteristics, not the situation in which teachers find themselves, has been a serious mistake. It has led to overestimating the influence of personal traits and underestimating the influence of the context in which teachers find themselves every day. Because of this *fundamental attribution error*, as it is called, policy makers have undervalued the power of the age-graded school, particularly the way it isolates teachers from one another, discourages collaboration, and influences daily teaching.[24] Moreover, policy makers have ignored what students bring to school. Contexts matter. So what happens in classrooms and in homes influences teaching, yet policy makers continue to focus on who teachers are and how they are trained. Teachers cannot carry alone the total responsibility for their students' well-being and achievement.

Teachers have no control over the knowledge, skills, attitudes, and habits students bring to school from home. They do not make policy decisions that establish the conditions within which they teach daily. They have not established the age-graded school and self-contained classrooms. State and district policy makers set goals, allocate resources, and establish structures. They introduce standards and assessments. They allocate resources that determine class size and where new technologies are deployed. They put in place new school structures such as blending online and conventional instruction, pay-for-performance plans, and professional learning communities.

Such policy decisions make a difference in whether teachers do their jobs well or not. Yet these consequential decisions, which shape the conditions under which teachers teach and students learn, are not made by teachers.

Another reason knowledge of complexities in teaching and learning that occur daily in the black box of the classroom is important is that advocates for particular policies from pay-for-performance plans to charter schools too often rely upon correlations to see into classrooms. If school test scores rise or fall, then teachers are first-rate or mediocre. Such associations imply causality to many observers but the relationship between test results and teacher effectiveness may or may not be connected; other factors may be involved. Consider a recent Fordham Foundation report on declining test scores among high achievers.[25]

The report uses trends in test score data to conclude that two of five "high-flying" students whose achievement was tracked from third to eighth grade between 2004 and 2009 dropped in achievement. They point to the effects on teachers and teaching of the passage in 2001 of NCLB. Such associations, as one critic pointed out in a review of this report, use a "black-box approach that assumes a link between its findings and NCLB-related policies."[26]

Such pseudo-causal linkages suggest that classroom dynamics are so simple that a federal law caused some high-achieving students to do poorly, again missing the complexity of teaching and learning, suggesting anew that teachers are solely responsible for test scores without any mention of policy makers putting in place an infrastructure or neglecting to do so that supports teachers in their classroom lessons. Yes, teachers, both in their personal characteristics and the contexts in which they teach, are central to helping students' well-being and academic achievement in school and—like any helping professional, from therapists to physicians to social workers—teachers need organizational supports and resources to do their job well, supports that only policy makers can provide. For these reasons, I believe getting inside the black box of past and present classrooms is essential.

Any examination of the black box that is the classroom, however, must begin with sorting out the soaring rhetoric of reform from what teachers actually do in their classrooms. Those who traffic in words— policy makers, civic and business leaders, print journalists, bloggers, wealthy donors, and champions of the latest reform—seldom distinguish between rhetoric, formal policy decisions, and the implementation of those decisions in schools and classroom. Without these distinctions, the black box will remain opaque. Baffling continuities will persist and puzzling questions will go unanswered.

Policy Talk, Policy Adoption, and Policy Implementation

By *policy talk*, I refer to the cyclical political rhetoric of past and present reformers, particularly their gloomy assessments, followed by overconfident and untested solutions to recurring problems. Hyperexcited emotional appeals were made about national defense during the Cold War with the Soviet Union between the 1950s and 1980s, and we hear echoes of such policy talk now with regard to fears of Chinese economic and military hegemony in Asia. So, too, have Americans heard dire predictions and fiery words, in the 1890s and again since the 1980s, about U.S. market competitiveness suffering because graduates are unprepared for jobs and global competition. Ditto for policy talk since the 1960s about high-tech innovations such as online instruction saving U.S. schools while whipping up support for a brave new technocratic world of schooling.

Policy talk is a form of rhetorical hyperventilating that repeatedly overstates problems and understates the difficulties of solving them. For years, it has focused on the personal characteristics of teachers without giving much attention to the teaching context. Such talk is important in framing problems and mobilizing actors to roll up their sleeves, but seldom lays out a specific agenda or blueprint for action. In short, fiery words do not a reform make.

Policy adoption refers to the conversion of excited policy talk into actual decisions governors, mayors, superintendents, legislators, and foundation officials make to solve the problems framed in the rhetoric (e.g., too many low-skilled students graduate high school is the policy talk; decision makers adopting a policy to end social promotion converts talk into action). Examples of policy adoption range from voters authorizing mayors to take control of schools (who then outsource them to private contactors), to school boards buying iPads for kindergartners, to the U.S. Congress and president approving NCLB. Like policy talk, these decisions often occur in cycles. Think of national efforts to transform teacher education institutions in the 1960s, 1990s, and even as I write these words, or school boards adopting "new" math curricula every few years as a solution to declining performance on math tests, or phonics going in and out of style as a way of teaching reading.

Policy implementation points to converting adopted policies into school and classroom practices. Policy implementation in districts, schools, and classrooms, however, is not cyclical like policy talk and action. It is linear. Schools as institutions have structures, cultures, and history. David Tyack and I called these patterns the *grammar of schooling*.[27] Seymour Sarason called these patterns the *regularities* of school organization and culture.[28] Some adopted policies do get put into practice, slowly and incrementally changing these regularities; trends in implementing policies do become noticeable as time passes. And when trend lines become visible, they bear the fingerprints of teachers.

Many efforts to design, adopt, and implement new programs stretch out over five or more years. When researchers, for example, observe classrooms to see how teachers use computers in activities and what math or reading lessons teachers put into practice, they find great variation across classrooms within the same school and between schools in a district. Some teachers pick and choose elements of the program after watching colleagues, others just ponder when to begin implementing, and still others ignore the policy. Because of school culture and organizational realities, change is gradual and episodic. But trends do appear over time. What happens in schools and classrooms, then, is a world apart from the hyperbole and gloom accompanying recurring policy talk and adoption of new policies.[29]

Over the years, I have tried to capture through metaphors these distinctions between policy talk, action, and implementation. Each metaphor not only projects an image that compares and contrasts differences between policy talk, deciding on policies, and putting them into practice but also projects a view of the organization. For example, the metaphor of links in a chain conveys an image of command-and-control organizations such as the U.S. military or NASA, where top-echelon officials give the orders and soldiers and astronauts obey their superiors—as in the invasion of Iraq in 2003 or NASA's Mission Control shuttle launches. Another metaphor—pushing forward strands of wet spaghetti—captures the difficulties of converting policies into actual performance in complex organizations where interdependent relationships and external factors create unpredictability and uncertainty in outcomes.[30]

In still another metaphor, I wrote about the hurricane of school reform. In the natural world, a hurricane whips up twenty-foot high waves, agitating the surface of the ocean. A fathom below the wave-tossed surface, water remains disturbed but the motion is far less intense than what occurs a few feet above. On the ocean floor, however, fish and plant life go on, uninterrupted by the uproar on the wind-ravaged surface.

I compared the hurricane whipping up the waves on the surface to reformers talking about schools failing to solve national problems of economic stagnation, social instability, and the loss of character in the next generation. That hyperinflated rhetoric inevitably leads to proposed solutions to the crisis.

A fathom below the surface, there is still turbulence but not the sheer magnitude of what is occurring above. Among school reformers, policy elites gather at White House conferences to debate solutions, blue-ribbon commissions make recommendations, academics write papers, and media pundits including bloggers circulate proposals for action to solve the problems. Specialists write curricula, units, and lessons. Publishers put out instructional materials. Action occurs.

Yet deep down on the ocean floor, life goes on, undisturbed by the roiling waters and huge waves on the surface. I compared that ocean floor to the nation's classrooms, where both change and continuity unfold in regular, undisturbed patterns.

Now I invoke another metaphor, the black box of the classroom, fitting into the policy-to-practice continuum. Metaphors—links in a chain, pushing spaghetti, hurricanes, and now the black box—can project images that capture crucial pieces of a complex phenomenon too often unnoticed by policy elites intent on changing complex institutions. I do know that mixing metaphors can be troublesome and hilarious, if not confusing. I do realize that asking readers to keep these different metaphors in mind as I describe and analyze school reform morphing into classroom practice may lead to chuckles and winces. I am willing to take that risk.[31]

I return now to the central question of this book: *With so many major structural changes in U.S. public schools over the past century, why have classroom practices been largely stable, with a modest blending of new and old teaching practices, leaving contemporary classroom lessons familiar to earlier generations of school-goers?*

In this book, I offer a three-part answer.

Part 1 examines three policy cases that have in common putting new structures in place to alter classroom practice: a high school that embraced new technologies between 1998–2011; the teaching of science over the past century; and the effects testing and accountability policies have had on teaching practices since 1990. I offer these cases to illustrate what decision makers were thinking when they adopted structural changes in teacher access and use of technology, new science curricula seeking inquiry and practical applications through hands-on classroom experiences, and holding students and teachers responsible for test score results. Policy makers assumed that these new structures would lead directly to desired classroom practices and student outcomes. They did not.

The chapters in part 1 contain much evidence that these new structures had limited influence on practice—far below what policy makers had promised—and in many instances unintended effects that raised serious questions about the worth of the structures and their minimal influence on practice. Given the policy logic driving these structural changes, without much effect on practice, there was little to no influence on student learning. These three cases, then, not only reveal flaws in the policy logic reform-driven decision makers used but also reveal how little they knew of institutional complexities in schools and classroom interactions between teachers and students.

In part 2, I compare and contrast practices in two helping professions—teaching and medicine. The point is to show how reformers established new structures to alter practice through changing people, adopting market-driven solutions, and embracing technological innovations in two different institutions, ones with substantial differences between practitioners. Yet these reform-driven policies have encountered similar responses from both teachers and doctors.

Part 3 summarizes common answers reform-driven policy makers, practitioners, and researchers have given the central question of overall continuity in teaching practices in the face of major structural changes such as the history and sociology of teaching, teacher resistance, and policy makers' errors.

I will analyze the above cases to see whether the familiar explanations challenge, amend, or converge with the century's worth of evidence I have collected and sifted through. I also examine closely and draw conclusions about contemporary policy makers' beliefs and the policy logic they have followed in adopting and implementing school reforms—that creating new structures and altering old ones will reshape what practitioners do and that, in changing daily practices, the desired teacher and student outcomes they seek will be within their grasp. Finally, I return to another look at metaphors for school reform and my explanation of what is inside the black box and how that knowledge is significant for policy and practice.

PART ONE

✦✦✦

Engineering Structures to Reform Classroom Teaching

THE FOLLOWING THREE CHAPTERS deal with policy makers' serious, long-term efforts to reform classroom teaching by changing school structures. In these cases, reform-minded policy makers deployed new technologies, altered the science curriculum repeatedly, and established new accountability and testing regulations. In each instance, policy makers' hopes ran high that these new top-down structures, when they were put into place, would alter teaching practices and improve learning, giving students the knowledge and skills to succeed economically and socially.

Desktop computers, followed by laptops, tablets, and handheld devices with accompanying software appeared in classrooms. Teachers used new science curriculum guides, textbooks, and materials. New state curriculum standards, tests, and accountability regulations focused on school outcomes raised the stakes considerably for students, teachers, principals, and district officials. Indeed, top-down, regulatory structural changes, like tidal waves, swept over schools and classrooms. Yet when the waters receded, were classroom practices improved? Did students gain the requisite knowledge and skills to thrive in a market-based society? I answer these questions in part 1.

Chapter 1

Restructuring Las Montanas and Technology, 1976–2010

Surrounded by hills that turn rich green in the winter and golden in the spring and summer (although skeptical East coast visitors might call it brown), Las Montanas (a pseudonym) is located on nearly fifty acres in the heart of Silicon Valley in the San Francisco Bay area.

In 1976, when Las Montanas opened its doors for the first time to thirteen hundred students, nearly sixty teachers, and five administrators, there was little doubt that the high school was innovative. Conceived and designed in the late-1960s as an open-space building, its 160,000 carpeted and air-conditioned square feet housed a large media center and administrative office suite as well as the Forum (a large open gathering place for students), two gyms, a cafeteria, a snack bar, and a faculty room. In addition to an array of regular classrooms, there were specialized rooms for music, drama, science, art, and vocational subjects. As enrollment waxed and waned over the years, portable classrooms were added and have become fixtures outside the main building.

Las Montanas also had a distinctive curriculum with an individualized program for its mostly college-bound clientele. Short courses, semester courses, and flexible weekly schedules gave students and teachers many options.[1]

If the building, curriculum, and scheduling were uncommon, so was school governance. The entire school was divided into three units, each with an administrator, one-third of the students from all grades, teachers from all academic subjects, and one secretary. Each unit was further subdivided into two "learning communities" led by a coordinator who was a teacher selected by both students and colleagues. In addition, every certified staff member, including the principal, advised a small group of students for fifteen minutes a day. Every Wednesday morning, the entire faculty would meet for updates on the week's issues and divide into their learning communities; school began one hour later and periods were shortened so that advisers could meet with their students toward the end of the school day.

Las Montanas, 1976–1998

Las Montanas embodied a multitude of structural reforms—the bricks-and-mortar building, curriculum, schedule, and governance that were expected to move teachers away from predominately traditional teacher-centered instruction toward creating student-centered lessons.

Beginning in the late 1970s, however, a series of events undercut these reforms. California voters approved Proposition 13, which significantly reduced funding for schools in the early 1980s. The legislature mandated higher graduation requirements and more testing in 1983, further modifying what could and could not be done in the state's high schools.

At about the same time, Silicon Valley was emerging as a national center of high-tech innovation, development, and production. Venture capitalists funded start-up companies that made multimillionaires of twenty-something engineers and programmers. Pressures on schools from parents and business leaders to adopt more technology accelerated. The state legislature and department of education promoted new technologies through grants and technical support. For Las Montanas and other high schools, district staff drew up technology plans for wiring schools, purchasing technologies, and deploying computers. A new infrastructure to alter what teachers did in their lessons and what students learned in schools emerged.[2]

With all of these changes in funding, new top-down state mandates, and new technologies, Las Montanas had changed considerably by the early 1990s. Counselors had been let go, class sizes ballooned, most staff members who had founded the school had left, and flexible scheduling was gone. The governance arrangements were still in place but exerted little influence on what occurred daily in school. More minority students now attended even as overall enrollment had declined. Moreover, standardized achievement test scores had slipped below both state and national averages.

In 1992, district officials appointed a new principal. Adrian Jones (all names are fictitious) envisioned Las Montanas as a high-tech magnet school that would draw teachers and students from the entire district and stem the hemorrhaging enrollment and teacher turnover. He recruited a cadre of young, reform-minded faculty intent on creating interdisciplinary programs that integrated information technologies into their daily work. In persuading experienced technology-oriented teachers to transfer from other district schools and attracting young, energetic teachers, he convinced foundations, district and state officials, and Silicon Valley entrepreneurs to invest in Las Montanas.

By the mid-1990s, staff, business leaders, parents, and students had hammered out a mission statement, schoolwide goals, and specific curricular standards that connected access and use of technology to student achievement. Jones had mobilized about one-third of the faculty to support a technology magnet school, and some teachers had designed and put into place interdisciplinary programs. This shift created fault lines among faculty, however, dividing teachers over the quality of the academic programs, lax disciplining of students, and how much of the new technologies should be used in classrooms. Nonetheless, within five years, enrollments in interdisciplinary programs had gone from less than 10 percent to about 40 percent of the students across all grades and academic subjects.[3]

And then the reform-minded Jones left for a different post, the five-year magnet grant was ending, and his successor, Lydia French, committed to Jones's vision, became principal. Moreover, the school population had continued to change. It was now nearly 70 percent minority (with 16 percent limited English proficiency) and 44 percent of the students were eligible for free and reduced-price lunches.

Under French, Las Montanas had received a major grant from a Bay Area reform group (Bay Area School Reform Collaborative—BASRC) to be a "leadership" school in the region. In addition, a state Digital High School grant provided more hardware and wiring for the entire school. Technology was the ticket, French believed, and she—like her predecessor—wanted to have the school become a technology magnet school for the district. She appointed Carl Hooper, a former vocational education teacher, as technology coordinator to shepherd the growth of technology through its infancy (Hooper remained coordinator through 2012, when he retired).

Although boosting the school's media center, technology, and inter-disciplinary programs and raising academic standards remained central to her plans for Las Montanas, French understood that many program features of a quarter-century earlier had disappeared. For example, only two teachers from the founding faculty remained. Furthermore, she and faculty leaders realized that although individual programs might shine, "efforts of individual programs have not been converted into systemic, schoolwide reform"—especially, French might have added, reforms that targeted improvements in students' academic performance.[4]

Test scores showed some improvements but were substantially below state and national averages. Furthermore, none of the statistics on student performance were broken out by ethnicity or race, therefore masking serious academic issues facing the faculty and administration. Chief among them were literacy for English language learners (ELLs) and the large numbers of minority students failing in each grade.

The principal and teachers, long aware of these academic deficiencies, attacked the problem. Much attention was given to implementing schoolwide standards established under the former principal in 1994, further expanding interdisciplinary programs, restructuring the ninth grade to help students perform better academically, and intensifying efforts to apply technology to teaching and learning. The state Digital High School grant, for example, focused on the ninth-grade interdisciplinary core program, which included a course in "computer productivity."[5]

The 1998–1999 Study of Technology Use at Las Montanas

In 1998, I proposed a study of Las Montanas to Lydia French, who welcomed this research. Two graduate students and I spent the academic year visiting classes, interviewing staff and students, and conducting surveys.[6]

So, what did we find in our 1998–1999 study about student and teacher computer access and use?[7] First, some data on use in the school and nationwide (see table 1.1).

As the table shows, Las Montanas was well ahead of the rest of the country average in both the number and use of computers. Unlike most schools, which might have computers in the classroom or a few labs,

TABLE 1.1
Access to and use of computers at Las Montanas and in the United States, 1998–1999

	United States	Las Montanas
Students per computer, schoolwide	6	4
Students per computer, library	114	16
Students with computers at home (%)	56	90
Teachers with computers at home	80	85
Teacher use at school (%):		
• Word processing	N/A	76
• Recording grades	59	58
• E-mail	N/A	85
• Searching Internet	24	68

there were ten computer labs scattered throughout the building, a few of which were designated for particular departments such as English. Note also the high student-computer ratio nationally in school libraries—now media centers—and the low ratio at Las Montanas. In the late 1990s, the technology coordinator and principal had deployed thirty iMacs to the Library Media Center (LMC) in addition to one mobile cart with six to eight computers. Both teachers and students used those computers (see table 1.2).

A closer look at those academic subject teachers who brought their students to the media center revealed that three departments (English, science, and social students) accounted for nearly 70 percent of all computer use in the media center. Moreover, even within those departments, an even smaller band of academic teachers—fifteen out of sixty on the entire staff—accounted for most media center use of computers.

These figures, however, give no sense of the lessons that teachers taught in classrooms, labs, and media center. Some examples follow.

Observing a Humanities Class

I observed Alison Piro teaching a humanities class in 1998 and interviewed her afterward.[8]

TABLE 1.2
Teacher use of high school media center, 1998–1999*

Percentage of faculty who brought classes to LMC	74
Median number of days students used computers in LMC	12
Median number of periods students used computers in LMC	34
Median percentage of yearly instructional time	5

*I counted use in only academic subject teachers (English, foreign language, math, science, and social studies). I did not count use by teachers in special education, vocational courses with computer-assisted design, multimedia and graphics software, or art/music/drama.

Shelley, an eleventh-grader is standing on a raised platform in the middle of the classroom, surrounded by students seated at their group tables. The classroom lights are turned off and the shades are drawn. The only light in the room comes from the overhead projector, which Alison Piro positions in such a way that it serves as a spotlight on Shelley. With these words, "The freedom we should demand . . . " Shelley begins her speech as ex-slave Frederick Douglass.

These few moments in Alison Piro's classroom captured the essence of Piro's teaching—dramatic, diligently planned, and even innovative in its use of technology (albeit in this case a low-tech machine). The environment was warm and safe and conducive to students' performance. Whether it was a literary reading, a film produced by students, a piece of art, or a slide show, performance was a central part of Piro's pedagogy, a strategy she believed allowed students to demonstrate their comprehension of the concepts and themes they had read and discussed.

With five years of teaching experience, Alison Piro co-planned and co-taught two periods of an eleventh-grade interdisciplinary humanities class a day with Alan Bloom, who took the lead on the social studies curriculum while she led the English lessons, although both agree that theirs was entirely a team effort. Each class had thirty-two students.

Piro was a leader in integrating computers into that curriculum. She believed in the power of technology as a teaching and learning tool, wanted to tap its potential, and credited it for improving what she did in lessons. "It's how you use the tool," Piro said. "If we are only using it to word process, then we may as well have typewriters."

In Piro's humanities class, students used the Internet to do research and write passages that accompanied visual presentations such as slide shows and films. She expected students to "conceptualize and actualize" ideas using technology as their medium. For example, after reading several works of utopian literature, groups of students had to create their own utopias and "sell" their utopias to their audience (their classmates).

Piro's students used computers about eight times a month. Typically, students worked in pairs or groups on projects that took up to two weeks. As Piro reported: "Our technology use tends to span several days. For instance, when we were doing our Utopian Society project, we were in the media center, using butcher paper, pencils, and pens for about three days before we ever got to the technology. Then we spent a whole day researching images on laser disc, video, and the Internet. Then we spent a whole other three days and a Saturday [producing films]."

According to Piro, computer use depended on the instructor's teaching and learning goals. She admitted that there have been times when she chose incorrectly. An essay, for example, may have been a more appropriate assignment than a computer project. She carefully considered what tool—an essay, a computerized slide show, a short-answer exam, a piece of art, a digitized movie, a research project using the Internet—would be most appropriate for engaging students.

Shadowing Students

By shadowing six students, we observed full days of lessons as we followed them through their scheduled classes. One day I trailed Hector to four of his classes. For each class, I introduced myself to the teacher and sat in the back of the room. Afterward, while walking to the next one, Hector and I would discuss what had occurred. Over lunch, we talked further about his courses, the home computer that he used every night, and other aspects of school. Here is what I observed in two classes.

French 1. Between 7:50 a.m. and 8:45 a.m., the teacher taught the whole group of twenty-nine students using a textbook lesson (*Discovering French*) and one-page handouts of a dialogue between two people. She asked seven pairs of students to come to the front of the room to read the dialogue aloud. About half of the class was engaged, while others were doing homework for other classes, quietly talking, or staring

27

into space. The teacher occasionally said "Shhhhh!" to get silence for those students reading the dialogue.

U.S. History. The social studies teacher led a whole-group discussion of twenty-five students on inductive and deductive reasoning. She used many concrete examples drawn from students' lives and world and national current events. Virtually all of the students, including Hector, were attentive, listened to one another, and engaged in the discussion. Afterward, Hector told me that today's class was typical of the rest of the week.

I had noticed a cart in the room holding a videocassette recorder, monitor, and four computers. I asked Hector about the machines, and he told me that the class had seen a video this week. From time to time, he said, some students would use the computers in class to do Internet searches on items being discussed. He said that for this class he would use his home computer to complete the homework.

Other Sources of Data

We polled about one-third of the school's students representing every academic subject and covering all grades in the high school. Students reported some computer use in English and social studies and little to none in math, science, and foreign language. Moreover, "use" generally consisted of typing up assignments, working on reports, and Internet searches.

When we inspected which classes students reported on, we saw that there was as much variation within a department as there was between departments. In the English department, for example, one or two teachers were especially heavy users of computers in classrooms and the media center, a few were occasional to rare users, and the rest were largely nonusers. This pattern was similar across departments.

From a teacher survey (95 percent of sixty teachers responding) and in interviews with academic subject teachers, over half said that their teaching had indeed changed because of their use of computers. Among the changes they mentioned were: planning more efficiently, communicating with colleagues far more often via e-mail, and securing information from the Internet. Second, they highlighted the importance of having an additional tool to use in their customary repertoire of teaching practices. Finally, they saw students' access to information—the

Internet as a worldwide library—as a phenomenal enhancement to their teaching.

A young social studies teacher who said that using technology has changed his teaching explained:

> [T]he technology has just given me more tools to use . . . One thing I think it has allowed me to do is to access certain students who need something kinetic . . . Like the students who made the video aren't the kind of students who are going to write and debate the question: *Does democracy really exist?* because there are other students who can debate with so much more power that they are intimidated . . . Here is a way for them to convey their message about the question and to feature it at the beginning of the [video]—something they are proud of that the rest of the class clapped [for] after they saw it. It really brings them into the class and allows their ideas to be viewed and valued.

When we shadowed teachers and students, however, we saw what classroom researchers have seen for decades. All but a few of the teachers at Las Montanas used a familiar repertoire of instructional approaches: lecturing, conducting a discussion, reviewing homework, working on assignments, and occasional use of technologies such as overhead projectors, videos, and computers. From teacher surveys and shadowing students, we found that in some classes students gave reports, worked in small groups, did seatwork at their desks or, in the media center, completed projects. For the most part, even in computer-based classes, teacher-centered instruction with a mix of student-centered practices was the norm.

This completes my summary of the 1998–1999 study of changes in access and use of new technologies at Las Montanas high school. In 2008, I returned to the high school to see what changes, if any, had occurred in teacher and student use of computers.

Las Montanas and Technology, 2008–2010

Before describing the follow-up study, I need to recount events that occurred at Las Montanas after the 1998–1999 study.[9]

Four principals entered and exited Las Montanas between 1998 and September 2010. They traveled a road that went from stationary computer labs to a 1:1 computing school, and then to the current half-mobile cart, half-1:1 computing.[10]

Lydia French presided for four years over the largely minority, thirteen-hundred-student school after it had been designated a district technology magnet. The school had a rich array of computer labs and a core of tech-savvy teachers. In these years, however, academic achievement had declined and neighborhood gang activities spilled over into the school. The most serious incident was the off-campus stabbing of a student. Parent and student perceptions of the school turned negative. Student enrollment dropped. Teacher turnover increased. Lydia French exited and Dorothy Bunch entered.

District officials worried about Las Montanas being able to continue as a high-tech magnet school as it struggled with low test scores and sinking enrollment. To improve the school's image and boost enrollment—it had fallen to about a thousand students—district officials cobbled together local and federal funds to make Las Montanas a 1:1 laptop program in 2002.

Dorothy Bunch and Carl Hooper, the veteran technology coordinator, created an infrastructure including faculty development to sustain this program and campaigned to attract students to the school. Each student received a laptop in 2003–2004. In early 2004, however, the rules of the game changed suddenly. After two consecutive years of low scores on tests, the state department of education put Las Montanas on academic probation. A few months later, Dorothy Bunch left and Carolyn Claus took over as principal.

Claus concentrated on fixing the school academically. While laptops were available, she made it clear to the faculty that her total attention was on improving test scores in language arts, math, and other academic subjects. Individual teachers could choose to use laptops in their classrooms, but the faculty must remain focused on ending academic probation.

With state funds, Claus hired academic coaches who helped faculty develop pacing calendars for covering content. Teachers constructed benchmark tests that assessed student progress. Newly purchased texts aligned daily lessons to state standards. By 2006, state scores had climbed sufficiently for the state to end academic probation a year early. Soon after, student enrollment increased, and teacher turnover fell.[11]

Once the school was removed from academic probation, technology coordinator Hooper, a faculty committee on technology, and individual teachers advocated a return to 1:1 computing in 2007. But serious doubts about the financial viability and worth of the program occupied the principal's mind.

Early on in her principalship, Claus, who had been an assistant principal at Las Montanas at the launch of the 1:1 computing program, expressed both financial and instructional concerns about the future of laptops. Because state funding for California districts had shrunk, local funds for purchasing new laptops (as student enrollment increased), replacing "retired" machines, and costs for maintaining machines had risen annually to over $500,000. With less state and district funds, Claus worried about finding that money in her budget every year.[12]

Claus also expressed concerns about what she and her three assistant principals saw in classroom lessons when they did ten- to fifteen-minute walk-throughs. Months earlier, Claus had also invited a team of district administrators to observe classrooms and report back to the faculty what they saw. In both instances of classroom observations, there was infrequent use of laptops for instruction. When teachers did have students use the machines, more often than not—according to the reports of both Las Montanas administrators and the district team—observers saw mostly traditional classroom instruction and low-level use of laptops such as taking notes, doing homework, looking up items on the Internet, etc.

In early 2008, these data, including rising costs for the program, were shared with faculty. When teachers were polled about continuing the 1:1 laptop program with modifications, a majority of teachers expressed unwavering support for the program, even amid faculty complaints about laptops distracting student attention during lessons.

Again in 2008, district contributions to the Las Montanas budget fell. Federal funds had dried up. With less and less external money available to give every high school student a laptop, Claus, concerned about finding replacement funds and limited use of technologies in lessons, offered the faculty varied options for a modified 1:1 program and polled them for their preferences. The principal then decided that for the next school year, 2008–2009, ninth- through eleventh-graders would receive laptops. Teachers of senior students would get access to laptops by signing up for three mobile carts, each holding thirty-two laptops. In

2009–2010, tenth- through twelfth-graders got laptops and ninth grade teachers had to sign up for mobile labs.[13]

For 2010–2011, with even further drains on the budget, Claus made clear to the faculty that laptops for every student were financially unfeasible because of enrollment increases and out-of-warranty laptops that could not be replaced. She again consulted with the faculty. The faculty split over whether to continue with as many students as possible receiving machines and having a few carts or moving to an all-cart program. With the faculty split over what to do, Claus made the decision, and Las Montanas became an all–mobile-cart high school.

A few months later, however, the superintendent asked Claus to take over a troubled high school elsewhere in the district. After six years, Claus left Las Montanas. In September 2010, new principal Dave Bastedo—a former Las Montanas math teacher and assistant principal—surveyed teachers about the all-cart program and found that teachers wanted laptops distributed to eleventh- and twelfth-graders, with carts reserved for ninth- and tenth-graders. After consulting closely with technology coordinator Carl Hooper and the faculty technology committee, Bastedo reversed Claus's decision.[14]

Overall Conclusions from Both Studies

Overall, from the 2008–2010 study, I drew three conclusions based on a combination of classroom observations, teacher interviews, student surveys, and Library Media Center data on use of mobile carts and those teachers who brought classes to the LMC for research, writing, and small-group work. In considering these conclusions, keep in mind the school's demography at two different points in time (see table 1.3).[15]

1. In 1998–1999, only a small band of academic subject teachers regularly used computers in their lessons; the rest of the faculty were either occasional or nonusers; by 2010, however, most academic subject teachers were regular or occasional users of electronic devices in classroom instruction.

2. Even with far more teacher and student use of computers in academic subjects in 2009–2010 compared with 1998–1999, and even with nearly total complete faculty turnover (only one academic subject teacher who had been on the faculty in 1998 was teaching in 2010), there was far more stability than change in how teachers taught academic subjects.

TABLE 1.3
Las Montanas student and teacher demography, 1998 and 2010

	1998–1999	2009–2010
Total students	1,158	1,073
Percent minority	70	82
Percent free and reduced-price lunch	44	57
Number of teachers	60	57
Percent minority	17	25*

Source: Las Montanas (pseud.), "Focus on Learning: A Self-Study Submitted to Western Association of Schools and Colleges," March 21–24, 2010, pp. 8–11, 13–18; *Student Accountability Report Card,* Las Montanas High School (pseud.), Grades 9–12 for 2009-2010, p. 3.7; Larry Cuban, *Oversold and Underused: Computers in the Classroom* (Cambridge, MA: Harvard University Press, 2001), 81.
*2008–2009.

3. Connections between student achievement and teacher and student use of laptops are, at best, indirect and, at worst, nonexistent.

Stated baldly, these conclusions drawn from two studies completed a decade apart may surprise readers. Below I present the evidence that led me to each conclusion.

1. In 1998–1999 only a small band of academic subject teachers regularly used computers . . . by 2010, however, most academic subject teachers were regular or occasional users of electronic devices in classroom instruction.

The Evidence

In 2008–2009, there were thirty-two academic subject teachers (English, foreign language, math, science, and social studies). Seven math teachers worked in classrooms where interactive whiteboards (IWB) had been installed.[16] The vendor had trained the math teachers to use IWBs. None of the seven math teachers who had ninth- through eleventh-graders furnished with laptops asked their students to regularly bring them to class; none of the seven math teachers used carts or took their students to the LMC. Although I observed individual students using their laptops to take notes and search the Web for information during math lessons, math teachers relied wholly on IWBs. Below is a description of the math lessons I observed.

In 2008–2009, ninth- through eleventh-grade students had laptops, while seniors had access to LMC computers; teachers with senior classes could sign out three mobile labs stacked with laptops from the LMC. My data on the use of the LMC and carts come from twenty-five academic subject teachers (less the seven math teachers). Of those, five were nonusers of the LMC and carts (two foreign language teachers and three from social studies). Of academic subject teachers, 80 percent used the LMC and carts (a decade earlier, 74 percent of academic subject teachers had used computers in the LMC and stationary labs).[17]

Of the twenty academic subject teachers who used LMC and carts in 2008–2009 (remember that five teachers were nonusers that year), seven teachers (in the English, social studies, science departments) accounted for 72 percent of use.

Further changes in the deployment of laptops occurred in 2009–2010. For this year, the principal, after consulting with the faculty, decided that incoming ninth-graders would have no laptops and the other three grades would. Thus, students who had laptops the previous year (tenth- and eleventh-graders) would have them for a second year in a row.

In addition, the five teachers who were nonusers of the LMC and mobile labs the previous year became users (in 2009–2010, however, four other academic subject teachers became nonusers). Overall, 85 percent of teachers used the LMC and carts. As in the previous year and the earlier study, a small band of teachers in English, science, and social studies accounted for the majority of laptop and desktop computer use in the LMC. Still, more Las Montanas teachers were using electronic devices regularly and occasionally than a decade earlier, including those seven math teachers who were observed using IWBs.

Consider Carol Donnelly, whom I watched teach biology in 2009. Donnelly has been a teacher for thirteen years, the last six at Las Montanas. She has been using laptops since 2003, when they were introduced at the school. When I observed her classes, she was teaching biology to honors students (one class), regular students (one class), and English language learners (ELL) in three classes. She used the same basic lesson for all of her classes, stretching out the content for ELL classes while going more in-depth in the regular and honors classes (e.g., research papers, PowerPoint presentations, science fair projects). She integrated laptops into her lessons once a week.

Every Wednesday, she told me, was laptop day. She brought a mobile cart from the LMC into her classroom. In one lesson I observed, Donnelly began the regular class with a review of the previous day's material on photosynthesis. Afterward, she had students open their laptops to watch animations of photosynthesis that she had loaded on their machines earlier. A pop-up quiz appeared after the animations. Donnelly walked around and checked student scores on the quiz. She then summarized the concept of photosynthesis by questioning students. Finally, she collected homework assigned the previous day.

At the beginning of her senior honors class, students usually worked on laptops for their science fair project. On that day, Donnelly lectured on the Calvin cycle of photosynthesis. Students took notes and then viewed the animations and took the quiz as the other class had. Closing activities were similar to the previous regular class.[18]

Sometimes a laptop lesson on Wednesday spilled over to subsequent days. Donnelly recalled a lesson on the plasma (or cell) membrane that took three days. She included exercises that came from Kerpoof multimedia software that had students draw and label parts of the plasma membrane.[19] She showed me a worksheet that she had created to accompany the lesson. She spends a lot of time finding Web sites, videos, and applications to use with her classes.

Donnelly also has students blogging. With a laptop camera, students liven up their blog page with photos they take of themselves and others. She reads the blogs and comments but gives no grades on entries. She told me about a prompt concerning Thanksgiving and turkey that mentioned tryptophan with links to URLs that described the chemical and what it does in the human body. Some students, she said, blogged on the chemical after reading the links she had provided.

When asked about benefits of laptops for her and students, she gave an example: "When I asked students to compare the features of a cell to anything they wanted—the high school, family, friends, sports team, etc.—they created stories, took photos off the Web, did an iMovie and a Keynote (Apple slide presentation software) presentation. I was surprised and pleased. I had not expected all of that to be done in one class period."[20] She added: "I have definitely changed my teaching. I do far more preparation now and give kids access to ideas and information they would not ordinarily find."

In addition to observing Donnelly and other science teachers during my two-year study of the school, I had collected eighteen observations of math lessons from five of those teachers. Administrators gave me copies of their walk-throughs, in which the principal or assistant principals spent ten to fifteen minutes watching a math lesson and jotting down notes on a form. My observations—which no administrator saw—were of the entire lesson (fifty-six minutes). Between my observations and those of administrators, I had lesson reports on all math teachers.

These experienced teachers (most had been teaching ten or more years), according to questionnaire responses, used computers daily at home and school. In class, they used IWBs daily; only a few combined the IWB with student laptops in class, and that occurred occasionally.

Like other academic departments at Las Montanas, math teachers were very aware of the California Standards Test (CST) and the consequences of low math scores. In 2004, when the school was placed on academic probation, the math department used district-developed benchmark tests to prepare for the annual CST.

To make concrete all of these data, I describe a geometry lesson taught in 2009 by veteran teacher Katie Lee.

Twenty-five tenth-grade students (mostly Latino, with a scattering of whites and African Americans) sat at desks arranged in rows facing the IWB and Lee's desk. On the walls were lists of what Lee expected in student behavior, posters about the importance of math in daily life, examples of student work, and assignments for the three different math classes that she taught. On the IWB was an agenda for the day's lesson.

After the tardy bell rang, Lee said: "You need to bring your laptops tomorrow to prepare for the next benchmark test." She then directed the class to do the warm-up posted on the IWB. These daily warm-ups, a staple of high school math lessons, can range from riddles to unusual tasks to specific problems related to the lesson. This warm-up dealt with the surface area of a prism.

All students worked on the warm-up. After five minutes, Lee asked a student to go to the IWB. Taking the stylus (an electronic pen), the student swiftly laid out the answer and how he did it. Lee checked out his answer on a calculator that appeared on the IWB after a tap of her pen. She asked how many students had solved the problem in the warm-up; most raised their hands. She then segued to the textbook homework for the lesson on "scale factor."

Lee penned a question on the IWB: "What is scale factor?" Some students called out answers, and others raised their hands. After listening to their answers, she gave further examples from the textbook. She tapped the IWB to use figures that she had entered from her laptop that morning on "similar solids." Laid out on the IWB were the words *Shape, Scale, Surface Area,* and *Volume.* She walked up and down the rows of desks as she explained each concept and gave examples, and took questions from three students who were using their laptops to look up math URLs that she had given the class earlier in the semester. I noted that nearly all of the students were attentive or whispering questions to nearby classmates about the words on the IWB.

Lee returned to the IWB to give an example of a cube with a 1:1 ratio on scale, surface area, and volume increasing to a cube with a 1:3 ratio on each. She explained the example, then asked: "Can you see a pattern?" A few students nodded their heads. She asked one of them, "What pattern do you see?"

The student responded; Lee then asked a student who had not nodded. This student said she was stuck. Lee then used example of a Baskin-Robbins ice cream cone, doubling and tripling volume and surface area with additional scoops. "What would the scale be?" she asked the class. A few students gave the correct answer.

Lee returned to the 1:3-ratio cube and asked, "What happens if it goes to 1:5?" She then directed the students to work in pairs for the rest of the period to answer that question. She walked around, answering questions and talking with individual students. Five minutes before the end of the period, she gave the assignment for the next day. Students worked until the buzzer ended the class.

Variations of this lesson in fifty-plus-minute periods in Algebra 1 and 2, geometry, and calculus were replicated in every math lesson I observed when shadowing students, when teachers invited me to sit in the class, or appeared in administrator observations.

Some teachers carried off the warm-up, review, students at the IWB working out problems, and other elements of the lesson with élan and engaged the class as Lee did; some of these teachers used "clickers"—devices that permitted students to answer a teacher question without waving their hands in the air. For example, students would work on a problem in pairs or individually. Then the teacher passed out "clickers" so students could answer a multiple-choice question posted on the IWB by voting whether the A, B, C, or D answer was correct. Students pointed at the IWB and clicked. The teacher then tapped a button, and the results for the entire class would be displayed in bar graphs so that the teacher and students could see what percentage of the class got or missed the concept embedded in the multiple-choice question. The teacher could then move on or re-teach the concept, depending on how many students had erred.

Other math teachers didn't use clickers and conducted each phase of the typical math lesson using the IWB and conventional asking of questions while calling on students to answer or letting students call out answers.

All data from interviews, surveys, LMC sign-up sheets, and classroom observations led me to conclude that more frequent and pervasive teacher and student use of laptops and desktops in academic subjects at Las Montanas occurred between 2008–2010 than a decade earlier.

2. Even with far more teacher and student use of computers in academic subjects in 2009–2010 compared with 1998 . . . there was far more stability than change in how teachers taught academic subjects.

The Evidence

With computer use practiced across most classrooms by teachers new to Las Montanas—nearly all of the academic subject teachers in 2009–2010 had come to Las Montanas since 1998–1999—an observer might expect that the manner of teaching would have changed significantly from a decade earlier. Yet I found that even with a different faculty and increased use of classroom computers in lessons, the mode of instruction remained largely teacher-centered or what some reform-minded critics might call *traditional* or *frontal* teaching.[21]

Earlier in the chapter, I described classroom lessons I observed in 1998 and characterized those lessons as largely teacher-centered with a mix of student-centered practices. In the 2008–2010 study, I gathered 116 classroom reports, of which 46 were lessons that I observed and the rest from administrators' classroom observations. The total classroom reports covered 95 percent of academic subject teachers.

Readers have already been introduced to science teacher Carol Donnelly and math teacher Katie Lee. Here I offer brief descriptions of lessons taught by English, social studies, and Spanish teachers I observed. I chose these descriptions because they typify the dominant manner of instruction and varied uses of technology across all academic departments.

English. Sandy Demeter sat at her desk in the front of the room as the twenty-seven ninth-grade students filed in. Desks were arranged in clusters of three facing the teacher and whiteboards.

Demeter's laptop sat next to the LCD projector. According to LMC records, she often brought her class into the LMC to work on projects with their own laptops or the twenty-five-plus LMC iMacs.

After the buzzer sounded, Demeter settled her students down. She asked the class to begin fifteen minutes of sustained silent reading (SSR) and to write a reflection on what they have read. Students took out their reading materials. After about ten minutes, some students began typing on their laptops. Chimes ended SSR, and students closed their laptops.

The teacher reviewed the week's assignments listed on the whiteboard. She then turned to the structure of the haiku that they began yesterday. She went over the seventeen-syllable haiku by pointing to the one she had written on the whiteboard:

Ms. D's wild classroom (5)
stares at the computer screen (7)
eyes going glassy (5)

She then asked each student to create two haikus in the next fifteen minutes. Because desks were clustered in trios, there was a great deal of talk among students both on- and off-task.

Demeter walked to each cluster of desks to check on student-written haikus, to quiet students, and to answer questions. She asked three female students to put away their makeup kits. Some students who had finished walked around, talking with other students. She asked two students to write their haikus on the white board. As room noise rose, she cautioned them with "Ladies and gentlemen, pleeeeease." Noise fell.

After twenty minutes and review of student-written haikus on the whiteboard, Demeter said: "Let's turn to page 422, and iambic pentameter in poems." She then diagrammed iambic pentameter on the whiteboard, using a line from a Robert Frost poem on the page she had referenced. She then stamped her foot to beat out the rhythm of the line. Many students stamped along with her. They tried another line together and practiced the rhythm.

About four minutes before the period ended, some students put their laptops and textbooks in their backpacks as they got ready for the buzzer. Noise level rose until buzzer sounded.

Modern World History. Jim Meister's room had rows of desks arranged in a horseshoe, facing his chair and podium in the center (see the photo in figure 1.1). His laptop rested next to the LCD projector. The twenty-eight tenth-grade students were in the middle of a weeklong simulation on fascism, communism, and authoritarian regimes that placed

FIGURE 1.1   Jim Meister's classroom

each student in the role of an aristocrat, worker, and peasant. This lesson took a break from the simulation.

Periodically, Meister asked students to bring their laptops to class for specific tasks. Not for this lesson.

Immediately after the buzzer sounded, Meister launched into the topic of Nazi propaganda under Hitler, using a Keynote presentation. He told students to take out their notebooks and copy the bullet points on each slide. As he lectured, he constantly moved among students' desks.

To illustrate how propaganda works, Meister asked students to believe only what he said and to forget what other history teachers or textbooks had said. He then explored with them the concept of believing only him—with Hitler in mind. They began asking questions. Meister then used examples of the United States owning the Blockbuster and Wendy's chains. He lectured right up to the buzzer that ended the period. Students were still taking notes.

Spanish. An experienced teacher who had come to Las Montanas five years ago, Rachel Minor welcomed twenty-seven ninth- and tenth-graders into her classroom. Four rows of three desks were arranged in a horseshoe facing a whiteboard. In the middle of the horseshoe was the teacher's desk. The teacher passed out laptops stacked on a cart to students.

Minor began class by saying, "Please turn your music off and take your earbuds out." She told the class to begin work on a vocabulary lesson that she had loaded onto their laptops the previous day and take the quiz at the end of the lesson.

As students got down to doing the digital worksheet, Minor walked around the classroom, checking screens to see what students were doing, answering questions, and prodding some students to get on task. Afterward, she went to her desk and opened her laptop. Periodically, she scanned the room and called out student names to see if they had finished the vocabulary worksheet and had started the quiz. After fifteen minutes, she walked up and down rows, telling the class they had a few minutes left.

Minor asked for class's attention—four students sitting around me in the back of the room had been chitchatting the entire time while working on the vocabulary sheet. They stopped talking.

Minor went over the worksheet. "You will need to know these words because for [our] multimedia project creating a travel brochure to a

Latin American country, these words will come in handy." She read each word, asked students what it meant, and told them to pronounce it aloud. Students called out answers in ragged fashion. After ten minutes, fewer and fewer student responded.

Minor then walked up and down rows to see if the students had completed their quizzes. Some students had put their earbuds back in. She began collecting laptops approximately eight minutes before the period was to end, thereby signaling students to put things in their backpacks, zip them up, and stand around the door waiting for the buzzer. Minor asked the students to sit down. They did. A few minutes later the buzzer sounded.

Patterns in Instruction

Across these five academic subjects (science, math, English, foreign language, and social studies) the pattern of teacher-centered instruction involving lecture, textbook, seatwork, and overnight assignments was obvious during 2008–2010. Within that overall pattern, student participation individually, in small groups, and in whole-class discussions varied among these teachers. In effect, each teacher had constructed a hybrid repertoire of old and new practices within the framework of teacher-centered instruction, a pattern I had documented in 1998–1999. Yet none of the teachers in this observation had been on the faculty then.

Part of the pattern I observed in 2008–2010, however, was far more use of technology in lessons than in the previous study.[22] Again, there was variation among subjects and teachers but it was clear to me—and data from student surveys, LMC sign-out sheets and classroom observations confirm this point—that frequency and pervasiveness of technology use (e.g., Keynote-aided lectures, IWBs, clickers, student note taking, digital worksheets, and video segments) had increased substantially since 1998–1999. I also noticed far less use of overhead projectors and videocassette recorders, both of which had been replaced by IWBs, PowerPoint, or Keynote) and other software applications.

That uptick in technology use in lessons might help to explain what most Las Montanas teachers had said on survey responses and in interviews: they had made changes in their teaching. Even though the Las Montanas faculty in 2008–2010 had turned over completely (except for one teacher) since 1998–1999, teachers in 2010 reported, as did teachers a decade earlier, that their use of computers and software applications had altered their classroom practices.[23]

Most academic subject teachers had, indeed, made changes in how they prepared for lessons and in using electronic devices for administrative and instructional tasks. But the underlying pattern of instruction, in this researcher's judgment, had largely remained teacher-centered. That is not a criticism, but a description of what I saw.

I based this conclusion about patterns in instruction on the data I collected from interviews, lesson observations, and documents over two different points in time in one high school. Contrary to what champions of high-tech devices and policy makers had assumed would occur with increased access to computers, no fundamental shift from teacher-centered to student-centered instruction transpired. What these teachers had done was mix old and new practices—they had made changes and created hybrids—blends of traditional and nontraditional instructional practices.[24]

3. Connections between student achievement and teacher and student use of laptops are, at best, indirect and, at worst, nonexistent.

The Evidence

A year after Las Montanas rolled out 1:1 computing in 2003, the state put the school on academic probation—a public act that startled and shamed parents, students, and staff. Shortly afterward, Carolyn Claus, the newly appointed principal, told staff that laptops would be set aside until the school improved its test scores and was removed from the state list of failing schools.

One would think that if the principal and faculty believed that daily use of laptops in lessons would result in higher test scores, then an all-out offensive to get teachers to integrate those machines into daily lessons would have been the first order of school business. But it was not.

Instead, as described above, with state grants in hand, the principal hired math and reading coaches, departments adopted benchmark tests, and teachers gave close attention to those test items that had confounded Las Montanas students. Within two years—the school had a year remaining to get off probation—Las Montanas was taken off the state list. Only afterward did the principal and staff roll out laptops for all students.

Nevertheless, at the time of writing, while gains in academic achievement have been substantial in some areas, the upward trend has still fallen below averages for the district and state and, of more importance, has skipped over some groups of students. Specifically, the gap between minorities and whites has widened in the very time period that 1:1 computing was implemented.

Take the state's Academic Performance Index (a composite number crunched from different state tests; the API index scores go from 0 to 1000, with 800 being the state target). Las Montanas' API in 2002–2003 was 594. The state placed the school on academic probation the next year and by 2005 the state had restored Las Montanas to its former status. Since then API scores rose to 688 in 2007–2008, stayed at that level for the subsequent year, and in 2009–2010 jumped to 713. When ethnic and racial groups are disaggregated, however, a drop in Hispanic students' scores occurred between 2007 and 2009. Moreover, the white-Hispanic test score gap widened in those years.[25]

In examining California Standards Test (CST) over the same time span, there have been gains and losses as well. The CST shows how well students do according to state content standards in English-language arts, mathematics, science, and history-social science. Students are either Not Proficient, Proficient, or Advanced.[26]

There has been an upward trend in percentages of students who scored Proficient and Advanced across the subjects between 2007 and 2010 (i.e., from 35 percent of students in English language arts to 42 percent; in math from 18 to 28 percent; in science from 32 to 41 percent; and in history-social science from 36 to 38 percent).[27]

To put these percentages in perspective, keep in mind that when 35 percent of Las Montanas students scored Proficient and Advanced in English language arts in 2007–2008, that meant that 65 percent of the students scored Not Proficient in the subject. Moreover, these increases still fell below the percentages of district and state students who were Proficient and Advanced. [28]

Finally, when these Proficient and Advanced percentages of students at Las Montanas are broken down by race and ethnicity, the gaps in performance are significant: for 2009–2010 in math, for example, 41 percent of the white students were Proficient and Advanced, while 28 percent of African American students and 18 percent of Hispanic students scored in those two categories.[29]

This profile of academic achievement between 2002 and 2010 suggests that anyone linking increased student use of computers in these years to significant gains Las Montanas students made in some content areas would have to bury some unpleasant facts:

- There was uneven progress across academic subjects.
- Gaps in test scores between white and minority students contracted and expanded.
- Most Las Montanas students scored below their peers in the district and state.

These facts mock any claim that 1:1 computing accounted for gains in school achievement. Based on this evidence, I found weak linkages between academic achievement at Las Montanas and the increased teacher and student use of electronic technologies.

Summing Up

In ending this chapter on the ebb and flow of electronic devices at one high school between 1998 and 2010, I can say with confidence that Las Montanas has changed a great deal since 1976, when it opened its doors for the first time. New structures had been assembled and then disassembled. The most recent policy-driven effort to put into place a new structure has been the creation of a technologically-driven school wired for the twenty-first century and equipped with devices that would engage students and fundamentally alter—yes, reform—how teachers taught, how students learned, and raise academic achievement. In each instance, there have been many changes at Las Montanas but they resulted in no fundamental reform in teaching practices and student learning.

Chapter 2

Restructuring the Science Curriculum, 1890s–2011

Snapshots of lessons in elementary school classrooms in the 1970s and 1990s capture the persistent struggle in which reformers have engaged for the past half-century over the purposes of teaching science to children and youth and the best way for students to learn the subject. Take one example, from an upper-grade elementary school science lesson in Lakota, North Dakota, 1970:

> Every student was working on his individual study project. Before beginning, he had written a proposal, stating what his topic was to be, what materials he planned to use, and how he planned to go about resolving the particular problem that he had set up. Typically, although not always, the boys leaned toward mechanical and electrical problems and the girls toward nature study. In almost every instance, the work was of an impressively high level. Almost staggering in its complexity was a project showing how an automobile ignition system works, with complicated diagrams of battery, switch, coil, spark plugs, distributor, rotary switch, and more.[1]

Another comes from an urban elementary school in the mid-1990s, where researchers interviewed and observed a veteran teacher with thirty years' classroom experience:[2]

> *Interview.* The intermediate grade science teacher stated that she had a "full science program." For her fourth- and fifth-grade students, she described using lectures and "hands-on" experiences as her primary instructional techniques. Throughout the interview she used the term "hands-on" eleven times in reference to her classroom.

She elaborated that "hands-on/minds-on" science meant "students could answer their own questions by doing some kind of investigation." She believed that inquiry was "more than children finding out or answering a question by the 'hands-on' process," rather it was needing to "accomplish the fact that they have a hypothesis, they do an experiment, and they come to a conclusion . . . "

[She] . . . mentioned a number of factors that influence her teaching; in particular, she mentioned that "what I really try to do is get critical thinking across to them." She also mentioned that she had several textbooks to supplement "lectures" and that the state achievement tests influenced the coverage of content matter in her classes . . . The primary barrier [to student achievement] was described as student capabilities. She elaborated on this point in some detail:

"The lack of self-discipline within the children [is a primary concern]. There needs to be more self-discipline and it would be nice if we had an aide. I know I'm dreaming but that would be nice . . . "

Lesson Observed. [The interviewed teacher] . . . was instructing fourth graders on motion. The lesson focused on reading information. She read most of the information to the students. Some brief demonstrations were included in the presentation.

These classroom vignettes distill the central role that teachers play in putting a new science curriculum into practice and illustrate the tensions that have existed for decades over the purposes of science education and how students should learn science. In other words, creating a new science curriculum—a well-intentioned initiative seeking to make major changes in classroom practices—doesn't necessarily reform teaching and learning any more than standing in a garage makes you a car or a truck.

Why is that? Surely, building a curricular structure out of an academic subject answers the basic question driving all formal schooling: *What knowledge, skills, and attitudes are of most worth to society and thus must be taught to the next generation?* Yet creating a curricular structure that answers basic content questions leaves other questions unanswered: Do teachers have the expertise to teach the essentials? How do we know that teachers have actually taught the required knowledge, skills, and attitudes? How do we know whether students learned what was taught?

These questions point to the hidden scaffolding that buttresses the visible curricular content and skills to be taught. By *hidden scaffolding,*

I mean the century-old structures of the age-graded school, timeless teacher-centered pedagogy, familiar assessments, and professional development. This scaffolding—basic structures that shape how teachers teach and students learn—determines whether the curriculum in elementary and secondary schools gets converted into lessons and students absorb the knowledge, perform the skills, and display the attitudes conveyed in those lessons. Those taken-for-granted structures seldom show up on the radar screens of those fervent about the reform potential of new science curricula.

Experts announcing a brand-new science curriculum or a blue-ribbon commission creating fresh science standards form only one part of a complex, interconnected structure built to improve teaching and learning. Think of building a new house. Architects design the house. Concrete contractors lay the foundation. Then carpenters put up 2×4 studs and braces and frame the walls; plumbers install pipes, sinks, and toilets; and electricians put in the wiring and outlets. The fundamental structure of the house is set. The family that moves into the house provides the furnishings and accommodates to the layout of the house. Over time, they make changes to its structure. They repaint the exterior; they replace the lawn with water-saving plants; they add WiFi and electronics that call for rewiring. These are important incremental changes; they will not, however, substantially alter the foundation, framing, basic wiring, or plumbing. The difference between incremental and fundamental changes I noted in the introduction apply to this analogy.

So where does a new science curriculum fit into the analogy? Those newly minted science curricula compare to the furnishings in the house. Couches, chairs, dining-room and kitchen tables, beds, rugs—both from the former home and newly bought—are fitted into the new home. When old science curricula are refurbished—let's say restructured—they fit into the traditional age-graded school, time schedules, and class sizes, as well as the existing buildings. The newly restructured science curricula, then, hardly alter fundamentally how schools have operated for decades. They furnish the age-graded school.

To illustrate the link between new science curricula (including the creation of science standards for teachers to use) and the fundamental structures of schooling, consider that over the past century, national and state commissions, scientists, academics, curriculum specialists, and teachers have repeatedly laid out new curricular designs in the form of science frameworks and standards to be taught. These formal standards, adopted by states and districts, have led to what researchers and practitioners have recognized as a de facto multilayered curriculum of science in the United States that has tried to shape what teachers teach and students learn without disturbing the deep, underlying structures that have been in place for many decades. Understanding these different layers of curriculum helps to make sense of the above statement that curricula furnish the age-graded school and the repeated failures of new curricula to significantly change how teachers teach and what students learn.[3]

Multilayered Infrastructure of Curriculum

The external and most visible layer is the intended (or official) curriculum. After extensive deliberation and committee meetings, state and district officials publish curricular frameworks and courses of study in academic subjects from kindergarten through high school.

Consider California. The first science framework in 1998 laid out content standards, grade by grade, as to what teachers should teach and what students should learn (and since then, there have been revisions to this framework).[4] The purposes of the science framework are stated clearly:

> Educators have the opportunity to foster and inspire in students an interest in science; the goal is to have students gain the knowledge and skills necessary for California's workforce to be competitive in the global, information-based economy of the twenty-first century . . . This framework is intended to (1) organize the body of knowledge that students need to learn during their elementary and secondary school years; and (2) illuminate the methods of science that will be used to extend that knowledge during the students' lifetimes.[5]

Note that the purposes of the framework seek to have students leave school inspired and interested in science, equipped with knowledge and skills to enter the workforce, and conversant with how scientists think and act. Multiple and competing aims drive this framework, a situation that has characterized science education reform for decades.

The California science standards are aligned to textbooks approved for teachers' use in elementary and secondary school lessons and, further, are linked to the California Standards Test given at grades 5, 8, and 10 and to the separate sciences (biology, earth science, chemistry, and physics) in grades 9 through 12. Thus, the standards are connected to instructional materials for teaching the subject matter, and assessment of whether the content has been taught and whether students have learned what was taught. This, then, is the intended curriculum.[6]

I say *intended* because, once adopted by the states, these curricular frameworks will have only a passing similarity to the science content and skills that teachers will teach once they close their classroom doors. Moreover, the science that students learn in kindergarten and elementary school will vary from what the frameworks contain and what teachers teach within the same school and across district schools. Finally, what gets tested will echo only in part what teachers have taught and what students have learned.

In short, in the real world of age-graded schools, pedagogy, assessment, and professional development are messy while the official curriculum too often sails above the clouds loosely tethered to what happens in classrooms. How can that be? The answer comes from other layers of the curriculum infrastructure.

If the official curriculum is the first layer, then the second is teachers, working alone in their rooms, choosing what to teach and how to present it. Their choices derive from their knowledge of the subject (elementary and secondary school teachers differ greatly in their knowledge of science), their knowledge of children and youth, their beliefs about how teachers should teach and children should learn, their prior experiences as students, their affection or dislike for topics in the framework and textbook, and their attitudes toward the students they face daily. In fact, researchers continually find that teachers in the same building will teach different versions of the same course while claiming that they are teaching to the state standards and to the prevailing desired pedagogy.[7]

Thus, the intended curriculum and what teachers teach may overlap in the matter of course title, key topics, and the textbook, but can differ substantially in actual subject matter and daily lessons (a discrepancy well illustrated in the teacher and researcher accounts cited above).

And then the taught curriculum overlaps with but differs significantly from what students take away from class. This is the third layer. Students absorb information and concepts from lessons. They also learn to answer teacher questions, review material, locate sources, seek help, avoid teachers' intrusiveness, and act attentive. *Collateral learning*, in

Dewey's phrase—or the *hidden curriculum*, as Philip Jackson put it—occurs when children pick up ideas from classmates, copy their teachers' habits and tics, imitate their humor or sarcasm, or strive to be as autocratic or democratic as the adults.[8] So, the learned curriculum differs from the intended and taught curricula.

What students learn does not exactly mirror what is in the tested curriculum. This is the fourth layer. Many studies have documented that science is one of the least engaging school subjects for students around the world, particularly after the age of ten. Disengaged students, to say the least, have less incentive to learn content and skills and perform well on tests. Moreover, classroom, school, district, state, and national tests, often using multiple-choice and other short-answer items, capture some—but hardly all—of the official and taught curricula. To the degree that teachers and students attend to such tests, portions of the intended and taught curricula merge. But what is tested is a limited part of what is intended in the published curriculum frameworks, taught by teachers, and learned by students.[9]

Finally, many of these tests seek to sort high-achieving students from their lower-achieving peers. The information, ideas, and skills contained in test items for such purposes represent an even narrower band of knowledge. Any newly published science framework, then, will be only the initial link in the structural policy-to-practice chain of intended-taught-learned-tested curricula that characterizes U.S. schooling.[10]

In summary, there are four curricular layers, not one unvarnished curriculum. The official curriculum, often derived from state curricular frameworks and national standards, is the external layer that reformers continually change in their effort to alter what teachers teach and students learn. But the official curriculum rests atop three other layers that assemble and distribute knowledge and skills in the age-graded school through pedagogy, assessment, and professional development: the taught, learned, and tested curricula. This multilayered structure furnishes the house that science inhabits.

I have omitted one important fact about this multilayered curriculum. Over the past century, old curricula in reading, math, science, history, and other academic subjects have been dumped and new curricula have been introduced repeatedly. To fit this important fact into the analysis of the multilayered curriculum, I move from the metaphor

(I warned you that I would be switching metaphors!) where I compare building a house to a new curriculum to a metaphor of ocean reefs. As coral is a mass of skeletons from millions of animals that, built up over time, accumulates into reefs above and below the water line, it gets battered and reshaped by the sea as it forms into islands. Inhabitants and ships cannot ignore its presence. Like a massive coral reef, the multi-layered curriculum is surrounded by a sea of prior efforts to reform curricula that influence the course of any contemporary reform. The reef is the historical context that contains the accumulated weight of previous innovations and mandates embedded in states', districts', and schools' formal subject matter, activities, and lessons. Yet many eager reformers in science education do ignore the coral reefs and pay little attention to the historical context for the new science curriculum and how it is taught.

These strata resting in a sea of historical reform spell the difference between effective and ineffective implementation of the official curriculum. Having a four-layered structure called curriculum that has been changed time and again is precisely how reform-driven policy makers end up again and again confusing change with reform. In changing the external layer of the multilayered curriculum, decision makers are confident that they have now improved—nay, reformed—the curriculum. They believe that teachers will teach more and better science, students will learn, and test scores will mirror those improvements. When the anticipated results fail to materialize in classroom lessons and student outcomes, confusion, disappointment, and disillusion occur among reformers, practitioners, and the public.

Not only does change get confused with reform, but also judging success and failure of new curriculum standards get thorny. For example, how can a published inquiry-based state curriculum that asks teachers to have students use materials and activities through which they will discover and understand science concepts be called a success when it varies a great deal among teachers implementing it and, furthermore, differs from what teachers report and what observers see in lessons? Or can the official curriculum be called successful when the state test comprises mostly multiple-choice items that require students to parse science terms recalled from memory rather than items that require students to interpret data and display deep understanding of concepts such as evolution or photosynthesis? Much of the confusion and ultimate disappointment over the introduction of new and reformed science curricula over the past century has been in connection with the discrepancies within and between the multilayered curriculum and the historical coral reef on which it rests.

External organizations and experts lay out the purposes, desirable curriculum, and content standards in the official curriculum. Then the official content standards are reduced to district courses of study, grade-by-grade standards, actual lessons for teachers to teach, and state and local exams that students take. The strata are all there, but there are gaps, discrepancies, and contradictions within and between the layers.

Reforming Science Curricula: Oscillating Between *Learning About* and *Learning to Do* Science

To firmly establish the size and pervasiveness of those reefs, there needs to be some elaboration of prior reforms. Looking back at the century-long struggles between scientists, educators, academics, and policy makers over the purposes of teaching science and how to teach science, *learning about* science as opposed to *learning to do* science, can draw the multilayered curriculum and its historical context together.

Well-intentioned and determined reformers historically have battled over the purposes of science education. Should teachers concentrate on teaching essential content to unknowing students or have students act as scientists, inquiring and solving problems? Should teachers focus on science content that is connected to students' lives or tethered to more general disciplinary knowledge? Should teachers concentrate on students becoming scientifically literate to deal with complex real-world issues that cut across disciplinary boundaries or stick to traditional subject matter?

Stating the tensions over the aims of a science curriculum in such either-or choices, however, does not do justice to nuances and compromises that specialists and practitioners have built to reconcile these conflicting purposes and then altered as new pressures arose and societal conditions changed. Nonetheless, in 1910, John Dewey foreshadowed these struggles for the next century when he said that "science has been taught too much as an accumulation of ready-made material with which students are to be made familiar, not enough as a method of thinking, an attitude of mind."[11] Dewey saw the split that continues to divide science education reformers over a century ago.

The history of science curricula in both elementary and secondary schools reveals time and again a preoccupation with students learning the content of scientific disciplines alternating with a strong focus on engaging students in the practice of scientific investigation and applying science to daily life—between *learning about* science and *doing* science. Generation after generation of reformers seeking to alter curriculum to find the hidden treasure of better teaching and learning have left a zigzag trail of crumbs that current reformers still follow but seldom reflect on.

The next two excerpts from classroom lessons from over a century ago illustrate these tensions over the purposes and methods of teaching science in schools.

In a Baltimore city elementary school classroom in 1893, an observer described the following physiology lesson:

> In answer to the [teacher's] question, "What is the effect of alcohol on the system?" I heard a ten year-old cry out at the top of his voice, and at a rate of a hundred miles an hour, "it—dwarfs—the—body, -mind, -and—soul,- weakens—the—heart, -and—enfeebles—the—memory." "And what are the defects of tobacco?" asked the teacher. In answer to this, one boy called off, in rapid succession, more diseases than are known to most physicians.[12]

The second example, also from 1893, comes from a third-grade student in an Indianapolis school reporting a science lesson:

The Bean
First we examined it. We found it was very hard, and smooth. When we looked on the side of the bean, we saw a little eye. The skin is wraped [sic] tightly around it. It is very glossy, and white. When it is put in water to soak, it gets quite large, and it is soft then . . . I broke it open, and found a little seed leaf inside. There were two seed leaves. When we got through describing it, we each planted our beans in a box that had sand in it. Frieday [sic] we looked at our beans. We found that they had pushed the sand off of them. They were white then. The teacher covered them over again. When we came back Monday, we found they had pushed the sand off them again and had grown quite large. Some of them had turned green. They left their coats down in the dirt . . . [13]

These examples show well how, at the secondary level, a similar shut-tling back and forth occurred between teachers transmitting informa-tion and students absorbing facts of specific disciplines (e.g., physical science, biology, chemistry) and applying science to daily life (e.g., bac-teria in one's mouth, how a thermometer works, tracking the growth of a bean). And they also show the persistent distinction between *learning about* science and *doing* science.

Consider the small number of high schools over a century ago. As enrollments in U.S. high school expanded—in 1890 just over 200,000 students attended high school; by 1918, the number had increased to over 1.6 million—reformers saw the primary task as making sense out of a high school curriculum that had grown into an unwieldy mishmash of courses. As one historian tartly put it, "The high school curriculum had begun to resemble a species of academic jungle creeper, spreading thickly and quickly in many directions at once."[14] Thus, reorganizing the entire high school course of study and linking its curriculum to col-lege entrance requirements was at the top of the to-do list for a newly created national committee of educators.

The 1893 report from the National Education Association's Com-mittee of Ten on the high school curriculum (the ten leaders were uni-versity presidents and secondary school principals) cut back the "jungle creeper" of classical courses that had spread over decades (e.g., Latin, Greek, history, mathematics, morals) and replaced many with practi-cal subjects (e.g., sciences, algebra, geometry, modern languages). These subjects were more relevant to a changing America and would, they thought, equip students with the intellectual skills essential for coping with that changing society.

The Committee urged that all students take academic subjects (English, modern and ancient languages, mathematics, sciences, his-tory, and geography) and that colleges accept students who completed a standardized high school course of study. A high school education, they believed, was an education for life; it didn't matter whether students desired to go to college or get a job—all students would take the same courses.[15]

For the first time, these educators recommended an array of science courses, such as physical science, chemistry, botany, zoology, astronomy, and physiology, as well as double periods of laboratory in science courses. The Committee believed that students taking these science courses and labs would develop mental habits of reasoning that would apply to both life and college.

Overall, the Committee suggested that districts allocate at least 20 percent of student course taking to the sciences. Its proposals for an official curriculum had no legal power, but many forward-looking superintendents and school boards voluntarily adopted many of the recommendations. By 1910, the model curriculum recommended by the Committee of Ten had, according to reports from the U.S. Commissioner of Education, led to substantial increases in students enrolling in science courses.

Even so, in 1900, just over 10 percent of fourteen- to seventeen-year-olds attended high schools, and the vast majority of those earning a diploma did not go to college.[16] But the percentage grew larger each decade as parents wanted their sons and daughters to stay in school beyond the eighth grade. That shift in school enrollments occurred because the United States was going through major societal changes—and reformers turned to the schools to solve these national problems.

In the midst of rapid growth of huge corporations controlling national industries and the burgeoning population of cities fed by ever-increasing migration from farms and from Europe, coalitions of civic and business leaders aligned themselves with emerging unions and top educators to criticize public schools for not equipping elementary and secondary school graduates with the necessary knowledge and skills to cope with urban ills and to succeed in an industry-based society. Calling themselves *progressives*, these reformers—the policy elites of that time—represented various interest groups pursuing divergent goals. They believed that schooling the next generation had to be more practical, more efficient, and more connected to the work world and life in cities, and do what so many urban families, overwhelmed by economic and social problems, could no longer do for their children.[17] This unalloyed faith in the power of school reform to solve social, economic, and political ills was present in the nineteenth century, remained strong through the twentieth, and today, though pitted with buckshot and frayed at the edges, remains sturdy.[18]

So those early-twentieth-century school reformers, strong in their righteous faith in schools as the vanguard of reform, heaped criticism on the official curriculum that the Committee of Ten had recommended. They believed that altering that exterior layer of the official curriculum would improve teaching practices and what students learned, producing a far savvier generation of adults who, in turn, would make a better America. They saw that, between 1900 and 1920, the increasing number of students who continued on to high school were far more diverse in background, motivation, and interests than those who attended school decades earlier; they decided that a one-size-fits all curriculum just wouldn't work. They believed that students needed a variety of courses that would prepare them for life, for jobs, and, yes, even for college in a world very different than the one previous generations of children and youth had faced.

Progressives Revise Curricular Structure

So again, a coalition of civic leaders and educators looked for closer connections between the political, social, and economic needs of society (i.e., what employers sought in workers and citizens' political duties) and what students did in schools. And, again, another NEA group, the Commission on the Reorganization of Secondary Education (CRSE), issued a report in 1918—popularly called *The Cardinal Principles of Education*—that moved 180 degrees away from the Committee of Ten's recommendations that all students take academic subjects.

Two years later, the Science Committee issued its report.[19] Written by progressive reformers, the CRSE report focused on differentiating the official curriculum to match the diversity of students—a curriculum geared toward getting students ready for work, understanding family life, appreciating good health and ethical character, embracing the duties of citizenship, and using leisure time in worthy ways. These were the goals of schooling for the twentieth century; they were called the *Cardinal Principles of Education*. But where among these Cardinal Principles were the academic subjects that so dominated the Committee of Ten's agenda?

The progressive educators who wrote the CRSE report largely assumed that most students entering high school had less interest in academic subjects and were probably unable to handle a traditional curriculum. Using intelligence tests administered in elementary schools, educators funneled students into different courses of study in the name of equal educational opportunity rather than force all students to take the same college preparatory courses. Here is where the comprehensive high school with its multiple options for students (what came later to be called *tracking*—still alive and kicking in 2013) became a reality.[20]

And science courses? The CRSE science committee report in 1920 expressed the dominant opinion of these progressive reformers:

> Science for the high-school students has been too largely organized for the purpose of giving information and training in each of the sciences, the material being arranged in accordance with the logical sequence recognized by special students of that science . . . The common method of science teaching too often has been of presenting the so-called essential with their definitions and classifications and of subordinating or omitting the common-place manifestations of science in home, community, civic, and industrial situations which make it easily possible for the learner to practice science.[21]

In subsequent years, "common-place manifestations of science in home" and elsewhere popped up in chemistry, physics, and biology courses. Specialists urged teachers to get students to work on projects such as building electric motors, eradicating mosquitoes in a community, and delving into the chemistry of food. In biology, for instance, curriculum experts recommended that teachers have their students see how colonies of bacteria were present in humans and animals and how they grow and spread in science labs. They recommended that colonies of bacteria be linked in classroom discussions and assignments to such direct questions to students as: Why wash your hands before meals? Why brush your teeth? Why cover garbage cans? Why quarantine hospital patients who have smallpox and diphtheria?[22]

By the 1930s, the sequence of science courses in high schools had become nearly standardized into general science, biology, chemistry, and physics. Pressures from progressive educators to engage students by making these courses more practical and more relevant to student lives prompted curriculum specialists to list what teachers might do in their lessons. One promoter of a more relevant physics course asked: "How can we justify the teaching of problems in heat when we barely have time to discuss the most important applications: the gasoline and diesel engines? Of what use is air pressure unless we study the airplane?"[23] Supporters of traditional science courses (those with far more academic and intellectual goals) dismissed such efforts to engage students as "kitchen chemistry" and "toothbrush biology." But for the moment, progressives held the winning hand.[24]

A smaller percentage of students than at the turn of the twentieth century continued to take academic courses leading to college, particularly laboratory sciences; instead, most students in the 1920s took a stunning array of practical courses. By 1923, for example, Los Angeles public schools provided eighteen different curricula, which included preparation for accounting, secretarial, agricultural, building construction, and automobile jobs. Newton, Massachusetts, offered fifteen different courses of study and St. Louis, thirteen.[25]

Through the Great Depression, when high school enrollments rose to over 50 percent of youth between fourteen and seventeen years old (4.8 million youth attended high school, up from 1.6 million a decade earlier), and those receiving diplomas had soared to over 25 percent, progressive educators continued to massage the official high school curricula and multiply the options that students had for earning diplomas.[26]

An unusual progressive venture was the Eight Year Study, in which thirty high schools were freed of college admission requirements, and special classes were set up for students who, with parental permission, attended progressive classes. Rather than lectures in each of the sciences, for example, students in these special classes would plan a science unit with the teacher, and then groups of students would choose the topics that they would investigate. A later generation of reformers would call this approach *project-based learning*.

At one of the thirty high schools, the campus high school of Ohio State University School, students in the class of 1938 reported how they studied science:

> Our tenth grade schedule set aside three hours a week for science. Under the guidance of two teachers, we chose the modern scientist's conception of the physical universe for the year's study. Through lectures and charts made by the teachers, we all got a brief survey of how scientists believe the universe was formed . . .
>
> We were then able to line up a long list of individual problems dealing more in detail with the study of our solar system and its operation. Each one of us was able to choose from this list the topic in which he was most interested. After about six weeks of work, largely in the library, on these different problems, we came together as a class. The following two months were spent listening to individual and group reports . . . One striking demonstration involved a walk

from one corner of the campus to another . . . Along this walk, two girls laid out our solar system to scale. This unquestionably showed us, in a way we will not forget easily, how small the world really is.

An examination made it possible for each one of us to rank himself in comparison with the class median of achievement. We all thought that the two months spent in reporting was too long a time for this and should be cut down in the future. This system of individual research and reporting was felt to be an inefficient way of getting the scientific information. It seemed desirable, however, as it taught us to seek out the material for ourselves, to compile it into a written paper and finally to present, orally, the most important facts to the whole class. These skills were deemed highly worth having, much more so than the few scientific facts we may have lost by this method of study. The last month of the year, we decided to undertake a study of our earth's structure and how it had been formed. This was mainly a lecture course . . . An examination on the material covered in the last month ended the year's work.[27]

Keep in mind, however, that even within the selected Eight-Year Study schools, not all students participated in progressive classes. The rest of the student body at these schools took college preparatory, commercial, and vocational courses consistent with most other high schools in the 1930s and 1940s.[28]

By the end of World War II, then, the comprehensive high school—with its many curricula targeting different groups of students—focused on community, health, societal, and personal issues facing children and youth. These courses—the intended curriculum—far outnumbered discipline-based academic subjects and dominated U.S. secondary schools through the early 1950s. Across thousands of schools, the degree to which most teachers taught lessons aligned to the progressive curriculum and students learned what was in those official courses of study (including science)—the taught and learned curricula—remains to this day debated by historians of education.[29]

Reforming Science Curricula Since the 1950s

The post–World War II United States saw a huge expansion of education at all levels as veterans returned to school and families migrated to the suburbs seeking a patch of lawn, space for growing families, and good schools. The progressive reforms of the previous decades, which had tracked students into different curricula for jobs, college, and other pursuits, soon came under attack from critics.

What drove these critics to their harsh polemics was the absence of academically demanding courses in this system. Where was the disciplinary rigor of trigonometry and calculus, physics, and chemistry? Where were the meat and potatoes of "good" schooling?[30]

University Experts Lead Reform of Science Curriculum

A new generation of civic, business, and educational leaders recognized that the sciences, math, and engineering had helped the United States achieve victory over Germany and Japan (e.g., through deciphering enemy codes, inventing radar, and developing the atom bomb). The decade after World War II ushered in a period of intense scrutiny of the American science curriculum. Policy elites saw weaknesses in the teaching of science in public schools and worried over the future production of scientists. The federally funded National Science Foundation (NSF) was established in 1950 to launch programs strengthening scientific research and support of education at all levels.[31]

In 1952, NSF held the first program to deepen college teachers' knowledge of the sciences they were teaching and develop new curriculum. In 1954, NSF sponsored the first summer institutes for retraining high school science teachers; over sixteen thousand teachers attended in the 1960s. Those who taught secondary teachers in these precollegiate institutes were drawn from university biologists, chemists, physicists, and mathematicians.[32]

For top policy makers and foundation leaders, the pipeline from kindergarten to graduate study, from school to careers in science, began in elementary and secondary schools. Not only did they want to improve the science knowledge and skills of precollegiate teachers, but these NSF leaders, donors, and scientists also wanted better textbooks, better classroom materials, and better lessons taught by informed teachers.

Academic experts in biology, physics, chemistry, and math, some of whom had worked in major projects during World War II, stepped forward to lead curricular changes. All of this energy and interest in precollegiate science occurred before the Soviet Union launched the space satellite *Sputnik* in 1957. That launch sent a thunderbolt through U.S. policy elites and redoubled the already existing efforts of the federal government, NSF, and donors to focus on getting schools to produce more mathematicians, engineers, and scientists. Educating the next generation of scientists, mathematicians, and engineers became urgent, and U.S. policy makers scrutinized public schools to determine how best they could defend the nation during the Cold War. In 1958, President Dwight Eisenhower signed the National Defense Education Act authorizing large expenditures on science and math curriculum and teacher training.[33]

With funds flowing into university science departments and eager academics wanting to help strengthen the teaching and learning of curricula, scientists flocked to new projects.[34] As cognitive psychologist Jerome Bruner remembered: "No curriculum project of the first five years after that [the Woods Hole Conference in 1959] was worth its salt unless it could sport a Nobel laureate or two on its letterhead."[35] These top-drawer scientists, joined by a smattering of teachers and curriculum specialists, created a series of new texts in each of the above fields that gathered between their pages the most up-to-date knowledge and, of equal importance, advanced ways for students to think like bench scientists while connecting content to real life problems.

Through NSF funding over a twenty-year period, courses in science christened the *new* biology (Biological Sciences Curriculum Study, or BSCS), chemistry (Chemical Education Material Study, or CHEM), and physics (Physical Science Study Committee, or PSSC; and later the Harvard Project Physics, which was later renamed the Project Physics Course) were written, published, and distributed to thousands of science teachers, many of whom had attended NSF summer institutes. While nearly all of these ventures in writing new texts were piloted in teachers' classrooms, one insider reflected, "My own experience with that process suggests the results of classroom try-outs had little effect on subsequent versions. Scientists were usually hesitant to accept the criticism of their 'science' from schoolteachers unless very convincing substantiating data were provided. More often than not, decisions on revisions were based on debates and arguments among the project staffs."[36]

The new science curricula had three features:

- *Varied and flexible*: The new biology (eventually there were three versions), for example, included not only a text but student lab manuals, films, overhead projector transparencies, supplementary readings, actual lessons, and tests. Using the latest technologies, the biology course came as a package of integrated learning aids, tests, and text that teachers could use.

- *Students did science*: In both elementary and secondary curricula, designers created science materials, activities, and tasks to engage in the scientific process—sometimes called *inquiry* or *problem solving* or *discovery*—by doing what scientists do and get at basic concepts in each discipline. Using actual science materials, students could solve problems, designers said. *Hands-on* science—referring to students using practical materials delivered in the curricular packages—became a mantra teachers and champions of the science curricula recited in manuals accompanying these texts and at precollegiate summer institutes. In the new chemistry, for example, the designers stated that "Successful laboratory work . . . means that the student not only collects data in the laboratory, but also supplies ideas to his data. The laboratory experiments are presented as problems to be explored, or if you wish, puzzles to be solved."[37]

- *Disciplinary themes rather than discrete topics*: For decades, too much science across the disciplines had been a disjointed collection of separate, often unrelated, topics that may have made sense to textbook writers but were inscrutable to many students who had to memorize fact-laden concepts. To get at the heart of a discipline, academics focused on themes. In the new physics, to cite one example, designers forged linkages between time, space, and matter as a central theme to the course.[38]

The thrust of newly designed science curricula for elementary and secondary schoolteachers was to capture the essential concepts of a discipline married to a process of *doing science*, that is, teaching students to inquire and do what biologists, physicists, and chemists do in their labs. Designers created curriculum that packaged both the content and the process of doing science into texts, materials, and aids that could be easily plugged into classroom lessons. Those academics who designed these courses hinted that these new materials would need only minor adjustments by teachers. These curricular packages, champions of the new courses whispered, were nearly "teacher-proof."[39]

Results in the Classroom

What happened, then, as a result of two decades of massive investments by funders, huge amounts of time spent by teachers in institutes, and enormous expenditures for texts and packages of materials in overhauling the science curricular structure in the name of inquiry and doing science?

It is clear that many districts adopted the new materials. A national survey in 1977 reported that 43 percent of districts were using in their high schools some version of the BSSC, 15 percent were using CHEM materials and 25 percent were using either PSSC or Harvard Project Physics.

What were the other districts using? Regular textbooks. The Holt series in biology, chemistry, and physics that had dominated the market before the restructuring of science curriculum in the 1960s still retained, depending upon the science, 35 to 50 percent of the textbook market in the 1970s.[40]

At the elementary school level, the most popular curricula—Elementary Science Study, Science: A Process Approach, and Science Curriculum Improvement Study—were being used in 32 percent of district elementary schools. While not a majority, these new texts and materials had become mainstay tools for teachers implementing different approaches to science. Moreover, many of the commercial texts that had dominated the market were reorganized around conceptual categories and used an activity-driven approach to science.[41]

What is much less clear is the impact of these new courses, materials, and training on teaching practices and daily classroom lessons. If shifts in teaching practice occurred—say from fewer lectures and demonstrations to more inquiry and hands-on science—the obvious question is: did student performance on tests and other measures in science improve?

Three major sources for determining what teachers did in elementary and secondary school science lessons are summaries of science classroom teaching, a national survey sponsored by NSF in the mid-1970s, and researchers doing district case studies of schools.[42]

For example, researchers analyzed nine studies of science teaching including national surveys and concluded:

There is more use of "hands on" and laboratory types of instruction [in elementary school science lessons] . . . However, a substantial number of teachers do not emphasize laboratory activities. Lecture-discussion is the most common learning activity, followed by student demonstration. Reports and surveys indicate a substantial number of teachers (probably about 30–40 percent) teach science largely as a reading/lecture class. At the secondary level, there is less lecture and more "student-centered activity" than there used to be but lecture and discussion is the predominant method used by teachers.[43]

Another group of researchers went into eleven high schools in the mid-1970s to watch teachers teach academic subjects, including science. They wrote case studies of what they observed and gathered from interviews. Robert Stake, who headed the project, found that the teacher was central to all classroom activity and the textbook was the primary authority of knowledge presenting as "what experts found to be true."[44]

Project researcher Mary Smith reported on a small Colorado city high school science program:

Introductory Biology—instructional methods are largely lectures, lab investigations, review sheets, occasional films, and guest speakers. The text used is from the Biological Sciences Curriculum Study. *Chemistry*—the text *Modern Chemistry* is used but the approach is traditional. The vast majority of class time is spent in lectures and laboratory experiments.[45]

Researcher Louis Smith summarized what he saw in a St. Louis suburban high school's science classes:

1. In most classrooms, a section of the blackboard with assignments for each day of the week.
2. Teachers' grade books literally full, cell-by-cell, of pages of numbers.
3. Teachers carrying a stack of laboratory notebooks home to be graded (in the evening) or into class to be returned (in the early morning before school).
4. Lab books full of red ink comments.
5. Frequent classroom byplay around the question, "Does it count?"
6. Reviews before tests, taking of quizzes and tests, returning and checking of tests.[46]

More than a decade after the federal government had sponsored a restructuring of the science curriculum across hundreds of urban, rural, and suburban districts, subsidized the publishing of new textbooks, and trained thousands of teachers in the new content and ways to teach that content, such observations of science classrooms provided ambiguous, if not gloomy, answers to the central question of what in the new science curricula was implemented and how it was taught.

Or consider the answers that Wayne Welch, a participant in the Harvard Project Physics and a long-time researcher of these science curricula, distilled from twenty years of making science curriculum. He offered four conclusions:

1. With enough funding and push from the federal and state level, the rich resources of scientific professionals could be organized and directed toward solving school problems.
2. The design of courses across the science curriculum had produced a panoply of texts, instructional materials, tests, and technological aids hitherto unseen by university academics and K–12 educators that fully dominated science policy talk and action in schools for two decades.[47]

These were the positive conclusions. The next two conclusions answered the tough questions above about the impact of this major effort to alter fundamentally science curricular structures on teaching and learning. In his words:

3. The educational system is extremely stable and efforts to change it have little effect.
4. Curriculum effects account for very little of the variance in student learning. In spite of the expenditures of millions of dollars and the involvement of some of the most brilliant scientific minds, the science classroom of today is little different from one of 20 years ago. While there may be new books on the shelves and clever gadgets in the storage cabinets, the day-to-day operation of the class remains largely unchanged. A teacher tells his or her students what is important to learn and so the class progresses . . .[48]

For those promoters of inquiry teaching in all of its different incarnations since the beginning of the twentieth century, the evidence of textbook-driven teachers of science assigning questions for each chapter, doing a few demonstrations, and having recitation-like question-and-answer sessions on scientific terms, such evidence from surveys, case studies of teachers, and interviews, must have been discouraging.[49]

Yet there is a puzzle here. Teaching practices, Welch and other researchers reported, have largely remained stable, a polite way of saying there has been little change and no reform of traditional classroom practices. Surely researchers saw many teachers using the new biology or new chemistry materials and different activities adopted by teachers, although not on the scale that reformers' policy talk and action would have anticipated. Thus, disappointment—but that is not a puzzle. Mystery enters when subsequent research on student outcomes associated with science curricular changes has shown some positive effects on elementary and secondary school students' achievement from two decades of curriculum restructuring.[50] If there were few changes in teaching practice, even with the use (or perhaps the non-use) of "teacher-proof" materials, then what would explain the seemingly positive results that a few researchers found?

I cannot unlock the puzzle other than to suggest that other factors may account for this incongruity. Perhaps, teachers were effective in their traditional ways of teaching science lessons with different texts and instructional materials. Student test scores might rise over time as teachers come to know the kinds of questions that appear on tests year after year. Shifts in students' socioeconomic status might influence outcomes. These increases in scores may, indeed, reflect classroom practices unobserved by researchers. Or they may simply be erroneous, resulting from flaws in the design and methodology of the studies. Whatever the case, the puzzle of stable teaching practices amid positive achievement gains remains. Beyond this puzzle is the larger issue of what science should be taught, why, and how. The answers remain contested.

Overall, the results of two decades of intensive curriculum restructuring have left much of the content, teaching practices, and student outcomes still caught in the issues that John Dewey raised a century ago over teaching *about* science and too little about how scientists *do* science.

Restructuring Science Curricula Again and Again

In the years since the major overhaul of science curriculum in the 1960s and 1970s, however, policy elites, seemingly untouched by these questions, puzzles, and the historical sea in which curriculum reform is embedded, have continued to restructure the science curriculum. This time, not the Cold War but economic rivalries for world markets and domestic economic changes have pressed federal and state decision makers to improve schooling for the nation's children while linking those improvements to workplace productivity and reaching a larger share in global markets.

The 1983 *Nation at Risk* report triggered an avalanche of policy rhetoric about U.S. students' low scores in math and science on international tests and Japan's economic success in outstripping U.S. manufacturers and companies in producing high-quality automobiles and electronic products. Again, policy elites exhorted schools to lift their graduation requirements, raise curriculum standards, produce more college-ready students who would seek careers in math, science, and engineering to not only outscore other nations on international tests but also spur scientific innovations that would increase workplace productivity and economic growth. No accident, then, that President George H.W. Bush convened the nation's governors in 1989 and produced a list of educational goals, among them "By the year 2000, U.S. students will be first in the world in science and mathematics achievement."[51]

A slew of reports were published by professional associations of scientists including *Science for All Americans*, released by the American Association for the Advancement of Science that made the case for each and every student becoming scientifically literate by the time they graduated from high school. Groups of teachers and scientists developed curricula in biology, chemistry, and other disciplines that focused on children and youth learning science actively rather than listening to lectures, doing lab sheets, and passively memorizing scientific terms and formulas.

But the notion of scientific literacy is complicated. As Jonathan Osborne has pointed out: "Science education wrestles with two competing priorities: the need to educate the future citizen about science; and the need to provide the basic knowledge necessary for future scientists." To Osborne, "Evidence would suggest that it is the latter goal that predominates—a goal which exists at least, in part, in conflict with the needs of the majority who will not continue with science post-compulsory education."[52]

Thus, ambiguity about the purposes of science education, that familiar split between learning and doing science, between absorbing knowledge and skills and doing what scientists do, continues to plague policy makers and confuse teachers.[53]

Political coalitions of business and civic leaders, university academics, and professional associations of scientists and practitioners lobbied for school reform, for restructuring public schools and, of course, for a new kind of science education.

Data from teachers who reported their instructional practices in the early 1990s showed again that "[familiar] practices, what others would call disparagingly 'traditional' pedagogy, in science education—the taught portion of the multi-layered curriculum—still prevailed. The holy grail of inquiry instruction for all students—however defined—seemingly remained beyond the reach of most science teachers."[54]

Of secondary school science teachers, 82 percent reported that they used textbooks at least once a week (math teachers said 90 percent and social studies teachers, 94 percent). Those texts were used by 75 percent of science teachers for homework (compared with 63 percent in math and 95 percent in social studies). When it came to lecturing at least once a week, 85 percent of science teachers did so, compared with 72 percent in math and 78 percent in social studies. As for teacher-student interaction, 91 percent of science teachers reported they held teacher-led question/answer sessions (what an earlier generation called *recitation*) at least once a week, compared with 83 and 88 percent, respectively, of math and social studies teachers.[55]

At about the same time, the National Research Council began developing new science standards and in 1996 published the National Science Education Standards (NSES). While the standards did not establish the content that teachers should teach, they did cover what should be learned, how it should be taught, and how to assess content and skills. Moreover, for the first time, attention was given to teachers' professional development, different ways of assessing students, and other elements usually missing from such documents prepared by professional elites. The emphasis throughout the published standards was on science teachers using inquiry, although a crisp definition of exactly what that meant was elusive.[56]

Consider the essential features of "Classroom Inquiry" laid out in the NSES:

• Learners are engaged by scientifically-oriented questions.
• Learners give priority to evidence.
• Learners formulate explanations from evidence . . .

- Learners evaluate their explanations . . .
- Learners communicate and justify their proposed explanations.[57]

As others have pointed out, translating these features into daily lessons and figuring out how to assess whether students have learned from inquiry-driven practices—especially if students are in low-income, largely minority classrooms—can (and do) drive teachers to distraction as they try to interpret what constitutes inquiry.[58]

Writing about inquiry is far easier than practicing it in classroom lessons. And, over the past century, whether the inquiry that gets put into practice in most teachers' classrooms shows up in tangible results insofar as test scores is an entirely different matter—as this chapter has illustrated. Case studies of science teachers, student reports of teaching practices, and international and national test score data on student proficiency in science have mirrored the uneven results of these top-down efforts at restructuring curricula in subsequent years—in these efforts, policy makers can seem like desperate blackjack gamblers doubling down on cards that might finally end their losing streak.

Take test scores. Between 1996 and 2005, on the National Assessment of Educational Progress (NAEP) overall science scores of fourth-, eighth-, and twelfth-graders have largely remained the same, rising a few points at the fourth grade and dropping a few in the twelfth grade.[59] On international tests, such as Trends in International Mathematics and Science Study (TIMSS) and Program for International Student Assessment (PISA), results since the early 1990s are less than stunning. U.S. elementary and secondary students score somewhere in the middle of the sixty-five participating nations, improving a tad in science on the most recent PISA test and scoring overall "mediocre to poor" on international tests.[60]

When one turns to classroom practices, eighth-graders across the nation reported in 2005 how their teachers taught science. As summarized by researchers:

> [S]everal instructional activities stand out as more commonly practiced than others. Reading a science textbook (64 percent), taking a science test or quiz (58 percent), and having a teacher conduct a science demonstration (55 percent) were activities that more than half of eighth grade students indicated occurred almost every day or once

or twice a week. Other popular activities . . . were hands-on exercises and investigations (49 percent), talking about results from hands-on exercises (47 percent), and working with other students on a science activity or project (43 percent) . . . [61]

In addition, only 23 percent of the eighth-graders said they discussed science in the news; 15 percent read a book or magazine about science, 13 percent prepared a written science report; and 7 percent gave an oral science report.[62]

Rhetoric about low scores on international tests is as heated as it has ever been. In the decade since the NSES appeared, the nation has experienced a series of heart-stopping events: the recession of 2000–2001; the terrorist attacks of 9/11; declaration of war on Afghanistan in 2001 and, two years later, the invasion of Iraq; the emergence of China as a global economic competitor; and the economic meltdown of 2007–2008, coupled with unemployment levels approaching double digits. Yet all of these shocks did not deter policy elites from a continuing focus on the importance of improved schooling as a way of dealing with economic and foreign threats to the United States. Here is President Barack Obama speaking in 2010 to the National Urban League on the role education plays in national policy:

> [E]ducation is an economic issue—if not "the" economic issue of our time . . . It's an economic issue when countries that out-educate us today are going to out-compete us tomorrow. Now, for years, we've recognized that education is a prerequisite for prosperity. And yet, we've tolerated a status quo where America lags behind other nations. Just last week, we learned that in a single generation, America went from number one to 12th in college completion rates for young adults. Used to be number one, now we're number 12 . . .
>
> We've talked about it, we know about it, but we haven't done enough about it. And this status is morally inexcusable, it is economically indefensible, and all of us are going to have to roll up our sleeves to change it.[63]

Little surprise, then, that, again, a strong bipartisan coalition of business executives, state superintendents, governors, and U.S. presidents has lobbied strenuously and persistently for national curriculum standards to make the nation globally competitive. After 1989, when

President George H.W. Bush launched a movement to set national goals, each subsequent president has pushed the concept of developing voluntary national curriculum standards. Success finally occurred with the National Common Core standards in English Language Arts and Math. Published in 2011, 45 states have adopted both. Science curriculum standards are to be the next Common Core standard.[64]

The National Research Council—which had published NSES fifteen years earlier—released its *Framework for K–12 Science Education* in 2011. In this report, an eighteen-member committee of top scientists and educational experts drawn from the National Academy of Sciences identified key concepts and scientific practices that all students should know by the time they graduate from high school. The prestigious group puts no gloss on the present state of science education:

> Currently, K–12 science education in the United States fails to achieve these outcomes, in part because it is not organized systematically across multiple years of school, emphasizes discrete facts with a focus on breadth over depth, and does not provide students with engaging opportunities to experience how science is actually done."[65]

The *Framework*'s purposes are:

> The overarching goal of our framework for K–12 science education is to ensure that by the end of 12th grade, *all* [original italics] students have some appreciation of the beauty and wonder of science; possess sufficient knowledge of science and engineering to engage in public discussions on related issues; are careful consumers of scientific and technological information related to their everyday lives; are able to continue to learn about science outside school; and have the skills to enter careers of their choice, including (but not limited to) careers in science, engineering, and technology.[66]

These multiple and competing purposes for the newest of the new standards in science, as this chapter has documented, have a long and tortured history.

Summing Up

The dream of improving science education by altering curriculum structures to get teachers to shift routine classroom practices to teach students to learn more and better science is well over a century old. In that time, clear patterns have emerged:

• *Persistent uncertainty over the primary purposes of science education, how best to teach the subject, and assess student learning.* Multiple and competing aims for science education have plagued policy makers, academic scientists, practitioners, and reformers of all stripes for decades. Time and again, different purposes have reverberated through the multilayered curriculum and echoed previous reform efforts.

The dichotomy about teaching *about* science as opposed to learning to *do* science has run like a tangled thread through past and present efforts to alter science curricula. Transmitting content to unknowing learners through texts, lectures, and demonstrations or learners dealing with questions that scientists ask continue to produce tensions in the ranks of policy makers, curriculum specialists, and practitioners —not to mention a blizzard of slogans. Should students become literate in science to imitate scientists or literate because, as citizens, they will have to deal with questions about climate change, pollution, health, technology, and statistical claims? No certainty on answers to this and similar questions is yet evident.

• *Plans for restructuring science curricula have consistently come from the top of the policy-making pyramid, not the bottom.* Listen to the drumroll of past plans to reorganize science education: the Committee of Ten (1893); the Commission on Reorganization of Secondary Education (1918); National Science Foundation grants and the National Defense Education Act (1950s); the National Science Teachers Association and National Academy of Sciences curriculum standards (1980s and 1990s); the National Research Council's *Framework for K–12 Science Education* (2011). Academic scientists, science educators, textbook publishers, and organized teachers advance their separate interests by lobbying top decision makers to make policies that support their positions. It has been uncommon that curricular changes in science education have either begun with or spread from teachers.[67]

• *Historically, top-down designs for restructuring science education have run afoul of the multilayered curriculum in U.S. schools.* The strata of official, taught, learned, and tested curricula have revealed time and again that changes in the first layer—the official or intended curriculum—may or may not show up in other strata. Without changes in teaching practices and tests, the chances of students learning what is intended approach nil.

In the past century of science curricular change, these patterns have become clear. Incremental changes have been made time and again, but fundamental reforms of actual classroom practices have often disappointed advocates pressing for better science education. Probing deeper at the fundamental structure of the age-graded school, for example, has been missing from reformers' agenda. Nonetheless, reform-driven designs for better teaching and learning continue.

In the past quarter-century, especially since the *Nation at Risk* report, the growth of state and federal authority over education, increasing influence of corporate practices, and an audit culture of accountability and testing has shaped the conduct of schooling. A decided shift among policy makers and voters has occurred in viewing schools as "good." Before, parents and educators worried about *process*—that is, how schools operate and teachers teach; today, they worry about *outcomes*—that is, signs of effectiveness such as test scores, graduation rates, and admits to college. That is the story of yet another set of structures superimposed on public schools that seek to substantially improve what and how teachers teach. I want to tell that story in the next chapter.

Chapter 3

How and Why Test-Driven Accountability Influenced Teaching Practice

Within the past half-century, popular and policy elite opinion on responsibility for student outcomes has shifted dramatically. Where once the center of gravity resided in parents and individual students being answerable for school behavior and achievement, now the school itself has become accountable for what students achieve. That marked shift in responsibility has been accompanied by new structures intended to hold students, teachers, administrators, and school boards individually accountable for academic performance. Changing how teachers teach and how students learn was an intended outcome of these accountability structures that began to take shape over three decades ago and are now fully a part of U.S. schooling.

Business-Driven School Reform, 1970s–Present

In the late 1970s, deeply concerned over U.S. consumers buying Japanese and German electronics and automobiles and the declining market share of U.S. companies in global markets, coalitions of business, civic, and foundation leaders turned to public schools as the lever for restoring economic growth and competitiveness. With the stark warning of national doom issued in the 1983 *Nation at Risk* report, these reform-driven coalitions lobbied school districts, state legislatures, and federal policy makers to reform U.S. schools.[1] They urged districts to build regulatory structures containing incentives and penalties aimed at meeting the twin demands of producing high school and college graduates who could help U.S. companies compete in global markets and increasing equal opportunity for those at the bottom of the achievement distribution—most of whom would be needed in fast-changing labor markets prizing knowledge and analytic skills. Both academic excellence and equity would be accomplished, designers of these structures claimed, through tightly coupling state curriculum standards to testing and holding schools and teachers accountable for what students learn.

In the 1980s and 1990s, these reform-minded coalitions continued to press state and federal policy makers to enlist schools in preparing the next generation of engineers, mathematicians, scientists, and knowledge workers to help the United States compete in global markets while lifting low-performing students into the academic mainstream. As James Fallows, writing in *The Atlantic*, put it: "Today's fears combine relative decline—what will happen when China has all the jobs? And all the money?—with domestic concerns about a polarized society of haves and have-nots that has lost its connective core."[2]

The 1994 reauthorization of the Elementary and Secondary Education Act—called the *Improving America's Schools Act*—contained these economic and equity expectations and expanded rules for states to follow in creating academic standards, annual assessments aligned with those standards at certain grades, and ways of determining Adequate Yearly Progress. By the late 1990s, a swelling reform movement mobilized by these business-minded coalitions lobbied states vigorously to put into place demanding curricula, more testing, and detailed accountability for students, teachers, and school administrators. As noted, these coalitions also endorsed acquiring and using high-tech devices in schools (chapter 1) and revising the science curriculum to produce more engineers and scientists (chapter 2).[3]

By 2000, nearly every state had adopted curriculum standards for what their students should know and administered tests to assess their performance. Schools were rated on the basis of these test scores and most states had regulations for closing and taking over low-performing schools. Two-thirds of the states mandated that students had to pass graduation tests, often called exit exams, before receiving a diploma. In thirteen states, cash payments or awards flowed to schools that met their targets and showed continuous improvement. All states required school boards to publish report cards that displayed data on students' test performance, rates for attendance, dropout and graduation, school discipline, student-teacher ratios, and financial information.[4]

Behind these standards-based reforms, then, is a swap informally negotiated between policy elites and those educators charged to implement these reforms. Federal and state officials prescribe the goals and objectives that schools must meet, such as academic performance and curriculum frameworks in science and math, while leaving the process—that is, how schools meet goals and benchmarks—to the districts themselves. Embedded in that bargain are two core assumptions:

- Teachers and administrators need both incentives and penalties to fully use their expertise in getting students to absorb the knowledge and display the necessary skills to succeed in school and graduate.
- Dangling money in front of and instilling fear in educators will jog practitioners to do what they are supposed to do.[5]

These assumptions, drawing from both private- and public-sector management theory, have propelled promoters of standards-based reform to advance a tough-minded, economically relevant version of schooling tinged with a bias against teacher unions and heavily reliant on accountability regulations that would also expand equal opportunity to students who had been marginalized in largely poor and minority districts year after year. That the reform will also jolt mostly white, suburban districts and their teachers into paying more attention to their low-achieving minority and non-English-speaking students has played to the strong equity impulse embedded in test-driven accountability policies. Both excellence and equity for all, entrepreneurial reformers said, was not only possible but also in our grasp.[6]

U.S. presidents and state legislators from both political parties endorsed the assumptions and bargain driving these educational policies. Under President George W. Bush, legislators embedded those assumptions into the next reauthorization of the Elementary and Secondary Education Act (NCLB) in 2001, thus guaranteeing that these state efforts would become national policy.

With the launch of NCLB, federal mandates flowed to states and into nearly all of the fourteen thousand school districts receiving federal funds. Every student in grades 3 through 8 had to be tested in reading and math. Districts and individual schools had to display student performance data by ethnic, racial, economic disadvantaged, special needs, and English proficiency categories. Every school and district had to make Adequate Yearly Progress (AYP), and schools that failed to make AYP in four consecutive years would be restructured and, if that failed to improve scores, closed. All students were to become proficient in reading and math by 2014. Every teacher had to be "qualified." Scores of additional requirements swept over states and districts. With NCLB, curriculum standards, testing, and accountability regulations had become massive regulatory structures that states, districts, schools, educators, and parents grew familiar with in the first decade of the twenty-first century.[7]

The implementation of NCLB created an educational system that some policy analysts characterize as *coercive* or *mean*—as opposed to *nice*—accountability. The hard-nosed approach, depending on what evidence is cited (and who does the citing), has increased (or decreased) reading and math test scores, revealed large academic achievement gaps between minorities and whites, labeled nearly half of the nation's schools failures by 2011, intensified teacher-centered classroom practices, and, possibly, weakened (or strengthened) tax-supported public education.[8]

Unmistakable to teachers, administrators, parents, researchers, and policy makers is that policy makers and reform-minded entrepreneurs have not only designed, adopted, and implemented new federal and state regulatory structures aimed at increasing the efficiency and effectiveness of public schooling, but they have also succeeded in influencing classroom lessons. In the second decade of the twenty-first century, business models emphasizing effective teacher and student performance permeate public schools.[9]

So What Happened in Classrooms?

According to reports from teachers, researchers, policy makers, and journalists, the structures of standards-based curriculum, testing, and accountability regulations strongly influenced school practices and classroom teaching in the 1990s and especially after 2005 when penalties for low performance under NCLB kicked in.

Teachers reported spending more classroom time preparing students for state tests. Principals reported that they allocated more time and resources for math and reading while taking time away from science and the humanities; adopted test-prep programs for their teachers; reclassified students eligible for testing; and even changed school lunches on test days to increase students' intake of calories. Kindergartens, many teachers and parents said, had become academic boot camps for first grade. Prodded by federal officials, districts' use of phonics spread into primary-grade classrooms. Observers of upper-grade classrooms reported increased lecturing by teachers and more homework assignments from textbooks. All in all, these reports draw a portrait of highly teacher-centered lessons targeting curriculum standards and annual tests with diminishing student choice of activities, cross-disciplinary content in lessons, project-based learning, and, in general, far less student-centered teaching.[10]

Are the reports accurate? Recent teacher surveys, case studies of classroom practices, and research panels analyzing the evidence from schools and classrooms concur on both positive and negative outcomes flowing from test-based accountability.[11]

Positive and Negative Results of Increased Accountability

While much of the media response to test-based accountability has been negative when recording what teachers, parents, and administrators have said and reporting the outcomes of research studies that investigated teaching practices, test scores, and failing schools, there have been positive outcomes. High-stakes testing, for example, has led to school principals, teachers, and students working hard, rededicating themselves to high-quality classroom teaching, and learning to make their schools successful. One Wisconsin primary-grade teacher told interviewers of her students who were having trouble reading:

> When Destiny couldn't pass the [text reading level] 7, I thought, OK, that doesn't feel like a reflection of the child I normally see. But this is what she did, so I'm going to have to take action based on it. I'm going to have to adjust my teaching. I'm probably going to do with her what I did with Matthew. For the last three weeks or so, I've met with him a second time, and I gave him extra books and just really worked on using the reading strategies. I feel like I can see that Destiny isn't doing that independently without my prompting, and she has to be able to do it by herself, so I need to get her there.[12]

Principals and teachers have focused on the state curriculum standards and tried different ways of teaching to reach all of their students. Another teacher from the same study said:

Everything we do [in our school] is driven by the frameworks of the testing, even though our kids aren't tested until third grade. We're supposed to be laying the foundation, the basics, for them. And if they don't get [it] in first grade then they are just piling more on in second grade and if they don't have it then, by the time they get to third grade and they take the test and they don't do well, then you're judged—your school is judged. So our school is looking at the data . . . You're still being judged that way. We're being held accountable for what we do.[13]

Some low-performing urban schools have turned around and become exemplars for others to copy. These schools have refocused their attention on curriculum, professional development, and allocation of instructional time to align teaching with both the strengths and gaps in student knowledge and skills.[14]

One example duplicated in many districts is the elementary school reading program called Open Court, which had been mandated for all Oakland, California, elementary schools and tilted decidedly toward teacher-directed phonics instruction. I observed lessons in two schools in 2005; among my observations were two teachers holding word-by-word scripts as they and their first-grade students repeated letter sounds in unison. Yet I also observed that teachers followed the Open Court manual and arranged the classroom furniture into a square where students faced one another; they organized reading, math, and writing workshop centers for small groups to follow up on earlier instruction—all indicators of student-centeredness.[15]

Nonetheless, amid success stories of turnaround schools, there are plenty of negative consequences of regulatory accountability. For example, a RAND study of NCLB in Georgia, Pennsylvania, and California between 2003 and 2006 surveyed district educators and reported some of the positives (e.g., providing extra instruction to low-performing students) but also found that:

[T]eachers also reported narrowing the curriculum toward tested topics and focusing on students near the proficient cutoff score, and some complained of lowered morale among their peers and lack of alignment between tested goals and their local curriculum materials. Administrators were generally more positive toward the reform than teachers, but both identified similar factors that hindered their efforts to improve student performance. These hindrances included inadequate resources and lack of instructional time, but they also included students' lack of basic skills and inadequate support from parents.[16]

The narrowed curriculum has occurred mostly across urban districts and schools trying to avoid the sting of failing state tests. A reduced curriculum means that district and school administrators reallocated more time for instruction in reading and math by subtracting time for instruction in other subjects or scheduled those students who have done poorly on state exams into classes where more time was spent on English language arts and math.[17]

Observing High School Classrooms

I saw the effects of the narrowed curriculum clearly in the two days that I observed lessons at Reagan High School in Austin, Texas. I visited the school for two mornings in 2007. One of eleven high schools in the district, Reagan's low test scores had placed it on a state list of schools that would be closed if scores did not improve. Mostly low-income (85 percent eligible for free and reduced-price lunch) and minority (67 percent Mexican American—one of three students were English-language learners—and 20 percent African American), district leaders moved swiftly to insure that the test scores of nine-hundred-plus students would improve sufficiently for the school to escape closure.

District office administrators replaced the principal, added staff, and, without consulting the faculty, adopted a new model for high school improvement (First Things First).[18] This schoolwide program divided Reagan into small learning communities (SLCs), focused sharply on academic instruction, and appointed teacher-advisers, called "Family Advocates," who worked with small groups of students weekly on non-academic topics. Within the school, the state-provided math coach helped teachers with classroom strategies and materials; both administrators and teachers met frequently to establish ways of tying daily lessons to state curriculum standards, textbooks, and those test questions Reagan students had missed.

Here is what I observed and heard from teachers and students during my two-day visit.

A few students were wearing T-shirts with their SLC's color and logo; most were not. Security aides patrolled the corridors, shooing students into classes. Some students had ID badges showing their name, photo, and SLC. Motivational signs ("Hard Work Pays Off") dotted the walls of both classroom buildings.

In the atrium of the Old Mall —an open area part of the original building—a very large wooden sign posted the attendance goal: "95% and Better!!" with space for a number to be inserted next to each class, freshman through senior. A nearby wooden sign said, "TAKS Countdown!!!!" (TAKS is the Texas Assessment of Knowledge and Skills test). Below it were the words "Days Left" and, below that, "Raiders Preparing to 'Rock' the Test!!!"

Scheduling SLCs, Family Advocacy groups, electives, and sufficient in-class time for engaging and content-rich lessons remained difficult, according to teachers and students. School administrators had arranged weekly common planning time for teachers, for example, in just two of the three SLCs. The school used a varied schedule during the week I visited. One day was block-scheduled for ninety-minute periods, and the other was divided into forty-one-minute periods.

Of the fourteen classes I visited, many were small (one had only eight students; the largest had twenty-one; the average had fifteen). Most students were attentive to the teacher and worked on assigned tasks. In half of the classes, at least one or two students had their heads down on their desk with their eyes closed. Some teachers said nothing to these students; other teachers asked them to pay attention or to go to the nurse if they were feeling ill. In none of the classes did I see any open conflict between teacher and students.

Teachers collected homework from some, but not many, students. When students read aloud in class, it was obvious that many had trouble with the text or worksheet passage. In one class, a late-term pregnant student helped the teacher set up the math class for group work;

in another class, the teacher worked individually with a gang member (according to the teacher) who was trying hard to pass algebra.

I saw lessons where the teacher wrote the daily objective on the whiteboard, reviewed homework, distributed worksheets, and had question-and-answer exchanges with students. Nearly all of the lessons were geared to the state test. In one class, for example, the chemistry teacher reviewed with students how to write formulas, since such items appeared on TAKS.

Three of the fourteen teachers conducted lessons different from the norm: one social studies teacher had a thirty-minute discussion based on text and supplementary readings about the use of gross domestic product as an economic indicator; a geometry teacher used six learning centers, where students in groups moved from one station to another to complete tasks that would be on TAKS; students used graphing calculators for some of the station tasks. In another class, the teacher had students teach each other concepts of genes and alleles—items on the state test.[19]

Observing Elementary School Classrooms

A more fine-grained portrait anchored in the daily life of students, teachers, and a principal in one school for an entire year fills in the missing details in otherwise abstract generalizations often made by researchers. Journalist Linda Perlstein spent the 2005–2006 school year at Tyler Heights, a largely low-income minority elementary school in Annapolis, Maryland. Under Tina McKnight, a veteran principal, Tyler Heights went from low-performing on the brink of being named a failing school to the fourth-highest-scoring—of 170 Maryland elementary schools with more than 70 percent of students coming from poor families—in the state.[20]

How did Tyler Heights do it? No surprise that the principal mobilized the faculty to focus units and lessons on state standards with close attention to the items missed on the state test. She changed schedules to set aside more time for teachers to work on reading and math; teachers practiced daily the skills essential to doing well on the Maryland School Assessment (MSA). Teachers helping one another within and across grades became common.

But for 2005–2006, there were weak fifth-grade and third-grade classes with brand-new students and low performers from previous grades. Could Tyler Heights be a high performer two years in a row or was the previous high-scoring year a fluke? Here is an excerpt from Perlstein's observations:

> On the second day of school in Miss Johnson's third-grade class, the teacher says:
>
> > "The stuff we learn in morning math meeting is going to be on the test . . . "
> > "When is going to be the test?" [student]
> > "March."
> > "What test?"
> > "MSA—it's hard," Miss Johnson said.
> > "How many pages is it going to be?"
> > "I love the fact that you're going to tie your shoes and stop playing with them," [Miss Johnson said to the student] . . .
>
> By the end of the school day, Miss Johnson's students . . . had listened to a William Steig story about a mouse named Amos and whale named Boris who became best friends forever after the elephant saved the mouse's life. They recited the days of the week and the months of the year, created number sentences that produced the answer twenty-nine, and figured out (with some help) that you got from ninety to eighty to seventy by counting backward by ten. They had written thoughts about friendship, the theme of the first reading unit, to be posted on the bulletin board: "*I wod want a frend is Nice.*" "*Do you always have to have friends and be playful?*" They had learned that they could play kickball only if they didn't argue during games, and the failure to follow playground rules would mean a recess spent against the brick wall.[21]

An important part of the MSA was "brief constructed responses" or BCRs. At Tyler Heights, teachers worked out a formula called BATS for students to follow in answering such items on the state test. On posters hung in every classroom:

> *B*orrow from the question,
> *A*nswer the question, use
> *T*ext supports, and
> *S*tretch [use phrases like 'so I think' or 'so I know']

Students were taught to fill their paragraphs with what the school calls "hundred-dollar words" and underline them for emphasis. They included transitions, such as "because," or "so I think." And vocabulary from the state content standards or MSA word . . . "character trait," "graphic aids," "dialogue." The children were instructed to review the words on flashcards in their spare time . . . They would boast about how many hundred-dollar words they managed to include in each BCR. "$900!!!" a proud child would write at the bottom of the page.[22]

After the MSA tests were over in April with nearly sixty days of school left, principal McKnight wrote to parents:

"Now we can get back to a more normal routine of learning . . . Our students have weeks and months of learning left in the school year. The MSA tests are over, but we are just beginning the rest of the school year." In Miss Johnson's third-grade class, Jamila wrote about the end of the tests:

Sunshine on the flowers
Perfume smell in the air
Roses bloom
Insects come
Nice flowers
Good day for Games[23]

In June 2006, the state released test scores to schools.

McKnight and teachers crowded around the computer as a state official in another location helped the principal remotely read the results. All grades scored well but McKnight and teachers were worried about the third grade. They scanned the numbers and saw that 90 percent of the students were proficient in reading and 90 percent in math. "It wasn't a fluke," Tina said. She stomped her feet like a drum roll as the teachers around her hugged and cried.[24]

From Observing Teaching Practices to Accounting for Student Outcomes

Many of the positives and negatives of test-based accountability structures are captured in these word portraits of Austin's Reagan high school and Annapolis's Tyler Heights elementary schools. But two questions arise in these reports from different sources, reports from educators, and anecdotal data on the influence of test-based accountability on classroom practices:

- How and why did test-driven accountability influence classroom practice?
- Did test-driven accountability cause gains in student achievement?

How and Why Did Test-Driven Accountability Influence Classroom Practice?

Neither teacher use of technology in classroom lessons nor science curriculum changes over the decades (described in chapters 1 and 2, respectively) changed classroom practices very much. Yet mandatory testing and high-stakes consequences for students, teachers, and schools attached to those scores did.

In those urban schools where fear of, and shame in, registering low test scores could lead to restructuring, firing of staff, and possible closure, teachers did teach content and skills that mirrored state standards in subjects being tested. Students did use software programs in computer labs or in 1:1 laptop situations that reviewed content on state standards and annual tests. Yet teachers taught and retaught that content in ways that were mixes of teacher-centered and student-centered practices (e.g., arrangement of classroom furniture, small-group work) or what I have called *teacher-centered hybrids*.[25]

Part of the explanation for why hard accountability has influenced classroom practice is the shotgun marriage of metrics to high-stakes outcomes for students, teachers, and schools, a phenomenon that social scientists uncovered decades ago. Since the mid-1970s, social scientists have criticized the use of specific quantitative measures to monitor or steer policies because those implementing such policies (e.g., police officers, army captains, teachers) alter their practices to insure better numbers. The work of social scientist Donald T. Campbell and others about the perverse outcomes of incentives was available but went ignored. In 1976, Campbell wrote, "The more any quantitative social indicator is used for social decision-making, the more subject it will be to corruption pressures and the more apt it will be to distort and corrupt the social processes it is intended to monitor.[26] He drew instances of performance measures being manipulated from police statistics on solving crimes, the Soviets setting numerical goals in industry, and the United States' use of "body counts" in Vietnam as evidence of winning the war. For public schools, Campbell said, "Achievement tests are . . . highly corruptible indicators."[27]

That was nearly forty years ago. Since then, researchers have identified examples of metrics being warped in diverse fields such as network television sweep weeks, college rankings by national magazines, and physicians' performance.[28]

Educational researchers also have documented the link between standardized test scores and teachers preparing students for test items, instances of state policy makers fiddling with cut-off scores on tests, dropout rates, and straight out cheating by a few administrators and teachers. The evidence confirms Campbell's insight.[29]

Since using technology in lessons and science curricular changes were not married to high-stakes metrics, they have had less impact on teaching practices than test-driven accountability.

Did Test-Driven Accountability Cause Gains in Student Achievement?

Whether test scores have risen under the carrot-and-stick strategy of accountability structures is unclear. Laura Hamilton and Brian Stecher pointed out in 2002 after a decade of high-stakes testing (but before NCLB mandates had taken effect) that "test-based accountability remains controversial because there is inadequate evidence to make clear judgments about its effectiveness in raising test scores and achieving its other goals." After a decade of NCLB, that verdict is still intact.[30]

Some researchers say there have been improvements in reading and math; others deny such gains.[31] Some authoritative groups see a few bright spots in test scores but lambaste the law for negatively influencing student outcomes. Ideological biases from the political left and right taint assessments of the law's impact.[32] Moreover, experts in evaluation and measurement who have analyzed large data sets in job training, welfare, and medical research, commonly find flaws in federal and state officials' use of test scores to make consequential judgments about individual and groups of students, schools, and districts.

What stuns many observers is official reluctance to fix the flaws. Consider researchers Steven Glazerman and Liz Potamites' assertion that accurately assessing how students and schools perform on existing state and national tests and attaching major consequences to test scores require, at a minimum: "[A] fair school accountability system or educational program evaluation—that is, one that holds educators accountable for what they can change—must measure student achievement in at least two consecutive grades. In order to hold all grades accountable, it would require some measure of student learning in all grades. In addition, it must acknowledge the role of factors outside the control of school staff, such as the family background of the students."[33] Regulatory accountability structures, including NCLB, fall far short of that standard.

The uncertainty and controversy surrounding the impact of the law should not surprise informed observers. Gauging the impact of a complicated federal law upon the complexity of a decentralized national system of 50 states, 14,000 districts, over 100,000 schools, nearly 3.5 million teachers, and 55 million students scattered across big cities, suburbs, and rural areas is, in a word, impossible. Too many changes have occurred simultaneously in national, state, and local school reform over the past decade to even pinpoint NCLB as the causal factor that made the difference in student results.

Consider state reform packages that were legislated in Kentucky, California, and Texas in the 1980s and 1990s. Not only were tests instituted and accountability regulations mandated, but these states also made substantial changes in curriculum frameworks, funding, early childhood programs, technology, and availability of school-choice options for parents.[34] Since a cascade of other reforms accompanied test-based accountability policies, attributing any gains (or losses) in scores simply to the carrot-and-stick regulations would be foolish. What do occur are associations—correlations—that can be made with a rise (or fall) of scores. To believe that correlations can be substituted for causation is doubling down on foolishness.

Imagine, however, an independent, well-respected, assessment meeting the standards of rigorous measurement showed that NCLB did, indeed, cause student scores in math and reading to have gone up. What would a president, governor, state commissioner of education, school board, or superintendent do to keep the scores ascending? None of these policy makers would know exactly *how* the increase had occurred. Sure, there would be plenty of theories:

Maybe fear really worked. If fear is the factor that worked, then close more schools. Then go ahead and evaluate teachers on student test scores. More sanctions would be necessary to keep progress going.

Or maybe it was the "qualified teacher" provision that was crucial.

Or maybe the scores went up because different families moved in or out of the schools where test scores soared.

Or maybe the results were positive because teachers prepped students well for the knowledge and skills embedded in state tests.

Or maybe . . .

Each "or maybe" and all in combination suggest that without knowing in what way hard accountability structures worked their magic to increase or decrease test scores, no straightforward strategy of improvement emerges from knowing that NCLB or any such structure caused gains in student scores. Of course, as of this writing, no such independent, well-respected assessment meeting the above standards of measurement has shown that NCLB produced gains in math and reading.

What Is the Future of Regulatory Accountability in the United States?

When NCLB was scheduled for reauthorization in 2007, the U.S. Congress heard variously from constituents, experts, and stakeholders that it should be reauthorized as is, amended, or ended. The anger and disappointment about NCLB expressed by teachers, administrators, parents, and testing experts, generally accompanied by appreciation for the effort to improve minority achievement, staggered legislators and probably accounted for the stalled reauthorization of the law. Without much support for simply renewing the law, Congress did nothing.[35]

With the election of President Barack Obama in 2008, the noise level for revising or ending NCLB increased, yet the law remains on the books largely as it was a decade earlier. Strong similarity between the Bush and Obama administrations in educational policies (e.g., support for federal-sponsored accountability, closing the achievement test score gap, use of test scores to evaluate and compensate educators, encouraging more charter schools) suggest that major elements of NCLB—as I write in 2013—will be retained, while a few parts, such as Adequate Yearly Progress and the 2014 mandate that all students test proficient in math and reading, will be revised, giving states far more flexibility than they have now in judging school performance.[36]

There is, however, an unfortunate punch line to my version of test-based accountability: missed opportunities. A punitive system of coercive accountability has produced unintended, even perverse, outcomes that designers of NCLB and similar legislation had evidently not foreseen—for example, intense focus on test preparation of students, reallocation of instructional time away from many subjects, administrators gaming the numbers, and, sadly enough, cheating.

Another outcome: with all of the money spent and staff time invested in developing and implementing curriculum standards; buying, administering, and grading tests, and collecting, analyzing, and disseminating test data and accountability reporting, only a fraction of time and resources have been devoted to building the capacity of teachers and principals to gain more knowledge and skills in their teaching and administering. Building an infrastructure of professional development and collaboration for teachers and principals is an essential part of any serious accountability effort (even though one analyst dismissed this as "nice" accountability, advocating instead "mean" accountability[37]). I discuss this approach in chapter 6.

Summing Up

From this account of the past three decades of standards-based testing and accountability influence on teaching practice, I have reached the following conclusions;

- *Current reformers have built structures for test-based accountability to change organizational and individual behavior, and many changes, both intended and unintended, have occurred.* High-stakes, test-driven accountability policies have ignored the official curriculum and narrowed the "taught" curriculum considerably to the point that teachers, particularly in low-income, largely minority schools, teach content and skills closely matched to what will appear on state assessments. More-over, subjects such as science, social studies, and the performing arts—academic content in most state frameworks—have received less teacher attention in classroom time allotted during the school day.

High-stakes, test-driven accountability policies have intensified certain teaching practices across K–12 schools in urban districts and some inner-ring metropolitan suburban districts; teachers have fil-tered these policies through their prior beliefs and experiences and, to differing degrees, have delivered teacher-centered lessons. Thus, these testing and accountability structures have affected teaching prac-tices but not necessarily in ways nor to the degree that policy makers believed they would. These structures did create many changes across the topography of schooling and classroom practice, particularly the intensification of teacher-centered practices but hardly altered funda-mentally (e.g., shifting to student-centered instruction or ambitious forms of teaching) what teachers did day in and day out.[38]

• *The structure of accountability regulations has been put into place and, to varying degrees, teachers have changed lessons by intensifying teacher-cen-tered practices but, thus far, these changes have yet to generate the gains in student achievement that policy makers promised.* Connecting these structural changes to gains in student test scores has yet to occur. The surge of simultaneous reforms in states where scores have gone up over time make it nearly impossible to attribute those gains to "hard" accountability structures. While there are associations of test score increases with the establishment of rewards and penalties of account-ability regulations, they remain correlations. One did not cause the other. Changes, then, in teaching practices that did occur as a result of regulatory accountability have yet to be causally linked to gains in student test scores.

The three chapters in part 1 on the uses of technology in one high school at two different points in time, repeated revisions in the sci-ence curriculum, and the onslaught of test-based accountability contain a consistent pattern of policy makers establishing different structures intended to shift dramatically what teachers do in their classrooms after they close the door. The policy logic of establishing these structures to reshape teaching practices was clear: new structures can fundamentally reform teaching practices and reformed teaching practices will yield positive results in student learning. The evidence reveals, however, that these new structures have had limited influence on practice, far below what policy makers had promised, and in many instances unintended effects that raised serious questions about the worth of the structures and their minimal influence on practice. Given the policy logic driving these structural changes, without much effect on practice, there was little to no influence on student learning. The mysteries of the classroom as a black box persist. That is the message of part 1.

In part 2, I turn to another helping profession, physicians, to see if establishing new structures to influence clinical practice occurred and then compare and contrast any changes with what has happened to teachers in the past quarter-century.

PART TWO

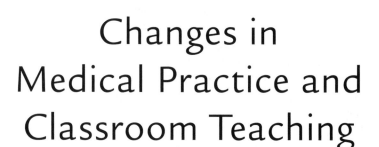

Changes in
Medical Practice and
Classroom Teaching

IN PART 2, I compare and contrast teaching and medical practice as another way of getting inside the black boxes of clinical medicine and K–12 classroom teaching. Analyzing practices of physicians and teachers may appear to readers as an odd way of finding out more about what occurs in doctors' offices and classrooms since so many differences separate the two professions, for example:[1]

- Most doctors go to school for eight years (undergraduate and graduate) to secure an MD and then spend another three to six years (of which most are supervised clinical practice) learning a specialty; most teachers in mainstream institutions spend five years (of which six months to a year are in supervised classroom practice) to earn a bachelor's and then a master's degree in education; most of those who receive alternative certification spend little to no time in supervised teaching prior to entering a classroom.[2]
- Doctors see patients one-on-one for as little as a few minutes; teachers teach groups of twenty to thirty-five students four to five hours a day.
- Medicine has been largely male-dominated until the past quarter-century, while K–12 schooling has been female-dominated for over a century and a half.[3]
- Most U.S. doctors get paid on a fee-for-service basis; nearly all full-time public school teachers are salaried.
- Evidence-based practice of medicine in diagnosing and caring for patients is more fully developed and used by doctors than the science of teaching accessed by teachers.[4]
- In terms of both social status and respect, polls rank doctors higher than teachers.[5]

While these educational, demographic, organizational, and societal differences are substantial in challenging comparisons, there are basic commonalities that bind teachers to physicians. First, both are helping professions that seek human improvement. Second, both have undergone profound structural changes in funding, technology, and professional autonomy intended to reshape the practice. These commonalities make comparisons credible, even with so many differences.

Helping Professions

The *helping professions*—from teachers to psychotherapists to doctors to social workers to nurses—use their expertise to transform minds, develop skills, deepen insights, cope with feelings, and mend bodily ills. In doing so, these helping professions share similar predicaments:[6]

Expertise is never enough.

For surgeons, cutting out a tumor from the colon will not rid the body of cancer; successive treatments of chemotherapy are necessary, and even then, the cancer may return. A primary care physician facing a chain-smoking patient knows that this high-risk behavior often leads to lung cancer—even the patient knows that—yet the doctor's knowledge and skills are insufficient to get the private equity fund CEO to quit.

Some high school teachers of science with advanced degrees in biology, chemistry, and physics believe that lessons should be inquiry driven and filled with hands-on experiences while other colleagues, also with advanced degrees, differ. They argue that naive and uninformed students must absorb the basic principles of biology, chemistry, and physics through rigorous study before they do any "real world" work in class.

In one case, there is insufficient know-how to rid the body of different cancers or stop a patient from smoking and, in the other instances, highly knowledgeable teachers split over how students can best learn science. As important as expertise is to professionals dedicated to helping people, it falls short—and here is another shared predicament—not only for the reasons stated above but also because professionals seeking human improvement need their clients, patients, and students to engage in the actual work of learning and becoming knowledgeable, healthier people.

Helping professionals are dependent on their clients' cooperation.

Physician autonomy, anchored in expertise and clinical experience, to make decisions unencumbered by internal or external bureaucracies is both treasured and defended by the medical profession. Yet physicians depend on patients for successful diagnoses and treatments. If expertise is never enough in the helping professions, patients not only constrain physician autonomy but also influence their effectiveness.

While doctors can affect a patient's motivation, if that patient is emotionally depressed, resistant to recommended treatments, or uncommitted to getting healthy by ignoring prescribed medications the physician is stuck. Autonomy to make decisions for the welfare of the patient and ultimate health is irrelevant when patients cannot or do not enter into the process of healing.

Similarly, K–12 teachers, who face captive audiences—among whom are some students unwilling to participate in lessons or who defy the teacher's authority or are uncommitted to learning—have to figure out what to do in the face of students' passivity or active resistance.

Structural changes have influenced practice.

But beyond serving in helping professions and facing similar predicaments, there is yet another reason why I compare teachers to physicians. Both occupations have undergone similar structural changes.

For decades, just as policy elites have tried to reshape teaching through creating, amending, and dissolving structures in order to improve student achievement, health care policy makers have tried similar ventures in medicine to improve the health of Americans.[7] The following chapters describe and analyze how new structures of funding, use of technologies, and managerial control through accountability mechanisms have affected professional autonomy, what physicians and teachers do in their black boxes, and whether those practices have improved overall health and achievement.

Chapter 4

Structural Changes and the Reform of Medical Practice

> *"During the 1930s, my grandmother saw a specialist about a melanoma on her face. During the course of the visit when she asked him a question, he slapped her face, saying, 'I'll ask the questions here. I'll do the talking.' Can you imagine such an event occurring today? Melanomas may not have changed much in the last fifty years, but the profession of medicine has."*
>
> —Eric J. Cassel, 1985[1]

Today, a stinging slap to the cheek of a patient who asked a question of her doctor would be extraordinary. Unfettered professional autonomy is no more. Shared decision making between doctor and patient has become the ideal.[2]

The story that Eric Cassel tells captures the doctor-centered medical practice that has existed for many decades. The growth of the medical profession since the late-nineteenth century and its structural control over entry and how doctors should practice enshrined physician autonomy to make medical decisions for patients. That autonomy was anchored in expertise first gained through undergraduate and graduate education followed by years of supervised clinical practice and then extended as doctors became solo practitioners or members of group practices and continued their education and attained additional certifications as specialists. Professional autonomy to determine diagnoses and treatments became a sacred commandment in the practice of medicine.[3]

As with the larger society over the past half-century, however, many changes—intended to be reforms—have occurred inside and outside health care that have redefined medical authority to make decisions and reshaped practice sufficiently to narrow physician discretion while increasing patient autonomy. Have such changes led to improved health for Americans?

In part 1, I described structural changes in technology, curriculum, and increasingly centralized control of schooling that occurred in tax-supported public education over the past century. In medicine, similar structural changes have occurred in funding, uses of technology, and managerial control. For most of the twentieth century, medical associations, through state certification, controlled access to physician services, established standards of practice, and suggested fees for physician services. Even with the growth of private insurers such as Blue Cross in the 1930s, doctors have had great discretion in deciding how to care for patients, which diagnoses and treatments to use, and what fees to charge.[4]

With Medicare legislation in the mid-1960s, the federal government created new structures to increase patient access to services and raise medical standards of practice. In providing equal access to health care, the legislation ended a glaring inequity tarnishing the American Creed.[5] Although these changes imposed substantial costs on the federal budget, such increased access would produce better health for the elderly and poor.

Since then, market-inspired medical policy makers have sought to reduce ever-escalating federal costs while improving patient care. Like educational decision makers determined to improve schooling, they seized different funding mechanisms (e.g., fee-for-service, salaried doctors, per-patient funding [or capitation]), new technologies (e.g., medical diagnostic and treatment, electronic health records), and managerial tools borrowed from the private sector (e.g., pay-for-performance and accountability mechanisms) to alter daily clinical decisions, increase efficiencies, and improve the quality of patient care.

Because these major structural changes interact with the basic predicaments that physicians face—the limits of their expertise, dependence on their patients in the black box of doctors' offices, clinics, and hospitals—untoward and unexpected outcomes have emerged.

Funding Medical Services and the Practice of Patient-Centered Care

The single reform that fundamentally changed the distribution of health care in the United States was Medicare legislation signed by President

Lyndon Johnson in 1965. Instead of privately funded health insurance for the middle class (e.g., Blue Cross), the federal government, in concert with states, now provided health care for the elderly and poor. Payment for medical services took the private fee-for-service arrangements that physicians had before Medicare (e.g., patients paying doctors for office and home visits, diagnostic tests, etc.) and extended them to all eligible patients under Medicare and Medicaid and private insurers. Even with the expansion of managed care and health maintenance organizations (HMOs) in the 1990s, 90 percent of primary care doctors' income derives from fee-for-service largely driven by payment for office visits.[6]

How doctors are paid and where they practice—regions where there is high and low spending for health care—influence the diagnostic and treatment decisions physicians make and the quality of patient care.[7]

Here is how that happens. Central to clinical decision making is a physician's judgment. Most diagnoses, treatments, and prognoses are informed by experience, intuition, and research-based guidelines, but many decisions about individual patients are often neither black nor white but cast in shades of gray.[8]

Consider treatments for lower-back pain or prostate cancer, or whether doctors should see patients with hypertension every three or six months. Different doctors in different places faced with patients with similar symptoms often come up with different answers to the same question. As one journalist put it: "Cardiologists in Davenport, Iowa, are quick to insert stents; cardiologists in Iowa City and Sioux City are not. They can't both be right. Some people with heart disease are getting the best treatment, and some are not. The same is true of debilitating back pain, various cancers and even pregnancy."[9] And that is where post-1965 fee-for-service enters the picture.

In 2006, the federal government and third-party insurers paid the nearly 700,000 physicians in the United States, both specialists and primary care, on the basis of patient visits to their offices and clinics and other services. Although only one-third of all physicians (209,000) are in primary care, they account for over half of all patient visits. Because of fee-for-service payments, volume of visits matters greatly to primary care doctors. Seeing more patients at the office, clinic, and hospital means more revenue for doctors who, unlike specialists, do not order as many diagnostic tests. This leads to squeezing more visits into the workday. The amount of time per patient—between ten and twenty minutes—means that some questions and some issues go unmentioned in the encounter or are hurriedly covered as both doctor and patient sense that their time together is brief. Moreover, insurers do not pay for doctors calling, e-mailing, or engaging in other non–office visit interactions with patients. Inadequate time to talk with and listen to patients has been a constant complaint of physicians.[10]

Even when doctors band together to figure out ways to benefit patients and save money, insurers rather than the primary care physicians reap the gains. One example will suffice:

> A physician group paid primarily on a fee-for-service basis instituted a new program to improve blood sugar control for diabetic patients. Specifically, pilot studies suggested that tighter diabetic management could decrease hemoglobin A1c levels by 2 percentage points for about 40 percent of all diabetic patients managed by the physician group. Data from two randomized controlled trials demonstrated that better sugar controls should translate into lower rates of retinopathy, nephropathy, peripheral neurological damage, and heart disease. The savings in direct health care costs (i.e., reduced visits and hospital episodes) from avoided complications have been estimated to generate a net savings of about $2,000 per patient per year, on average, over 15 years. Across the more than 13,000 diabetic patients managed by the physician group, the project had the potential to generate over $10 million in net savings each year. The project was costly to the medical group in two ways. *First, expenses to conduct the project, including extra clinical time for tighter management, fell to the physician group. Second, over time, as diabetic complication rates fell, the project would reduce patient visits and, thus, revenues as well. But the savings from avoided complications would accrue to the insurer or a self-funded purchaser* (italics added).[11]

In short, fee-for-service, in this instance, acted as a *disincentive* to deliver the highest-quality care for patients.

And this core funding mechanism affects patients daily as they negotiate a complicated health system rhetorically committed to patient-centered practice but entangled in public and private insurers reliant on fee-for-service. Consider the case of "Ms. Martinez," a composite vignette of actual patients' experiences in an urban health care system.

Ms. Martinez, a divorced working mother in her early 50s with two children in junior high school, was new in town and had to choose an insurance plan. She had difficulty knowing which plan to select for her family, but she chose CityCare because its cost was comparable to that of other options, and it had pediatric as well as adult practices nearby.

Once she had joined CityCare, she was asked to choose a primary care physician. After receiving some recommendations from a neighbor and several co-workers, she called several of the offices to sign up. The first two she called were not accepting new patients. Although she knew nothing about the practice she finally found, she assumed it would be adequate.

Juggling repairs on their new apartment, finding the best route to work, getting the children's immunization records sent by mail, and making other arrangements to get them into a new school, Ms. Martinez delayed calling her new doctor's office for several months. When she called for an appointment, she was told that the first available non-urgent appointment was in 2 months; she hoped she would not run out of her blood pressure medication in the interim.

When she went for her first appointment, she was asked to complete a patient history form in the waiting room. She had difficulty remembering dates and significant past events and doses of her medications. After waiting for an hour, she met with Dr. McGonagle and had a physical exam. Although her breast exam appeared to be normal, Dr. McGonagle noted that she was due for a mammogram.

Ms. Martinez called a site listed in her provider directory and was given an appointment for a mammogram in 6 weeks. The staff suggested that she arrange to have her old films mailed to her. Somehow, the films were never sent, and distracted by other concerns, she forgot to follow up. A week after the mammogram, she received a call from Dr. McGonagle's office notifying her of an abnormal finding and saying that she should make an appointment with a surgeon for a biopsy. The first opening with the surgeon was 9 weeks later.

By now, she was very anxious. She hated even to think about having cancer in her body, especially because an older sister had died of the disease. For weeks she did not sleep, wondering what would happen to her children if she were debilitated or to her job if she had to have surgery and lengthy treatment. She was reluctant to call her mother, who was likely to imagine the worst, and did not know her new coworkers well enough to confide in them. After calls, she was finally able to track down her old mammograms. It turned out that a possible abnormal finding had been circled the previous year, but neither she nor her primary care physician had ever been notified.

Finally, Ms. Martinez had her appointment with the surgeon, and his office scheduled her for a biopsy. The biopsy showed that she had a fairly unusual form of cancer, and there was concern that it might have spread to her lymph nodes. She felt terrified, angry, sad, and helpless all at once, but needed to decide what kind of surgery to have. It was a difficult decision because only one small trial comparing lumpectomy and mastectomy for this type of breast cancer had been conducted. She finally decided on a mastectomy.

Before she could have surgery, Ms. Martinez needed to have bone and abdominal scans to rule out metastases to her bones or liver. When she arrived at the hospital for surgery, however, some of this important laboratory information was missing. The staff called and hours later finally tracked down the results of her scans, but for a while it looked as though she would have to reschedule the surgery.

During her mastectomy, several positive lymph nodes were found. This meant she had to see the surgeon, an oncologist, and a radiologist, as well as her primary care physician, to decide on the next steps. At last it was decided that she would have radiation therapy and chemotherapy. She was given the phone number for the American Cancer Society. Before 6 months had gone by, Ms. Martinez found another lump, this time under her arm. Cancer had spread to her lung as well. She was given more radiation, then more chemotherapy . . . [12]

Even when well-intentioned physicians, nurses, and medical personnel are committed to patient-centered practice, when fee-for-service dominates public and private insurers, the system for many patients—including Ms. Martinez—becomes unsafe, ineffective, untimely, inequitable, and uncaring. Current funding of medical services within the U.S. health care system does shape how primary care and specialty physicians practice. That includes the pervasive use of new medical technologies.

New Medical Technologies and Patient-Centered Care

Physicians have steadily adopted new technologies from the early-nineteenth-century stethoscope to the X-ray decades later to late-twentieth-century computer tomography scans. Such rapid adoption of new technologies has been (and is) common in medicine. What is uncommon is that medical technology, in concert with new structures of funding through public and private insurers, has in the past half-century come to dominate clinical practice among specialty doctors (but less so among primary care physicians whose revenue is largely generated by office visits). How come?[13]

Public and private insurers pay doctors not only for visits to offices, clinics, and hospitals but also for the diagnostic tests they order (e.g., blood work, sonograms, X-rays, scans), and the treatments they deem best in light of an emerging diagnosis. They also prescribe more medications and screen healthy patients for possible diseases (and schedule more tests for such screenings), since the system of payments from private and public insurers encourages such practices. Fee-for-service payments depend on the number of patient visits, diagnostic tests, and treatments covered by insurers.[14]

Surveys of physicians, in part, confirm this practice of securing additional tests beyond what may be necessary for the patient. Consider—in a recent survey of primary care physicians, 28 percent said they ordered more tests or referred patients to specialists—their operational definition of *aggressive care*. When asked why, physicians responded that they feared malpractice litigation, had to meet clinical performance measures set by insurers, and had insufficient time with patients. Recently, a group of nine medical groups of specialists tried to counter this trend by laying out recommendations that would reduce diagnostic tests (e.g., imaging tests for many cases of lower-back pain).[15]

To see how fee-for-service infiltrates daily clinical practice, do the following thought experiment. Suppose you want to build a house for your family. You will need experts, expensive equipment, and materials. And you have to coordinate all of these. However, instead of hiring a general contractor to oversee masons, carpenters, electricians, plumbers, and other specialists, suppose you paid electricians for every outlet they recommended, carpenters for the cabinets they thought you needed, plumbers for all the faucets they wanted to install, and masons for walks they thought you should have. In the end, the house would have hundreds of outlets, scores of cabinets and faucets, and a plethora of winding walks. The expense would be astronomical, and the house would be in dire trouble a few years later.[16]

Physicians, researchers, and policy makers say that lack of coordination and mindfulness in building such a house is what has occurred with fee-for-service dominating private and public payments to most physicians. One doctor pointed out that in the analogy, primary care physicians would act as general contractors in coordinating health care for patients. But family medicine and primary care practitioners are shrinking in numbers, while economic incentives through fee-for-service nudge specialists to order diagnostic tests and prescribe treatments using the latest technologies.[17]

When specialists form groups or hospitals invest in the latest equipment (e.g., imaging machines) and procedures (e.g., arterial stents), incentives to use both often multiply. For cardiologists, inserting stents to keep arteries open is a huge moneymaker ($30,000–$50,000 per procedure). As one medical researcher said: "In many hospitals, the cardiac service line [stent] generates 40 percent of the total hospital revenue, so there's incredible pressure to do more procedures."[18]

Financial incentives are especially evident in shaping clinical practice when the federal government puts its fiscal muscle behind certain medical technologies. For example, in the 1960s, a machine was invented to cleanse blood of the impurities caused by kidney failure. It saved lives but was so expensive that only the wealthy could take advantage of it. In 1973, the U.S. Congress amended Medicare to cover full costs of dialysis for patients who would otherwise not have been able to afford it. Dialysis is now a common treatment.

Electronic Health Records, Patient Care, and Cost Control

Now consider another new technology that the federal government has pushed by offering numerous cash incentives: electronic health records (EHR).[19] Keeping patient information in a single electronic record allows physicians to better coordinate treatment preventing errors in diagnoses and prescription of contraindicated drugs, among other benefits. In short, electronic health records are supposed to improve quality of patient care and cut costs. Yet physicians have been slow to adopt them.

In the 2009 American Relief and Recovery Act (often called the *stimulus bill*) federal policy makers budgeted nearly $40 billion over the next decade to get hospitals and physicians to convert paper patient records into electronic form. The law requires that by 2014, all hospitals, physicians, and medical agencies directly serving patients will have implemented EHR. That promise comes after forty years of reform-minded physicians in hospitals and medical schools pushing computerized health records to little effect; at the time the bill was passed, studies showed only 9 percent of hospitals and 17 percent of physicians using EHR in 2008. Two years later, those percentages had increased to 35 and 33, respectively. And in 2011, over half of physicians report they are using some form of EHR in their practice. These figures include those centrally administered health care organizations such as Kaiser Permanente, the Mayo and Cleveland Clinics, the U.S. Veterans Administration, Geisinger Health System, Intermountain Healthcare, and similar entities. In all of these organizations, doctors are salaried rather than paid under fee-for-service plans and teams of medical staff collaborate on patient care.[20]

While there is a great distance to cover and many more dollars to spend, slow progress toward the 2014 deadline is being made. And according to many physicians, EHR has improved quality while cutting costs. As Cleveland Clinic doctor Randall Cebul said: "I recently treated a patient who had frequent episodes of fainting spells. Using my clinic's EHR, I was able to quickly pull up her medical history, which included recent diagnostic tests, and make an appropriate treatment decision. Without an EHR, my decision would have been delayed and I would have had to order redundant tests, ultimately wasting thousands of dollars."[21]

Maybe not. A recent study showed that, at the same Cleveland Clinic, costs had not been reduced. After a decade's experience with EHR and $100 million investment in hardware and software at the Clinic, the study was amplified by the report of an investigative journalist, Emma Schwartz, who concluded that no cost savings had occurred.

Schwartz cited the example of one patient who could now step on a scale at home and prick a finger for blood. The results were recorded on the patient's EHR at the Clinic, where his physician could monitor his diabetes without seeing him face-to-face. Beyond this one reported case, Schwartz heard from Clinic doctors that the quality of diagnoses and decreased errors in medical decisions added up to improved quality of care in their hospitals, one of the oft-repeated objectives of EHR initiatives. But after almost a decade, "cost savings have not materialized and hospital officials are not certain when they will," according to Schwartz.[22]

One report from an investigative journalist, however, will hardly slow the federally fueled financial incentives to get more doctors and hospitals to use EHR as a way of improving quality and cutting costs.

Another recent study using a national population of primary care physicians cast doubt on the effectiveness of EHR in reducing physicians' orders for diagnostic tests such as MRIs and CT scans—one of the major advantages of EHR touted by its champions. Researchers examined nearly twenty-nine thousand patient visits to approximately twelve hundred physician offices in 2008. They found that, contrary to the predictions that EHR would reduce costs, doctors with access to EHR ordered 40 to 70 percent *more* imaging tests and more blood tests than doctors who lacked access to digitized records.[23]

The benefit of using digital records or technology in medical practice is not the issue. There is general agreement that EHR is worthwhile and will occur. Differences over the pace of adoption and the extent of use will arise but are tangential. As the lead author of the above national study said about EHR: "I'm a primary care doctor, and I would never go back."[24]

The issue, then, is the overall fragmented, decentralized structure of an entire healthcare system still dependent upon fee-for-service. As Steve Lohr, a *New York Times* journalist who wrote a series of articles on EHR, said: "An electronic health record is a tool, one that will be used by people in response to the incentives they are given. The American health care system is predominantly fee-for-service. Doctors and hospitals are reimbursed delivering more treatment, so we get more of everything— tests, surgeries, pills."[25]

EHR and similar technologies, contrary to the hype (and recall the heated hyperbole from vendors and high-tech reformers around teacher use of computers in classroom lessons) is not the answer to achieving significant cost reductions and improved patient care. According to Lohr, most experts agree: "[B]ig savings in American health care . . . will come from making sure people with chronic conditions like diabetes and heart disease manage their conditions, stay healthy and out of hospitals." This is the clinical practice that will reduce costs and add years to people's lives.[26]

Reshaping Medical Practice Through Integrated and Accountable Care Structures

The picture I have drawn thus far is too bleak, painting physicians as merely following revenue streams in a national Rube Goldberg contraption of private and public reimbursement of medical delivery rather than exercising professional judgment to help patients lead healthy lives. When one examines the full range of physician groups and individual clinicians in how they practice medicine on a daily basis, a different picture emerges that leavens the cheerlessness I have so far portrayed. It is a picture of very busy primary care and specialist physicians stretched for time to spend with patients, using new and old technologies to inform their decisions, balancing empirical data with intuition-enhanced experience in making judgments while coping with the inevitable uncertainty that surrounds diagnoses and treatments for individual patients. It is a picture in which national groups of doctors recommend that patients ask key questions and go further to urge members of their groups to reduce expensive diagnostic tests in situations where they are either unneeded (e.g., imaging for lower-back pain) or use lower-priced ones (e.g., an ultrasound rather than a CT scan for a patient who may have appendicitis).[27]

Adding to this brighter picture are policy analysts and medical researchers who point to Kaiser Permanente (California), Mayo Clinic (Minnesota, Florida, and Arizona), Cleveland Clinics (Ohio), Geisinger Health System (Pennsylvania), Intermountain Healthcare (Utah), Grand Junction (Colorado), Palo Alto Medical Foundation (California), and other entities as organizations that work on preventing illness and delivering integrated care to their patients. They are nonprofit, largely employ salaried physicians, and are patient-centered. They have figured out how to use medical technologies selectively in the interest of reducing uncertainty in diagnosing and treating patients even though they operate in a fee-for-service environment that rewards quantity in delivering care. These integrated care organizations and their successors—*accountable care organizations* (ACOs) in the 2009 Affordable

Care Act—avoid treating sick people as electronic "iPatients." They have worked at defanging the financial incentives that account for extravagant use of new technologies while lowering overall costs and delivering high-quality care. Whether their patients are healthier and live longer than others with similar conditions who go elsewhere for medical attention is unknown.[28]

Much has been written about integrated care at Mayo Clinics, Kaiser Permanente, and other similar organizations. Accountable care organizations, however, are recent inventions. Collections of medical care providers including primary care doctors and specialists, nurses, pharmacists, social workers that are paid by public and private insurers to care for a group of patients instead of being paid for each office visit and each test ordered, ACOs are talked about frequently but less often described when it comes to patient care.[29]

Consider Fannie Cline, a sixty-nine-year-old retiree living on Chicago's South Side. Cline has Type 2 diabetes accompanied by frequent dizzy spells that took her repeatedly to the emergency room of a nearby hospital. A few months after her last visit to the emergency room, a registered nurse and care manager from Advocate Health Care, a doctor-led ACO managing Illinois hospitals and clinics caring for over 200,000 patients insured by Blue Cross, began visiting Cline. This nurse talks with and listens to Cline, advises her on diet and exercise, orders meals, and schedules appointments with doctors and a social worker. With fewer dizzy spells and no stays in the hospital, Cline now spends time with her friends, remarking, "It is nice to have someone call you in between your visits to the doctor's office to see how you are. If my blood sugar is elevated and I feel off balance, she will ask me what I have been eating lately. She might say, 'Maybe you need more oatmeal and fruit.'"[30]

Led by primary care physicians who collaborate with other professionals, ACOs seek to reduce costly hospital visits and keep patients healthy. Whether these structures will survive in a feverish cost-cutting environment, even after the U.S. Supreme Court has ruled that the Affordable Care Act is constitutional, is yet unknown. Nonetheless, the quest for both specialists and primary care physicians to be collectively patient-centered and deliver high-quality medical diagnoses and treatments while preventing further illnesses remains a more realistic pursuit than fully automated and remote diagnoses and treatments that futurists paint for clinical medicine.[31]

Integrated care organizations and ACOs offer a model to both primary care and specialist physicians for ways of leading, rather than following, cost-constrained clinical practice. Understanding that health-care costs have to be reduced and that the overall systemic structures of fee-for-service drive up costs, shrink doctors' discretion to make judgments by standardizing decision making, and add little value to the quality of care, many physicians have criticized the pervasiveness of high-tech diagnostics, including EHR, on more basic grounds than cost, uncertain outcomes, and standardization. Such doctors talk about the importance of the relationship between patient and physician and how new medical technologies have too often replaced traditional, slower ways of gathering information from patients and in doing so have undercut the trust and confidence patients have in their physicians, thus compromising healing and caring for the ill.

For many doctors, physical diagnosis—touching a patient's body to ascertain normal and abnormal functions—is becoming a lost art, seldom practiced after it is taught in the first two years of medical school. This is because once students enter the clinical phase of their training, they see that daily practice means "getting tests ordered and getting results, having procedures like colonoscopies done expeditiously, [and] calling in specialists," according to Abraham Verghese. Verghese points out that beyond the importance of carefully touching the body of the patient to diagnose illnesses, there is the ritual of a physical exam, one that often establishes trust between the patient and the doctor. After examining an elderly woman in his hospital ward, he comments, "Rituals are about the crossing of a threshold, and in the case of a bedside exam . . . is the cementing of the doctor-patient relationship, a way of saying: 'I will see you through this illness. I will be with you through thick and thin.'"[32] Caring and trust, the precious ingredients of the doctor-patient relationship, do not appear in the metrics used to assess medical effectiveness; also missing from the Medicare incentives that reward doctors' use of high-tech tools are listening to the patient and spending time doing a physical exam.

Integrated care organizations such as Mayo and Cleveland Clinics and ACOs like Advocate Health Care are examples of a new medical model of conservative testing and shared decision making between doctor and patient in the diagnosis, treatment, and prevention of illness. However, these organizations account for only a small fraction of the medical care dispensed in the United States. For the vast majority of primary care and specialty doctors working in offices, hospitals, and clinics, I now turn to those structures and metrics that policy makers and managers use to establish and monitor physician accountability for medical diagnoses and treatments.

Reshaping Medical Practice Through Pay-for-Performance

Public and private insurers, in efforts to reduce costs, increase quality care, and produce healthier Americans, now exert managerial control over those financial incentives rewarding physicians' practices and procedures. They have created pay-for-performance plans that assess how well medical organizations and doctors' practices produce outcomes consistent with evidence-based clinical guidelines. Imposing accountability through pay-for-performance—as has occurred for teachers and administrators in schools—highlights even further the predicaments and dilemmas that physicians face in caring for their patients.

Largely propelled by top government policy makers deeply concerned by accelerating health-care costs, an accountability movement has grown over the past two decades to measure, report, and reward doctors' performance in hospitals, clinics, and office practices. As educational policy makers seeking to improve public schooling have done, health-care decision makers have borrowed from the profit-driven corporate world. These educational and health-care-policy makers assumed that market competition and economic incentives for individuals and organizations would produce, as they have in the private sector, more innovations, greater efficiency (i.e., lower costs) and better outcomes for students and patients. Furthermore, they assumed that:

- Performance metrics validated by research studies could be identified.
- Doctors in hospitals, offices, and clinics would be motivated by socioeconomic rewards to put these measures into practice.
- Achieving those performance measures would alter the larger health-care structure sufficiently to reduce medical errors, cut costs, attain a higher quality of patient care, and lead to better health outcomes.[33]

Acting on these assumptions, the Centers for Medicare and Medicaid Services (CMS) and private insurers identified numerous pay-for-performance measures confirmed in large part by evidence-based medicine; they then implemented these measures in hospitals, clinics, and doctors' offices. For example, there are process measures for hypertension and heart disease where, periodic readings of patients' blood pressure and blood sugar levels are taken. But single readings do not tell physicians whether the patient is bringing these diseases under control. So *intermediate outcome measures* that focus on patients' actual blood pressure and blood sugar levels over time are noted to indicate whether the patient is improving, stable, or deteriorating.

Then there are *final outcome metrics* that record what happened to patients who received treatment in hospitals, went to another facility, or returned home. Complications after surgery such as infections, strong reactions to chemotherapy that require readmission into hospitals, or death are examples of such measures. There are also patient-reported outcomes, such as satisfaction with medical treatments in hospital and the quality of care received. CMS and private insurers identified scores of such measures as a basis for allocating or withholding payments to hospitals, groups of physicians, and individual doctors.[34]

As one would expect when attaching high stakes to metrics in a helping profession such as medicine (or schooling) where there are many stakeholders (e.g., insurers, employers, doctors, medical staff, patients), views on pay-for-performance measures diverge, especially since insurers have published "report cards" displaying rankings, percentages, and results of these different measures for organizations and individual doctors. Divergent views of performance measures and report cards are inevitable when one examines the complex terrain that physicians inhabit and the predicaments they inherently face: expertise is never enough, making decisions amid uncertainty is common, and dependence on the patient for improvement is essential. No surprise, then, these metrics and their outcomes, thus far, have generated strong and mixed reactions.[35]

Many policy makers, administrators, and doctors are satisfied that the measures are consistent with findings derived from evidence-based medicine and their experiences with patients. They welcome efforts to raise the quality of care and reduce costs. While many specialists and primary care doctors agree with the policy initiative, they still question the measures because they know that these metrics—even when evidence-based medicine endorses them—seldom pick up individual differences between patients who have similar diagnoses. Or as one doctor put it: "Human beings are not uniform in their biology."[36]

One pediatrician whose practice includes adolescent girls tells the story of what happened to him when one of his insurer's measures of quality care is a requirement to test all sexually active girls for chlamydia, a sexually transmitted infection. Since insurers do not and cannot read every single medical chart, they use a proxy measure to determine whether a girl is sexually active: they check to see if patients take birth control pills. That proxy complicates matters greatly, because the pediatrician's patients don't take those pills for contraception, but for acne and menstrual pain.

The pediatrician asked a colleague: "So do I skip the testing for chlamydia and fail my quality standards? Or do I order a test that the patient doesn't need and that will probably not be covered by her insurance?" He ended his story by saying: "I'm all for quality. I just don't think this is quality."[37]

The current report card of another primary care physician, who has been highly ranked in the past on these measures from the local health insurer, left her dismayed: "The quarterly report card sits on my desk. Only 33 percent of my patients with diabetes have glycated hemoglobin levels that are at goal. Only 44 percent have cholesterol levels at goal. All my grades are well below my institution's targets. It's hard not to feel like a failure when the numbers are so abysmal."[38]

She pondered the report card and told a colleague: "[They] focus on diabetes in pristine isolation [when] my patients inconveniently carry at least five other diagnoses and routinely have medication lists in the double digits." Moreover, she noted, one of her patients has diabetes that can be controlled but has failed to come into the office regularly even though staff had contacted her many times. The doctor told her colleague that the patient "just can't afford to take that much time off from work," and asked, "Does that make me a worse doctor?"[39]

These recent policy efforts to create structures of accountability through establishing performance measures and dispensing monetary rewards to those who reach the benchmarks end up steering clinical practice (and teaching practice as well) toward standardization. The physicians (and teachers) I have described are caught in multiple predicaments of helping professions. They are enmeshed in the struggle that has been going on for decades over the worth of their intuitive judgments versus empirical evidence when uncertainty reigns and the abiding quandary of being dependent on patients for success when the metrics make the doctor wholly responsible for outcomes. Now the full-court press policy makers, saturated with data, have mobilized to standardize medical decision making to increase efficiency and effectiveness.[40]

Eliot Friedson, a sociologist who studied the rise of professionalism in medicine, saw elements of this struggle for the mind and heart of physicians a quarter-century ago. In 1988, he wrote:

> The basic issue may be put very simply. If officially approved diagnostic categories and treatment and management procedures are narrowly defined and enforced, this does not merely limit the physician's autonomy. It also treats patients as standardized objects rather than idiosyncratic individuals. It forces many patients into Procrustean categories and excludes others from treatment entirely unless they can afford to pay out of pocket. It is true that the closer the methods of controlling cost and quality come to resemble those employed in the industrial production of goods, the lower the monetary cost per standardized unit. But such 'efficiency' is gained at the cost of transforming most patients and their problems into industrial objects and withholding services from others.[41]

This clash is historic in the sense that there have always been tensions between using data to make decisions and intuitive, experience-based decision making both in medical and teaching practice. It is not either-or, since both often come together in making decisions. A balance, however, must be found between them. But in the United States today, with its ever-rising health costs and the enormous increase in technological access to information, what dominates the corporate sector, federal government, the military, police, judiciary, and education are data-driven decisions. These new structures for making physicians and teachers accountable through incentives and metrics fully display these converging forces.

As with attempts to use metrics in other institutions that try to capture the effects of teachers, social workers, police officers, military personnel, and federal and state policymakers, the task may at the onset seem manageable and quantifiable but, over time, especially when high stakes like money, social status, and promotion accompany the metrics, unintended, even perverse, outcomes often result. The fact is that attractive incentives corrupt measures. I pointed to the work of social scientist Donald T. Campbell in the mid-1970s about the perverse outcomes of incentives, and his observation that using quantitative indicator for social decision making will corrupt the social processes it is intended to monitor.[42] I also offered many examples of the untoward consequences of performance measures attached to testing and NCLB. In clinical practice, evidence of a similar corruptibility is slowly mounting.

Consider that many of the measures used to rank and reward doctors come from guidelines drawn from extensive research studies that are designated as best practices; for example, patients getting regular mammograms, Pap smears, and screening for high cholesterol, diabetes, high blood pressure, and colon cancer. Health insurers want physicians to use these evidence-based practices to standardize delivery of quality care, improve health of patients, and reduce medical costs, yet actions of patients are not taken into account.

Health insurers, at the same time, also evaluate and pay doctors on the frequency with which they use these evidence-based practices. Billions of public and private dollars are now invested in evaluating and paying doctors for hewing to best practices. Policy makers believe that were individual incentives distributed on the basis of performance, employees, teachers, and now clinicians will work harder and do the right things for their customers, students, and patients. Customers then would be satisfied with what they purchased; students would gain in achievement; patients would lead healthy lives.

A few medical practice examples will help underscore this point. Medicare requires—as a quality process measure—that doctors administer antibiotics to a pneumonia patient within six hours of that patient's arrival at the hospital. However, as one physician notes: "The trouble is that doctors often cannot diagnose pneumonia that quickly. You have to talk to and examine the patient and wait for blood tests, chest X-rays, and so on." What's worse, he continues, is that "more and more antibiotics are being used in emergency rooms today, despite all-too-evident dangers like antibiotic-resistant bacteria and antibiotic-associated infections."[43] So the measures themselves actually endanger patients. Another perverse outcome is physicians delivering suboptimal care to cheat on their results. For example, surgeons will from time to time choose reasonably healthy patients for heart bypass operations and ignore elderly ones who have three to five chronic ailments to insure that results look good.[44]

Medical researchers also know about the effects of low-income, underinsured, and non-English-speaking patients on the rankings doctors receive on the quality of care they render, especially if rewards or penalties are attached to such rankings. One study involving 125,000 patients revealed that doctors who cared for older or sicker patients were ranked higher (probably because of frequent follow-up, behaviors that received higher scores) than those doctors who cared for minority and underinsured patients who saw doctors irregularly. Which patients doctors care for, then, affects their rankings in pay-for-performance plans.[45]

In light of emerging evidence that untoward, even contrary, outcomes occur when cash incentives accompany measures, these pay-for-performance plans have brought to light a previously hidden assumption: doctors are totally responsible for what happens to patients and patients, perversely, play no part in healing. A "no-excuses" assumption drives pay-for-performance plans as it has in schools and classrooms. In the quest for physician accountability, the historic predicaments that doctors have faced in patient care have been systematically ignored. In effect, doctors have not only been blamed for causing the problems of rising health care costs, committing errors in diagnosing and treating patients, and dispensing differentiated care to the ill based on geography and socioeconomic status, policy makers establish accountability structures with metrics for evaluating, ranking, and paying physicians that will remedy both problems.

Summing Up

In 2013, medicine is no longer a doctor-centered profession. A half-century earlier, physicians had unfettered authority to diagnose and treat illnesses in the patients who came to them. It was certainly not a golden age of medicine by any means, given the mortality and morbidity rates of Americans and racial, ethnic, and social class inequalities of the time, but a period characterized by immense doctor discretion in decision making.

Since the mid-twentieth century, U.S. clinical practice has shifted slowly and unevenly from a physician-centric occupation to one where the ideal of medical practice is to be patient-centric. It is now an occupation, however, where a doctor's autonomy to diagnose and treat is considerably constrained. Certainly, the physician's authority—grounded in expertise and experience—remains strong, but few would doubt that the center of gravity in medical practice has moved toward insurers, policy makers, and patients.

The shift occurred because of structural changes in funding, increased use of new technologies, and heightened managerial control to achieve physician accountability for actions taken in hospitals, offices, and clinics. Those changes, however, can scarcely be called fundamental reforms in clinical practice. Fee-for-service remains dominant; issues of wide variation in quality care and even access to adequate health care persist. Overall health outcomes for Americans compared with other nations have certainly improved since the early twentieth century, but there is little evidence available that the structural changes in funding, technology use, and physician accountability have influenced the health outcomes of Americans.[46]

Although clinical practice has changed in its particulars, it has not yet erased abiding predicaments that shadow the profession. There is more diagnostic testing, more information available to patients, and better treatments for chronic diseases that were once acute and swiftly lethal. Yet there is less face-to-face time between physicians and patients. Yet inequalities in access to and use of medical care between the poor and wealthy and between minorities and whites persist. Yet occupational predicaments of helping professions endure in the medical profession, as expertise remains insufficient to erase uncertainties in diagnosing and treating the ill. Yet the uneasy tensions over the mix of empirical findings and intuitive judgments in medical decision making continue. And the inevitable physician dependence on patients for improved health still remains.

The current concentration by public and private insurers on accountability for health-care organizations and individual doctors has produced report cards on scores of measures and formal pay-for-performance plans. Even though the insurers have only glimmers of what occurs in the black box of practice, physicians are being held responsible for what happens to patients in ways they had not been a half-century earlier. Policy makers, blaming physicians for the high cost of health care and less-than-stellar patient care, ask them to solve these problems through evidence-based medicine, patient-centered practice, and pay-for-performance solutions. Yet—the final *yet*—have these structural changes led to the desired outcome of healthier Americans? Here, then, is a conundrum peculiar to helping professions in the early twenty-first century. And, as we'll see in chapter 5, that also goes for public school teachers.

Chapter 5

Structural Changes and Reforming Teaching Practices

In chapter 4, we saw how the funding of health care since Medicare and Medicaid became law in 1965 has altered the medical landscape. The mix of private and public insurers pursuing a largely fee-for-service approach in an environment where health-care costs increased annually has influenced physician autonomy and clinical practice in both intended and unintended ways. Seeking to control costs and improve quality care through alternative funding plans and pay-for-performance schemes, insurers have tried to standardize diagnoses and treatment plans. What remains unclear is whether any of these structural reforms have improved clinical practice and therefore led to healthier Americans.

In this chapter, I examine whether reforms in funding, technology use, and managerial control has had similar effects on K–12 teaching practices.

Funding Schools and Teaching Practices

Unlike medicine, where physicians' autonomy has been directly influenced by fee-for-service payments and their practice indirectly affected, the funding of public schools since the mid-twentieth century has had only indirect effects on both teachers' discretion and teaching practices.

Because education is a state responsibility, each state varies in how its schools are funded. Every state but Hawaii devolves authority to districts for operating public schools; for instance, California has over one thousand school districts. Generally, about half of public school monies come from a combination of state taxes and fees on individual income, sales of products and services, and corporations. Just under half comes from property taxes levied on homeowners by local districts, and about 8 percent comes from the federal government. States distribute these funds on a per-pupil basis for general and special programs. Because revenues and property taxes vary greatly between the states, per-pupil spending for basic education range from a high of $11,000 in New York to a low of nearly $4,000 in Utah.[1]

Because over three-quarters of the annual cost of providing schooling in a district is in teacher compensation, those districts with limited capacity to raise monies through property taxes have much less to spend on salaries and benefits. As a result, they suffer constant staff turnover and are forced to hired inexperienced staff, decreasing overall school effectiveness. Not so in high-wealth districts. There, teachers receive above-average salaries and benefits, allowing them to retain a stable teacher corps with minimal attrition.

Such inequities between districts have spurred court challenges over the past four decades, demanding that a "sound basic education" for all students be provided and wide differences in funding smoothed out. Plaintiffs and defendants have argued for decades over what exactly an "adequate" education is and what such an education would cost for both regular students and those who come to school with social, physical, and psychological disabilities. Because inequities in funding often stem from the widely divergent property values in high-wealth and low-wealth districts, different states have legislated funding mechanisms where wealthier districts shift funds to poor districts (often called "Robin Hood" laws). Texas, for example, has struggled with redistribution of state funds for decades, as has New Jersey with its Abbott decisions.[2] Equity in funding schools and determining the cost of a sound basic education remain contested in the early twenty-first century.

Two significant structural innovations in funding schools have occurred in the past quarter-century: funding to reduce class size and the creation of charter schools. While these innovations do not correct the resource inequities or settle the differences over an adequate education, they each have, according to promoters, the capacity to change teaching practices and improve student academic achievement. To the extent that these funding innovations—often accompanied by the rhetorical hype of second-order or fundamental reform—succeeded, they have been portrayed as not only altering classroom practice but also improving it and student learning.

Reduction of Class Size

Large classes of fifty-plus students were common in early-twentieth-century schools, especially in cities. Class size fell throughout the past century to around thirty students in elementary and secondary classrooms in the 1960s, dipping to twenty-five and rising to thirty-five in times of budgetary retrenchment. Beginning in the 1980s, state efforts to reduce class size to twenty students or fewer per classroom, especially in primary grades, led legislatures to fund smaller class size. The aim was to alter teaching practices and lift student achievement.

Research studies had established that smaller class sizes produced gains in test scores spurred many of these efforts. For example, the Tennessee experiments in reduced class size in elementary schools—a small class was thirteen to seventeen students; a large class was twenty-two to twenty-six students—did yield achievement test score gains, particularly for low-income and minority children. Most reduced-class size efforts, however, seldom reached the class-size threshold that Tennessee had created.[3]

The theory was that small class size would permit teachers to engage students more fully, use particular classroom practices such as small group and individual instruction more easily, and, as a consequence, improve student academic performance on tests. The theory had a few holes in it.

One of the largest efforts to cut class size took place in California in the mid-1990s. The state legislature invested $1 billion to downsize primary-grade classes of around thirty students to about twenty. Parents, teachers, and school boards applauded the effort and sang the praises of the legislature and governor. Note, however, that California created classes that were close to the "large" ones in the Tennessee experiment.

But when researchers examined the outcomes after five years of reduced class size in California, what did they find? According to a RAND research report:

We tracked achievement gains in cohorts of students with different amounts of exposure to CSR [class size reduction] from kindergarten through third grade. Whether we used statewide average scores or conducted a more refined school-level analysis we reached the same conclusion. We found no association between small differences in exposure to CSR (i.e., the total number of years a student had been in reduced size classes) and differences in academic achievement.[4]

And what about teaching practices in reduced size classes with about twenty students, compared with larger classes? From self-reports of how teachers taught their lessons and direct observations of lessons, the researchers concluded:

> For the most part, teachers in reduced and non-reduced size classes reported using selected instructional activities with equal frequency. In mathematics these activities included using a calculator, using mathematics in the context of other subjects, doing mathematics worksheets, using patterns to discover mathematical relationships, and practicing computational skills. In language arts, the activities included having guided discussion about reading, discussing new or difficult vocabulary, working in a reading book, and listening to the teacher read stories.[5]

Another researcher examined studies covering U.S. and international efforts to reduce class size since the 1970s, including the Tennessee and California studies noted above. He found very small effects on achievement and little to no change in classroom practices of teachers in small and large classes. Even with all of the embellished talk from reformers about fundamentally altering classroom teaching, at best, there were only first-order or incremental changes in how teachers taught.[6]

Charter Schools

Discouraging as these results on test scores and teaching practices would be to champions of reduced class size, results from funding charter schools, another innovation that promised shifts in teaching practices and gains in student achievement, would give heartburn to their advocates.

Since 1991, when Minnesota launched the first charter schools, the movement to create publicly funded charters freed from district rules where parents can choose to send their children had spread to forty states and the District of Columbia, enrolling almost 2 million students (nearly 4 percent of all public school students) in over five thousand schools (over 5 percent of all public schools). Charters are located mostly in cities, and some urban districts have a majority of their students attending charter schools; for example New Orleans (nearly 70 percent) and Youngstown, Ohio (over 52 percent).[7]

The theory driving charter schools is that untethering schools from district policies, including union contracts, for three to five years would give them the budgetary and organizational autonomy to steer their own innovative course and increase the academic quality in terms of teaching practices and student achievement. Charters would also be accountable to the market—parents and students choosing to attend or exit—and to stipulations in the charter itself to perform well academically and be fiscally responsible. If there were serious lapses, charter renewal would be forfeited. Thus, flexible curriculum, eager teachers, parental choice, accountability, and public funding would combine to create schools where a new organization, hardworking innovative teachers, and satisfied parents would produce higher student achievement than would have occurred in regular public schools.[8]

After two decades, the number of charter schools continues to grow. Parental demand for choices in schools remains high. There is evidence that charter schools differ from regular schools in organizational practices (e.g., block scheduling, extended school day, teachers staying with same students two or more years; small group instruction). Yet, in the face of this growth and difference in structures, charter and regular teachers both say—surprisingly, given the theory driving charter schools—that they exert little influence over curriculum and instruction.[9]

Because most reformers believe that effective teaching practices result in improved student achievement, have teachers in charter schools, freed from district rules and prescriptions, practiced their craft differently from their peers in neighborhood schools? So far, the evidence says that with even more teacher autonomy and flexibility in charter schools there is little difference between their classroom practices and those of regular public school teachers.[10] Researchers who examined classroom practices across charter and non-charter schools concluded that, "as charter schools implement innovations in governance, management, and other organizational practices, charter schools are embracing curricular and instructional approaches *already in use* (original italics) in other public schools that are considered as traditional 'basic' approaches to instruction."[11]

Such findings leave holes in the theory driving charter schools. Like their counterparts in regular public schools, charter school teachers mainly use traditional classroom practices such as scripted lessons and lectures, textbooks, worksheets, homework, and question/answer/evaluation exchanges, seasoned by certain student-centered practices such as small-group work, student discussions, and independent projects.

A look at Knowledge is Power Program (KIPP), which as of 2011, managed 109 charter elementary and secondary schools in twenty states serving over thirty thousand students, shows that classroom practices are unmistakably teacher-centered.[12] KIPP is not, of course, representative of all charter schools in its practices. Aspire, Green Dot, and other charter management organizations have schools in their networks where classroom instruction vary considerably but still remains within the tradition of teacher-centeredness.[13]

Keep in mind that these elementary and secondary school charters are geared to preparing children and youth for college. That is their unvarnished mission. Frontal teaching, direct instruction, extended days, and no-nonsense approaches to student behavior are the norm. So variation among teachers in different networks of charter schools is within a narrow band of teacher-centered practices. It is important to keep in mind that when I use that phrase, I intend no connotation of such practices being appropriate or inappropriate, effective or ineffective. Nor do I suggest that teachers studied were not constantly changing activities and assignments; they did so, but within the framework of teacher-centered instruction.

A classroom example, one that is representative of a particular charter school network with which I am familiar, helps to fill in the general picture. In 2011–2012, I visited thirteen teachers in four charter high schools of the Leadership Public Schools (LPS) network. While these teachers included many hybrids of student- and teacher-centered activities in their lessons, most of their practices, some of which I saw as innovative, landed on the teacher-centered side of the instructional continuum. Here is a geometry lesson that I observed in March 2012.

Observation: A Geometry Lesson. The class of twenty-nine students, mostly Latino with a sprinkling of other minorities and whites, had already begun the lesson. Students sat in seven rows of four desks, each facing the front whiteboards and a screen. The teacher's laptop was on one desk at the front of the room. Inspirational quotes, student work, and math-related posters dotted classroom walls.

The student objective for the day was written on one side of the white-board. On the other side were listed school rules. Below the lists was the agenda for this lesson:

1. Launch
2. Presentation
3. Practice
4. Conclusion
5. Exit Ticket

Each student had a four-page worksheet with "Launch," "Presentation," "Practice," and "Conclusion" sections. Under each section was printed the objective: "I CAN calculate the surface area and volume of a sphere" with questions and problems to solve. For example, the Launch section—an opening activity, usually a problem or task that students begin as soon as they enter the room—contained multiple questions about a basketball, such as "The amount of leather used to make the outside of the ball represents _____ because _____."[14]

When I arrived, the teacher was leading students through the Practice questions on the worksheet: "Find the approximate SA (surface area) and volume of the following sphere" (a picture of a sphere is on the worksheet). The teacher walked up and down the rows as students worked, keeping a constant patter of statements, directions, and questions: "I like that idea, show Christian your solution; I think it will show that it is efficient." At one point, he said to a student: "I challenge your calculation. Show me how you did it."

The teacher clapped his hands in quick rhythm—a signaling system—and brought the activity to a close. Students stopped. He then said: "Let's see if you guys know what you are talking about."

The teacher moved to the Exit Ticket part of lesson, a software app that LPS teachers had designed using recycled iPods. Students got their mobile devices and logged in. There were two questions on the printed worksheet for students to answer; they went to work. "Definitely use your notes for the formula you put down," he told the class.[15]

He walked around the classroom looking to see what each student was doing. He held an iPad in his hand loaded with software to monitor students' work on iPods. More patter from the teacher as he cruised the rows: "You're annotating makes me happy. I love the evidence I'm seeing."

He stopped to answer a student's question. He then asked the class, as they were working, "How many of you did I have last year?" Half of students raised their hands. "Wasn't I a royal pain in having you line up items as you write up a problem and its solution? When you get to college, you leave out a symbol, a semicolon, you torpedo the entire solution."

As he scanned the classroom, looked at his iPad to see what students were doing, he turned to a student and said, "Alex, we're talking math; that's your warning."

Teacher clapped again. "Let's move to Conclusion." He told the class: "Read the problem silently and after three minutes, talk to your neighbor on how you did it." Shortly thereafter, another quick handclap.

"Let's do another poll on answers." Students used their iPods. "OK," teacher said. "Ten voted for this answer and two voted for the other. The two are correct. Why are these two right? Check with your neighbor. Talk it out."

There was a noticeable surge of energy in the class after the teacher pointed out the error. Pairs of students talked to one another. Teacher waited and then said: "Alex, explain the answer." After Alex talked through the explanation, teacher clapped and said, "Eyes up here." He went over the homework and reminded students of a test in two days. The bell rang, ending the class, but the teacher held the students until all of the iPods were returned to the tray in front of the room. Then he dismissed the class.

Like this geometry class, the other lessons I observed across the four high schools "hugged the middle" of the instructional continuum, with mostly teacher-centered activities mixed with student-centered ones. Moreover, this teacher integrated new technologies into his lesson to help students and him learn more.[16]

In these charter school classrooms, I saw a great deal of instructional coherence across academic subjects.[17] Similar goals, lesson activities, demands on students, and pacing of tasks during hour-long classes were evident in the observations, while variations existed in teacher managerial style, temperament, and humor. Moreover, in these schools, cultural norms clearly made mastering content and skills in order to get into college the highest priority. Those norms showed up in classroom banners of each teacher's alma mater, epigrams posted on walls that exhort students to work hard, and frequent exchanges between adults and students over the importance of doing well in academic subjects to get into college.[18]

My classroom experience, observation of teachers in public school classrooms, and research studies persuade me that greater variations in lesson goals, activities, pacing, and schoolwide norms—in short, less instructional coherence—exist in public school classrooms than in KIPP, Aspire, Green Dot, and Leadership Public Schools. All of these public charter and regular classrooms, however, clearly featured teacher-centeredness tinged with practices that gave a gloss of student-centeredness to lessons.

No surprise, then, that with the schools having such similar teaching practices, when student achievement in public schools and charters are compared the record is, at best, mixed. Some studies compare charters to regular public schools on state test scores; others have compared test scores of those students who got into charters through lotteries and those who didn't. In both kinds of studies, charter schools showed either a slight edge, were equal to, or did less well than comparison groups of public schools.[19]

Public funding of charter schools since the early 1990s introduced new options for parental choice and autonomous organizations that compete with public schools for students. These structures, however, are like empty trucks; they can transport different pedagogies to students. Although charter schools, like public schools are caught up in the reform slogan of "All students should go to college," charter school teachers who come voluntarily to their posts have far more theoretical autonomy than their public school cousins. Nonetheless, they have adopted the college-for-all approach and prepare their students using teacher-centered practices mixed with occasional student-centered activities. But as noted above, charter schools, as far as current evidence indicates, do not regularly outperform non-charter schools in student achievement. Thus, regardless of new funding structures for charter schools, regardless of different levels of teacher autonomy in their classrooms, teachers in both charters and regular schools largely use similar practices.

Instructional Technologies and Teacher Practice

Recall the geometry lesson described above, where iPods and an iPad were integrated into instruction. Does the similarity in teaching practice include new technologies? I now turn to instructional technologies (IT).

As described in chapter 4, the structure of fee-for-service funding has greatly influenced the use of those new technologies. Physicians have adopted new medical technologies with great speed, and have clearly integrated screening and treatment technologies into caring for patients. Individual doctors and physician groups determine which new technologies, from imaging machines to electronic health records, should be purchased, for what purposes, and where they should be placed. While physician autonomy has shrunk in the past few decades, it is still the doctors in emergency rooms, clinics, and hospitals who order tests and prescribe treatments—not the administrators.

For teachers, new structures (and much funding) have been put into place to use IT in daily lessons. Buildings have been wired. Machines have been bought. But teachers—and this is an important difference between physicians and K–12 teachers—do not make the decisions to adopt laptops, tablets, or smartphones for classroom instruction. Unlike clinics, hospitals, and doctors' offices, where physicians generally decide on screening tests and treatments, school boards base the decisions on superintendents' recommendations, sometimes consulting with teachers informally or as members of district advisory committees. Of course, most teachers have home access to personal computers and mobile devices, but for classroom instruction, policy makers and administrators make the purchasing and deploying decisions. To what degree the absence of teachers' input in choosing new technologies influences the use of IT in classrooms has seldom, if at all, been studied.

So, do teachers integrate IT into their practice?

In chapter 1, I described how Las Montanas High School moved from computer labs in 1998 to 1:1 laptops between 2004 and 2011. By and large, principals and district administrators decided which technologies would come to Las Montanas and when. Teachers were on a schoolwide advisory committee, and a cadre of enthusiastic faculty wanted new technologies, but those teachers were a minority within the staff. Still, I did observe over that period greater IT use by teachers and students in lessons, but only modest changes in classroom practice. The changes teachers made in adopting new technologies fortified familiar teaching practices. Beyond this one high school, I now examine use of new IT hardware and software across U.S. elementary and secondary classrooms.

Kindergartners using iPads, middle school students collecting data with their handheld devices on ant colonies, and teams of twelfth-graders making videos for their senior projects appear often in media reports about computer use in U.S. schools at the end of the first decade of the twenty-first century. Commercial and teacher Web sites and blogs recount innovative teachers integrating technology into daily lessons through student wikis, personal blogs, and other imaginative ways. Like much of the policy talk about computers in classrooms, reports of individual teachers' use of IT ripple across the nation, exciting high-tech advocates to think teacher and student engagement is common in most classrooms. Furthermore, those advocates believe that students engaged with devices gain in academic achievement. Neither is the case, however.[20]

Media reports and research literature on classroom use of desktop and laptop computers are filled with glowing stories of motivated students and teachers. Yet when researchers and journalists observe classrooms, they often see students and teachers using those new technologies simply to support conventional approaches in daily lessons. Typed homework, Internet searches, PowerPoint or Keynote presentations, and taking notes as teachers lecture are commonly noted.[21] Even more discouraging to advocates is the meager evidence that technologically engaged students do well on measures of student achievement. At best, the evidence is mixed and, at worst, lacking.

What accounts for these disappointing results? First, there is the novelty effect to explain student engagement with high-tech. New devices—think clickers in an algebra class or iPads for kindergartners—motivate students initially; but as time passes, the effects wear off.[22] Second, major studies have repeatedly shown weak to no linkage between these devices or software and substantial changes in teaching practices or improved test scores. The lack of clear and strong evidence, however, has hardly slowed (nor will it slow) the rush to buy these devices and software for classroom instruction.[23]

For champions of creatively integrating computers into daily lessons, such uses do disappoint, since many truly believe that new technologies can transform traditional teacher-centered practices into student-centered learning. They also believe that student achievement will improve as students dip into individually tailored online lessons. Technology advocates holding those beliefs have been given a decided boost by recent cuts in educational spending forced by the Great Recession of 2008. With fewer dollars available, policy makers and administrators, looking for efficient and inexpensive ways of delivering courses and lessons, have turned to online learning in K–12 schools. Driven by smart and zealous entrepreneurs, donors, and venture capitalists who seek openings in the K–12 educational market, online instruction—a staple in higher education for nearly a half-century—has entered elementary and secondary schools.[24]

Here is what former New York City chancellor Joel Klein, now CEO of a high-tech division of Rupert Murdoch's News Corporation, had to say about new technologies:

> As someone who led America's largest school district for 8 years, serving over 1 million children, I believe technology can radically transform the way students learn by customizing instruction, and by helping teachers focus on each student's areas of greatest need . . . Technology's greatest potential is as a vehicle for students to learn more deeply and individually, unleashing them from the limitations of learning in step with 25 or more peers with different needs and strengths . . . If we commit to rigorous, analytical education technology, the payoff for student learning and for society will be much larger.[25]

In his arguments for more technology use in schools, Klein echoes those abiding beliefs held by promoters of laptops, tablets, and online instruction: (1) students will be engaged in one-to-one learning tailored to their individual academic needs with stellar online teachers, tutors, and software banks filled with customized lessons and (2) engagement with such lessons will lead to gains in student achievement.

What Klein and many enthusiasts for online instruction in K–12 are less explicit about is that online teaching costs are far lower per student than regular instruction in brick-and-mortar public schools where one teacher meets with twenty-five, thirty, or more students. At a time of rampant budget cuts, the idea of online instruction, with its lower instructional costs—once programs are up and running—and seemingly positive effect on student achievement, spurs champions of Web-based instruction such as philanthropist Bill Gates to tout this high-tech solution for delivering quality instruction.[26] One of the outcomes of this vision, then, is that over time, there will be fewer teachers in classrooms.

Blended Schools

These reasons for boosting online instruction come together in such initiatives as the School of One, Carpe Diem, and Rocketship schools—all hybrid schools. The combination of individualizing instruction through online lessons and having a teacher available to help and teach group lessons in the same school—called *blended learning* or *hybrid* schools—defuses some of the criticism leveled by both parents and teachers at for-profit cyber-schools (e.g., Agora, a charter school) offering a full-time menu of online instruction. Nonetheless, the cost of such hybrid schools, after initial outlay for high-tech equipment, remains lower than the costs of fully staffed regular schools, a fact evident to anyone who can read a budget.[27]

Blended instruction often means a combination of students in a computer lab working individually on lessons for anywhere from 25 to 50 percent of the school day, with the rest of the time spent in classrooms with teachers. Most hybrid schools enroll largely minority and poor elementary school children. Rocketship is one such organization. Here are the observations of a journalist who looked at the computer lab portion of a Rocketship school in San Jose, California:

> The Learning Lab at Los Sueños Academy, in downtown San Jose, is not unlike the computer labs you'd find at many elementary schools—it's just much bigger. Tightly packed computer cubicles, 100 in all, form long rows along the 2,000-square-foot open-plan room.
>
> The size of the lab reflects the outsize ambitions of Rocketship Education, the Palo Alto–based nonprofit organization that runs Los Sueños and four other charter schools in San Jose. In fact, the lab is the financial and academic key to Rocketship's ambitious mission. Cofounder John Danner aims to expand rapidly by using fewer teachers and paying them better—all while transforming how they teach.
>
> The 100 minutes a day that Los Sueños students spend in the Learning Lab supplement the five hours of classroom instruction required by California law. But the time spent in the Learning Lab also replaces one out of four teachers per grade in every Rocketship school. That adds up to about five fewer teachers per school, at an average savings of $100,000 per teacher (including the cost of benefits), or $500,000. Rocketship uses that money to pay for the aides in

the Learning Lab, two additional administrators at each school and 20 percent higher pay for teachers . . .

At any time of the school day, the Learning Lab at Los Sueños is at least three-quarters full. The students wear headsets and their eyes are on the monitors. The window shades are drawn. Construction paper in green and purple (the school colors) decorates the walls of every station.

After shaking hands with a learning specialist as they enter the room, the young "Rocketeers" go straight to their stations and log on. Except for some antsy kindergartners and first-graders, students stay more or less focused on their monitors. The few who dawdle or pester a neighbor get a reminder—or if they persist, a red written warning. There are purple slips, too, for exhibiting Rocketship core values: persistence, responsibility, empathy, and respect. The lab is overseen by five aides. Typically, the kids spend 60 minutes in front of a computer, splitting the time between math and reading.

In an area carved out in the center of the room, classroom aide Katya Silva tutors five fourth-graders who were identified as below basic in reading. Today, they are reading "Mrs. Hen's Plan," a two-page story about a hen's efforts to hide her egg from a farmer. The day's goal is to focus on words related to cause and effect. After students take turns reading aloud, some haltingly, they underline clue words—*as, so, because*—that can help them decipher meaning. A mother of two children at Los Sueños, Silva was an active volunteer before she was hired as a Learning Lab specialist at about $13 per hour. Some of the specialists are new college grads exploring teaching as a career, though neither a BA nor certification is a prerequisite.

The scripted lesson plans that Silva uses—four per day, 16 per week—are written at Rocketship's home office in Palo Alto for each group's selected intervention. The students are chosen based on the results of unit tests or their reading levels, and in consultation with their classroom teachers. Silva and the other aides work under the assistant principal, who sets group goals (for example, giving students three positive expressions of feedback every five minutes) and meets individually with them weekly . . .

On this particular December day, soft-spoken Arrianna Cardenas, like other second-graders, warms up for the first 10 minutes by doing simple addition and subtraction drills on Equatia, and then turns to word problems on a different program, TenMarks . . .

> Los Sueños uses an assortment of seven programs, four for math and three for reading, including Rosetta Stone for its least-proficient English learners. Of the math programs . . . TenMarks stands out for correlating its content to match Rocketship's detailed standards and sequence of instruction.
>
> That alignment will be essential as Rocketship pursues the next step in blended learning: integrating what students do in the Learning Lab with what they learn in class—and giving classroom teachers a role in determining online content for their students . . . [28]

Learning labs and regular classrooms comprise the blended school. In 2012, I visited a second-grade classroom where twenty-eight children were sitting in a half-circle on the floor. Their energetic teacher (a second-year Teach for America recruit) asked the children to answer the question whether immigration to the United States was good or bad. This question launched a teacher-directed project from which student teams were to find answers. The teacher was going over the different activities that each team would work on in their project. A chart next to her listed a hierarchy of cognitive skills. The taxonomy was like a ladder going from the bottom rung of remembering facts to the top one of using critical thinking when making judgments. The seven-year-olds knew from previous lessons each rung of the ladder.

I watched as the teacher read from a slip of paper describing an activity (e.g., pick a way to solve the immigration problem) and then ask the children to talk to their teammates and decide in which cognitive domain on the chart the activity should be put. After a few moments of students talking to one another, she asked group members where she should stick the slip of paper. Students waved their hands to be called on each time. After each domain had an activity pasted on it, the teacher asked the children to form into their pre-assigned groups and discuss how they would begin their project (she had assigned roles for each student to perform in their small group such as leader, timekeeper, etc., with different colored dots at their desks). The students went into groups and began discussing their project.

In this lesson, I saw a novice teacher engaged in ambitious teaching with seven-year-olds. How much the students understood of Bloom's Taxonomy to apply it to the project they were working on and answer the overall question on immigration, I have no idea. What I saw was twenty-eight students wanting to please their teacher and engaged in the part of the lesson.[29] To determine whether Rocketship charter schools, or similar ventures, with their pedagogical blend of online instruction and classroom teaching make a difference in student achievement is far too soon to tell, although that seldom stops promoters from making such claims.[30]

Online Instruction

Most claims for online instruction have a hollow ring because there is so much variation in who students are, different programs, the quality of instruction, and design of research studies. Students receiving online instruction range from home-schoolers to those enrolled in the International Baccalaureate diploma program and Advanced Placement courses to those students who have failed courses and sign up for credit recovery. Included now are elementary school students who combine Learning Labs with classroom instruction.

Web courses also differ in delivery; some emanate from virtual schools with a curricular menu of software and teacher-directed courses; others are courses in which teachers hold real-time discussions online, with periodic face-to-face contact.

And the quality of online instruction varies. While current technology permits online and offline discussions among students and between teacher and students, the nature of the setting nearly always results in short bursts of telling, checking for understanding with multiple-choice questions, mini-lectures, video and YouTube segments, and PowerPoint slides. In short, I am describing teacher-centered instruction but with much variation in presentation and activities.

There are stars among instructors who relish the work, plan thoughtfully, and use the limited face-to-face interaction and discussion threads creatively. They offer many stories of student success. Software designers have also created programs that both entice and push students through carefully sequenced lessons sufficient to teach complicated concepts clearly and crisply. But most online instructors and software programs plod along well-worn roads that only highly motivated, independent students can traverse to finish the journey.

Then there are the flawed research design and methodologies used to determine whether a particular technology, computer-assisted instruction, a new math software, laptops, iPads—whatever the new "new thing" is—has produced gains in student test scores. Horse-race type studies—which technology is better, old or new?—that compare, say, those laptop-equipped students with those lacking the devices have been done for well over a half century and have been shown, time and again, to be faulty for not taking into consideration other factors that could explain gains in student achievement, such as the teacher's pedagogy, students' socioeconomic status, and other instructional materials, among a host of others.[31]

Even if those who advance online learning as the "disruptive innovation" that will replace regular schools or those advocates of blended learning spread their gospel, these facts are incontrovertible. The truth is that, with so much variation—in students, how online instruction is delivered, teaching quality—and flawed research designs, attributing achievement gains to online instruction is nearly impossible. Claims about online learning revolutionizing teaching and student learning are, to put it generously, just that—merely claims.[32]

There is little question that teachers not only use new electronic technologies in their classrooms but also have increased their usage over time. There is also little question, given the evidence, that most technology-using teachers have adapted new devices to existing classroom routines. Those adaptations in teaching practices, however, have yet to cross the threshold where any gains in student achievement can be accurately credited to teacher use of new technologies.

Reshaping Teaching Through Managerial Use of Student Test Scores

Thus far, in looking at whether structural changes in funding and technology use have reshaped teaching practices, what I and others have found has disappointed reformers whose high hopes for reduced class size for young children and charter schools have yet to produce clear-cut shifts in the mainstream teacher-centered pedagogy dominating U.S. classrooms and gains in student achievement. When it comes, however, to changes in how teachers are evaluated and paid, new structures in holding schools and teachers accountable for student outcomes have had effects on classroom practices, albeit not always in the intended directions that policy makers sought.

As chapter 4 described, top government policy makers and private insurance companies, deeply concerned over ever-rising health-care costs and unwilling to rely on doctors to restrain expenditures, built structures over the past quarter-century to hold physicians accountable for actions they took in diagnosing and treating their patients. These structures leaned heavily on a research base of randomized clinical trials built up over decades on diagnostic screening procedures to the effects of drugs on an array of diseases. Combining evidence-based medicine with incentives and sanctions, public and private insurers have measured, reported, and rewarded doctors' performance in hospitals, clinics, and office practices.

In applying managerial practices drawn from outcome-driven corporations, these medical policy makers and insurers established structures relying on performance-based metrics. They assumed that creating economic incentives for individuals and organizations would increase innovation, lower costs, and improve patient care. They identified numerous measures, confirmed in large part by results from clinical trials, and implemented those evidence-based measures in hospitals, clinics, and doctors' offices. As I pointed out, the various physician report cards and pay-for-performance plans have yet to yield the promised innovations, high-quality care, and reduced costs.

Reform-driven educational policy makers have made a similar set of assumptions in constructing accountability structures and metrics to manage how schools are to be judged successful and teachers are to be evaluated and paid. In doing so, however, these decision makers lack the research base that physicians have had available in evidence-based medicine.

While some social scientists and educational researchers have used randomized control group studies to uncover what caused phenomena in schools and classrooms, such studies have been the exception, not the rule. Ethical considerations, cost, and the complexity of schools, teaching, and learning reduce experimental-control research designs.

Qualitative research studies using surveys, interviews, case studies, and ethnographies are not designed to draw causal inferences; moreover, they cannot, given the questions asked, the samples drawn, and methodologies used. Qualitative studies ask different questions and provide rich data for exploring other issues that are missing from experimental-control designs. As a consequence, unlike the research base available to physicians—who can draw from a literature of random-ized clinical trials and use results for diagnosis and treatment of com-mon and uncommon illnesses (e.g., Cochrane Collaborative)—only a small and emerging body of knowledge drawn from randomized con-trol-experimental studies about teaching, learning, and effective schools yet exists that policy makers and practitioners can tap (e.g., the U.S. Department of Education, What Works Clearinghouse, and the Camp-bell Collaborative).[33]

That slim database, however, has not lessened the current passion of policy makers and politicians for using test scores to evaluate teacher performance (and pay higher salaries). Smart researchers and officials are determined to reengineer teaching to make it closer to the "flight of a bullet" rather than the "flight of a butterfly," in the words of Philip Jackson.[34] Yet in seeking the Holy Grail, they have ignored the fact that researchers and policy makers have already slogged through a century of unsuccessful efforts to make teaching scientific.

Not many contemporary reformers can recall Franklin Bobbitt in the 1920s, Ralph Tyler and Benjamin Bloom in the 1950s, Nathaniel Gage in the 1970s and 1980s, and many other researchers who worked hard to create a science of curriculum and instruction. These scholars rejected the notion that teaching can be unpredictable and uncertain—the flight of a butterfly. They believed that teaching could be rational and pre-dictable through scientifically reengineering teaching and learning in classrooms.

In *How To Make a Curriculum* (1924), for example, Franklin Bobbitt listed 160 "educational objectives" that teachers should pursue in teach-ing children, such as "the ability to use language . . . required for proper and effective participation in community life." Colleagues in math listed three hundred objectives for teachers in grades 1–6 and nearly nine hun-dred for social studies. This scientific movement to graft "educational objectives" onto daily classroom lessons collapsed of its own weight by the 1940s, and was largely ignored by teachers.[35]

By the early 1960s, another generation of social scientists had advanced the idea that teachers should use *behavioral objectives* to guide lessons. Ralph Tyler, Benjamin Bloom and others created taxonomies that provided teachers with "prescriptions for the formulation of edu-cational objectives."[36] Again, teachers generally ignored these scientific prescriptions in their daily lessons.

In the 1970s and 1980s, Nathaniel Gage and other researchers sought to establish "a scientific basis for the art of teaching." They focused on teaching behaviors (how teachers asked questions, which students are called on, etc.)—the process of teaching leading to the products of effective teaching, student scores on standardized tests. This line of research, called *process-product*, continued the behavioral tradition from an earlier generation committed to a science of teaching. Using experimental methods to identify teaching behaviors that were correlated to student gains in test scores on standardized tests, Gage and others came up with "Teachers should . . ." statements that were associated with improved student achievement.[37]

The limitations of establishing a set of scientifically prescribed teaching behaviors soon became apparent as critics pointed out how many other factors (e.g., teacher knowledge and beliefs, the content of the lesson, students themselves, the classroom environment, the school) come into play when teachers teach students. Again, teachers generally ignored the results from process-product studies.[38]

And here in 2013, reengineering teaching through science again seeks the flight of the bullet. Evaluating and paying teachers on the basis of student test scores through value-added measures (discussed in detail below) dominates policy talk and action.

In establishing new accountability structures that used squishy metrics and attached high-stakes rewards (e.g., cash bonuses for individual teachers) and sanctions (e.g., no diploma for failing high school students; teachers fired for being ineffective), educational policy makers have plunged into a battleground where the search for teacher effectiveness has generated anger, fear, and lowered morale among those who work daily in classrooms and, at the same time, generated political gains for elected policy makers.

Value-Added Measures for Evaluating Teachers

Recall that under President George W. Bush, the Teacher Incentive Fund made grants to districts for overhauling their teacher evaluation systems. After Barack Obama became president in 2009, the U.S. Department of Education launched Race to the Top, a multibillion dollar competition between states during a recession when school budgets were cut. To win, states had to meet certain conditions to collect federal dollars. One of those conditions was that they had to create new systems of teacher evaluation that included student test scores. Furthermore, in another federal initiative to turn around failing schools, the U.S. secretary of education dispensed School Improvement Grants to districts to overhaul schools with persistent low academic achievement. One of the strategies for turning around such schools included using student test scores to evaluate teachers.[39]

Philanthropists have pursued similar policies. The Bill and Melinda Gates Foundation awarded grants to six districts to create and establish "fair and reliable measures of effective teaching," including the use of student test scores.[40] Yet even with all this federal and private money being spent, the question remains whether these structures and metrics have reshaped classroom practices.

In most organizations, supervisors measure and evaluate employees' performance. Consequences, both positive and negative, flow from the judgments they make. However, in public schools, negative consequences don't flow very much. Supervisors have commonly judged over 95 percent of all teachers "satisfactory." Such percentages clearly do not distinguish between effective and ineffective teaching. The reform-driven agenda for the past decade that included testing, accountability, expanding parental choice through charter schools, and establishing a Common Core curriculum across the nation now includes in its to-do list distinguishing between good and poor teaching.[41]

The current generation of reform-driven policy makers, donors, and educational entrepreneurs are determined to sort out good from mediocre and poor teaching if for no other reason than identifying those high-performers who have had sustained effects on student learning and reward them with recognition, bonuses, and high salaries. They are equally determined to rid the teacher corps of persistently ineffective teachers.[42]

Identifying the best and worst in the profession in ways that teachers perceive as fair, improving the craft of teaching, and retaining their support for the process has, in most places, thwarted reformers—but not enough to stop policy makers and donors from launching a flurry of programs that seek to recognize high performers while firing time-servers. Such policy makers, donors, and media have concentrated on using students' annual test scores. Some big city districts have not only used scores to determine individual teacher effectiveness but also permitted publication of each teacher's "effectiveness" ranking (e.g., Los Angeles Unified School District, New York City). Because teachers see serious flaws in using test scores to reward and punish teaching, they are far less enthusiastic about new systems to evaluate teaching and award bonuses.[43]

Behind these new policies in judging teaching performance are models of teaching effectiveness containing complex algorithms drawn from research studies done a quarter-century ago by William Sanders and others called *value-added measures* (VAM).[44] How do value-added measures work? Using an end-of-year standardized achievement test in math and English, VAM predicts how well a student would do on the basis of the student's attendance, past performance on tests, and other characteristics. Student growth in learning (as measured by a standardized test) is calculated. Thus, this thinking goes, how much value—the test score—the teacher adds to each student's learning in a year can be measured. Teachers are then held responsible for getting their students to reach the predicted level. If a teacher's students do reach or exceed their predicted test scores, the teacher is rated effective or highly effective; teachers whose students miss the mark are rated ineffective.[45]

Most teachers perceive VAM as unfair. Fewer than half of all teachers (mostly in elementary schools and even a smaller percentage in secondary schools) have usable data (e.g., multiple years of students' math and reading scores) to be evaluated. For those teachers lacking student test scores, new tests will have to be developed and other metrics will be used. But will they be based on similar measures? If so, the results will be flawed. Teachers know that other factors such as student effort and family background play a part in their academic performance. They also know that other data drawn from peer and supervisor observations of lessons, the quality of instructional materials used by teachers, student and parent satisfaction with the teacher are weighed much less or even ignored in judging teaching performance.[46]

Moreover, student scores are unstable year to year; that is, different students are being tested as they move through the grades, so teacher "effectiveness" ratings are based on different cohorts of students. What this means is that a substantial percentage of teachers might be ranked "highly effective" in one year and ranked "ineffective" in the next. False positives are common in such situations. Furthermore, many teachers know that both measurement error and teaching experience (i.e., over time, teachers improve, but they still have bad years and good years) account for instability in ratings of teacher effectiveness. Finally, many teachers see the process of using student scores to judge effectiveness as pitting teacher against teacher, increasing competition between teachers rather than collaboration across grades and specialties within a school; such systems, they believe, are devised not to help teachers improve daily lessons but to name, blame, and defame them.[47]

Yet with all of these negatives, many teachers, principals, policy makers, and parents are convinced that something has to be done to improve evaluation and distinguish between effective and ineffective teaching.

Evaluating Teacher Performance in Washington, D.C.

In Washington, D.C., IMPACT, a system of evaluation and pay-for-performance, was inaugurated by former chancellor Michelle Rhee in 2009. This system reveals both the strengths and the flaws in VAM.

The *Teaching and Learning Framework* for IMPACT lays out a crisp definition of "good" teaching in what D.C. teachers call the *nine commandments*:

1. Lead well-organized, objective-driven lessons.
2. Explain content clearly.
3. Engage students at all learning levels in rigorous work.
4. Provide students with multiple ways to engage with content.
5. Check for student understanding.
6. Respond to student misunderstandings.
7. Develop higher-level understanding through effective questioning.
8. Maximize instructional time.
9. Build a supportive, learning-focused classroom community.[48]

IMPACT uses multiple measures to judge the quality of teaching: 50 percent of an annual evaluation is based on student test scores; 35 percent on judgments of instructional expertise drawn from five classroom observations by the principal and *master educators* (subject-based expert teachers); and 15 percent on other measures. Using these multiple measures, IMPACT has awarded six hundred teachers (out of four thousand) bonuses ranging from $3000 to $25,000 and fired nearly two hundred teachers judged as "ineffective" in its first year of full operation (for those teachers with insufficient student test data, different performance measures were used).[49]

Here is a description of one classroom being observed by a master educator:

A case in point is the lively classroom of Andrea Stephens (not her real name), a first-grade teacher at a racially mixed elementary school in Northeast D.C. Master educator [Cynthia] Robinson-Rivers is conducting an informal observation as Stephens teaches a lesson about capital letters, punctuation marks, and the short "a." Stephens is kind, firm, and engaging, and she wins points for gestures like asking a reluctant pupil if she could "get one of his smiles," making him feel valued. But she is apparently not engaging enough. Several students are not paying attention; one is a mugger and a performer, and he can't sit still. After several attempts to quiet him, Stephens gently pulls him up next to her, holding his hand while she addresses the rest of the class. The general atmosphere suggests to Robinson-Rivers a need for better management. "The children weren't completely out of control," Robinson-Rivers says. "But if they aren't facing you it can suggest a lack of interest." The session reveals other perceived shortcomings, despite Robinson-Rivers' respect for Stephens as "a warm, thoughtful practitioner." It was too teacher-directed, Robinson-Rivers says; it failed to make the objectives fully clear, and it didn't make the most of limited instructional time. "If the pacing is too slow, you can lose valuable time from the lesson," Robinson-Rivers says. "If in a 20-minute morning meeting the kids participate in a variety of engaging activities, it's much easier to maintain their interest and enthusiasm." Stephens also falls short on Teach 5 [one of the "commandments"]—checking to see whether students actually understood her. "There was no way to know whether the shy girl or the boy who spoke little English understood or not," Robinson-Rivers says. Instead of having all the pupils answer in unison, she suggests that Stephens cold-call on individual students, or have all the boys or all the girls answer in some non-verbal way. "It's hard because teachers do think they are checking for understanding. But it's actually an easy one for professional development; you could just say there are three easy things you can do." Stephens, whose overall score for the year was in the "effective" range, is open to evaluation and receptive to feedback—she even asked for an extra observation—and in this regard, master educators say she is fairly typical.[50]

IMPACT does sort out effective from ineffective teachers according to its nine commandments of good teaching. That the use of VAM and other indicators rewards and punishes teachers is also clear. Questions, however, about teacher turnover (Has IMPACT reduced attrition among effective teachers?) and student performance (Has IMPACT improved test scores?) have gone unanswered thus far. Allegations that teachers and administrators have erased student answers and otherwise fiddled with tests further cloud the picture of IMPACT's influence on teaching practice and student achievement.[51]

Among teachers and principals, the degree to which IMPACT has influenced daily teaching is disputed. According to some teachers, there are colleagues who pull out special lessons when principals and master educators appear for thirty-minute unannounced visits. Other teachers tremble and panic when an evaluator walks into their classroom, and the lesson becomes a shamble. Yet there are many teachers who relish the feedback they get from conferences after observations and assert that they have made changes and their lessons have improved. While the workload demanded by teacher observations has become unmanageable for some principals, others have welcomed the role of instructional leader. Still others find IMPACT destroying their ways of supervising and improving teaching in their schools.[52]

Other Districts Experimenting with VAM

What has occurred in Washington, D.C., with new curriculum standards, new tests, and IMPACT mirrors what has occurred in those urban districts across the country—Memphis, Tennessee, has recently adopted IMPACT—that have put into place testing and accountability structures described and analyzed in chapter 3. Since the early 1990s and especially after the passage of NCLB, most urban schools across the nation have narrowed their curriculum, leaving less time for non-tested subjects, intensified teacher-centered instruction with more lessons devoted to preparing students for tests, and, in general, reduced instructional time for reaching all of the curricular standards they are expected to meet over the school year.[53]

Even with teacher perceptions of unfairness and a climate of competition and fear surrounding performance-based evaluation, as well as researchers' reservations about both VAM's validity and reliability, there are teacher unions and groups of teachers who have worked with district superintendents to come up with multiple measures that include the use of student test scores to evaluate teacher performance. In Charlotte-Mecklenburg, North Carolina; Pittsburgh, Pennsylvania; Hillsborough, Florida; and Chattanooga, Tennessee, the Gates Foundation and other donors have funded programs that bring together research on teaching effectiveness and teacher evaluation procedures using student test scores as one of a cluster of measures to gauge teaching performance.[54]

Districts such as Montgomery County, Maryland; Hillsborough; Cincinnati, Ohio; Chicago, and many others use a framework for teaching developed by Charlotte Danielson, *22 Components of Great Teaching*.[55] Many of these districts and others (e.g., Denver, Colorado) have worked closely with their teacher unions to develop instruments, choose teachers to observe peers, and ensure that the effort considers issues raised by teachers.

Even with evidence of solid collaboration in a scattering of urban districts, divisive issues separating teachers and district administrators from using student test scores as even one of multiple measures in judging teacher performance persist. One acknowledged flaw in VAM, for example, is that student scores for a teacher vary from one year to another, resulting in some teachers moving from "effective" to "ineffective" ratings and back again in another year—or being fired. VAM algorithms, then, using imperfect data and making subjective decisions on what to include and exclude in the complex equations, are hardly "objective" indicators of a teacher's actual performance, given the continual appearance of false positives. As noted above, there are plenty of other unresolved difficulties when it comes to using VAM for up to 50 percent of a teacher's rating.[56]

Nonetheless, policy makers and researchers have argued for using these faulty and even unreliable value-added data to evaluate and pay individual teachers because even blemished measures are far better than the current system in which 95 percent of teachers receive satisfactory ratings. Furthermore, promoters of VAM argue that performance ratings in other occupations are similarly flawed but still give managers a better approximation of true performance than existing checklists or subjective ratings. An imperfect half loaf of bread is better, they say, than an unattainable and perfect full loaf. The unasked question, of course, is: *For whom is it better—teachers, principals, district officials, students—to use test scores as a measure of teacher performance?*[57]

Policy makers and researchers have used such rationalizations when introducing new medicines (as long as clinical trials honor the "do no harm" principle for treating the ill). Ditto for new technologies. Often companies push enhanced prototypes out the door as alpha and beta versions of hardware and software, leaving consumers to cope with and report glitches to vendors.

Even with all of the rationalizations, qualifiers, and acknowledgments of imperfections surrounding value-added measures, IMPACT and similar ventures evaluating individual teachers are at best beta versions subject to many technical glitches and unreliability. Saying "Oops!" when new technologies stumble means inconveniences and annoyance; but when—not *if*—new systems of evaluating teachers take wrong turns, they damage individuals. When errors are made in evaluating teachers, inaccurate data and false positives ruin careers and publicly shame teachers who do not merit such humiliation. Serious harm is done.

Finally, imagine the chaos that will ensue when value-added measures are used to evaluate individual teachers after states adopt Common Core standards and the new tests that will accompany those standards. The literature of testing is clear: in such an instance, student scores often dip. So when the new tests for Common Core standards in K–12 math and English-language arts are introduced in 2014, the additional years necessary to accumulate sufficient data to evaluate individual teachers may well lead to the entire system of VAM collapsing of its own weight or sinking slowly into neglect and oblivion.

In time, different versions of "good" teaching, each with their own "commandments," may be used to evaluate individual teachers as the technology of this methodology eliminates the abundant flaws and noise that accompany VAM. Even were that to occur, however, without teacher participation in the design of the evaluation, inclusion of multiple measures that include classroom observations, surveys of parent/student satisfaction, and protection from errors in judging performance, this unreliable approach to evaluation (and teacher pay) will continue to instill fear, promote teacher competition rather than collaboration, erode morale, and, ultimately destroy current school reforms by alienating the very people who work daily in classrooms.

There is a policy alternative, however. Using improved versions of VAM to reward and sanction schoolwide performance rather than individual teachers offers a higher probability of teacher collaboration, a sharing of knowledge and expertise among teachers to improve student learning and well-being. Recognizing that schools are the basic unit of improvement is consistent with the research literature on effective schools and commonsense experience with how people pull together organizationally to achieve worthwhile goals.

The history of efforts to reward school staffs rather than individuals has shown both promise and pitfalls in various districts across the country. But it need not be an either-or choice. VAM, along with other indicators, can be used for schoolwide performance rewards and sanctions while individual teachers can be evaluated with multiple measures, including student performance indicators that teachers and administrators jointly agree on.[58]

The point of all this is to be clear that, yes, some aspects of teaching can be improved through scientific studies, when teachers work together giving constant attention to classroom work, academic performance, and student well-being. Empirical findings have time and again improved teaching from decoding skills in reading to classroom management. VAM has possibilities and should continue to be developed for schoolwide performance. But what has been learned from science is not the lion's share of what constitutes daily teaching. As Philip Jackson said in 1968: "Teaching is an opportunistic process [where] . . . neither the teacher or [his] students can predict with any certainty exactly what will happen next. Plans are forever going awry and unexpected opportunities . . . are constantly emerging. The seasoned teacher seizes on these opportunities and uses them to . . . his student's advantage." [59]

Surprise and uncertainty greet teachers daily even for their best-planned lessons. Experienced teachers know this in their bones as they finesse or stumble during a lesson. They improvise on the spot, changing an activity, a task, a question without foreknowledge of whether the change will work. The unpredictability of classroom life requires artistry that few researchers—especially among the VAM-obsessed with their lengthy algorithms—care to (or cannot) include in their equations because there are no metrics to connect such unpredictability and artistry to students' test scores.

Those who still dream of engineering classrooms into mechanisms where empirically derived prescriptions help teachers become effective have failed to grasp that inside the black box of daily teaching is a mix of artistry, science, and uncertainty.

Summing Up

In comparing and contrasting medical practice and classroom teaching in part 2, I found that new structures of medical funding, technologies, and managerial control have constrained physician autonomy and have had some influence on practitioners in diagnosing and treating patients. Fee-for-service funding continues to dominate compensation in clinical practice. Rapid adoption of new diagnostic and treatment technologies, for example, is linked to insurer payments, as are performance report cards and metrics tied to individual doctors' pay.

But such measures do not necessarily result in overall cost reductions or improvements in the quality of patient care. All these structures provide evidence of how policy talk and adoption of policies creating structures influence what professionals and nonprofessionals say and think about how doctors practice but fall short of describing what actually occurs when patients and doctors interact. Yet—and this is a very important *yet*—the fundamental relationship between doctor and patient, the basis on which illness is treated and better health can emerge, the very heartbeat of clinical practice, remains firm. Fee-for-service has affected but not yet altered that relationship. Furthermore, whether those structural changes and anticipated and unanticipated effects on medical practice have led to healthier Americans—the desired outcomes of structural changes—remains contested.

For teachers, new structures in these very same areas have clearly influenced policy talk and action but examining the impact of classroom implementation of these policies shows that, other than changes that intensified existing classroom practices, there have not yet been substantial shifts in how teachers teach. That is, accountability and testing have fortified, not altered, teacher-centered instruction. And even these changes cannot be causally linked to gains (or losses) in student achievement.

Policy makers believed that making changes in funding for reduced class size policies and establishing charter schools would considerably alter daily classroom practices. According to many research studies, it did not. The promise of new technologies, from laptops to handheld devices, to shift dominant teacher-centered lessons to student-centered ones went unfulfilled, again, according to surveys of teachers and researchers' forays into classrooms. While promoters and policy makers continue to attribute the use of new technologies to changes in teaching practices and gains in student test scores, research has yet to show that new devices and software have caused either to occur.

Changes in practice did result, however, from putting into place testing and accountability structures, including new efforts to evaluate and pay teachers that relied on students' test scores. But the changes were not in the direction that reformers sought. Instead, studies point to teachers making changes that intensified teacher-directed lessons aimed at preparing students for standardized tests, meeting state curriculum standards, and spending much less time on nontested academic subjects. And again, these changes in classroom practices have yet to be causally connected to gains or losses in academic achievement.

So in these two chapters, where I compare medical and teaching practice, both commonalties and differences emerge.

- While insurers' funding through fee-for-service has influenced how both specialists and primary care physicians diagnose illnesses and use new technologies, the fee-for-service structure did not alter core medical practices or the primary relationship between doctors and patients. Similarly, for classroom teachers, new funding approaches, science curricula, and technologies had only a slight influence on daily lessons. At best, then, these structures in medicine and schooling have had far less influence on the physician-patient and teacher-student relationships than reformers had sought.
- Accountability structures and metrics that concentrate on patient and student outcomes have not substantially changed clinical medicine or mainstream classroom practices. In both professions, practitioners have challenged and raised significant issues about the direction and outcomes of implementing these structures.

- Overall health outcomes for Americans in morbidity and mortality and student achievement outcomes have yet to show substantial positive effects that can be attributed to these structural changes.[60]

These comparisons and contrasts between two helping professions aimed at improving individuals' lives reveal the complexity of practicing in institutions dedicated to human improvement. Reform-minded policy makers and donors, well-intentioned as they are in using business plans and models of change borrowed from other organizations, seek improvements in how doctors and teachers practice. Time and again, however, they have come to reckon with the fact of *dynamic conservatism*—the complexity of institutions adopting changes to maintain their stability.[61]

It is common in even the most traditional of community institutions that changes are made in order to *sustain* principles and practices that give that institution its character. What reformers dead set on transforming traditional institutions often forget is that complex organizations have plans for reformers as much as reformers do for organizations.

PART THREE

Unlocking the Black Box of the Classroom

FEDERAL, STATE, AND LOCAL POLICY MAKERS—from U.S. presidents and governors to legislators and district school boards—have the authority to create, amend, and dissolve structures of school governance, organization, curriculum, and instruction. Policy makers have used that authority to make both first-order and second-order changes in schools again and again in the past century. They did (and do) so because they believe that structures will alter in significant and desired directions what practitioners do daily in their classrooms. And, most important, those changed classroom pedagogies will lead students to learn successfully what society expects of its graduates to have when entering civic life and the labor market. That logic of structures changing practice has driven past and current reformers for decades.

Yet case studies of structures placing new technologies in schools, repeatedly revising the science curriculum, and establishing testing and accountability rules have underscored that these policy arrangements have had mixed effects, some intended and other unintended, on teaching practices. None of these structures substantially altered the dominant patterns of classroom teaching, although hybrids of old and new teaching practices have emerged.

The case of medical practice over the past half-century since Medicare and Medicaid became law reveals that public and private insurers using fee-for-service funding did influence some clinical decisions of specialist and primary care physicians. Overall, however, adept doctors, like teachers engaged in helping professions, made some changes, but few fundamental shifts occurred as a result of policy makers establishing new structures. Clinical practice in both professions remained a blend of continuity and change.

Why has stability and change persisted in these helping professions? Chapter 6 answers this question.

In sketching out the past thirty years of school reform, where structural changes were constant yet shifts in classroom practice were, at best, incremental, I offer explanations for why there was so little fundamental reform in teaching. I then fashion an explanation that makes most sense to me before looking around the corner of the upcoming decade as to what might be done with different structures that respect teachers' expertise and build on their willingness and commitment to improve practice through working closely with colleagues.

Chapter 6

Why So Many Structural Changes in Schools and So Little Reform in Teaching Practice?

The path of educational progress more closely resembles the flight of a butterfly than the flight of a bullet.

—Philip Jackson, 1968[1]

Questions:

What's the difference between sending a rocket to the moon and getting children to succeed in school?

What's the difference between a surgeon extracting a brain tumor and judge and jury deciding guilt or innocence for a person accused of murder?

Answer:

Sending a rocket to the moon and extracting a brain tumor are complicated, while getting children to succeed in school and arriving at verdicts are complex, closer to the "flight of a butterfly than the flight of a bullet."

According to multidisciplinary scholars and practitioners, complicated procedures like brain surgery and rocket launchings require engineer-designed blueprints, flowcharts breaking actions into step-by-step tasks, well-trained staff, and exquisite combinations of computer software running carefully calibrated equipment. Think, rocket landing on the moon in 1969, doctor-controlled robotic arms doing brain surgery, and the U.S. "shock and awe" invasion of Iraq in 2003.[2]

A complicated system assumes expert and rational leaders, top-down planning with a "mission control" unit pursuing scrupulous implementation of policies in a clockwork-precise organization. Complicated systems use the most sophisticated math, technical, and engineering expertise in mapping out flowcharts to solve problems. Work is specified and delegated to particular units, and outcomes are monitored. Confidence in performance and predictable results is in the air the organization breathes.

Yet even those sophisticated systems fail from time to time; for example, the *Challenger* shuttle disaster, the Three Mile Island nuclear meltdown, and the *Deepwater Horizon* oil spill.

Like complicated systems, complex systems such as legislatures, the courts, health-care, and schools are filled with hundreds of moving parts, but many of the parts are human, and these players have varied expertise and independence. Moreover, missing in such systems is a "mission control" that runs all these different parts within ever-changing political, economic, and societal surroundings. The result: constant adaptations and compromises in design and action.

Recall the U.S. president, Congress, lobbying groups, and scores of interest groups trying to pass a health-care reform bill into law during 2010 in the midst of a slow recovery from the Great Recession of 2008. Blueprints, technical experts, strategic plans, and savvy managers may be necessary but are insufficient to get complex systems with hundreds of reciprocal ties between people to operate effectively in constantly changing and unpredictable environments. These weblike, complex systems of interdependent units adapt continuously to turbulent surroundings. They are constantly changing just to maintain stability.

Hospitals, courts, and schools—even with their façades of command-and-control mechanisms, flowcharts, and policy manuals filled with detailed procedures—are constantly buffeted by unpredictable events and interrelated factors over which participants have no control. Picture a hospital emergency room; judges presiding over successive arraignments; and, yes, teachers teaching first-graders, algebra courses, and Advanced Placement U.S. history in the black boxes of classrooms.

These complex social systems have time and again foiled reform-driven policy makers' efforts to get doctors, judges, lawyers, and teachers to change their routine practices in any substantial way. I now return to the central question of this book to connect the complexity of school systems to classroom practices: *With so many major structural changes in U.S. public schools over the past century, why have classroom practices been largely stable with a modest blending of new and old teaching practices leaving contemporary classroom lessons familiar to earlier generations of school-goers?*

To document the complexity of the K–12 school system, look at figure 6.1, a representation of the external political factors and organizational forces that frequently impinge, sometimes unexpectedly, on what occurs in classrooms. Such figures, of course, give the mistaken impression that these stakeholders are static when, in real life, they are constantly using policy talk drenched in reform rhetoric as they lobby school board members and interact with administrators, teachers, and each other producing a tangled web of interdependent players in a complex system aimed at human improvement.

Now look at figure 6.2, which tries to capture the different factors—again, not static but in dynamic tension with one another—within a

FIGURE 6.1
External influences on the classroom

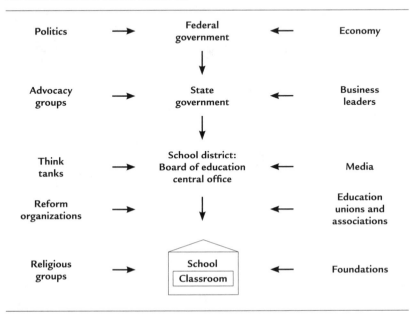

FIGURE 6.2

The classroom as a complex system

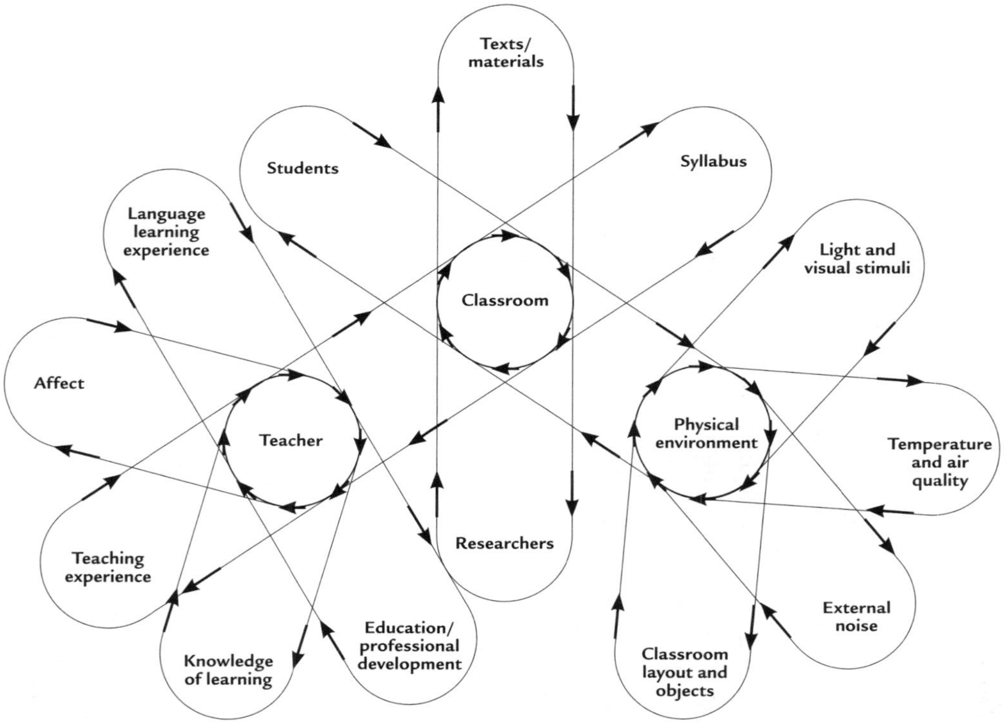

classroom. In the helping profession of teaching, the interdependence of teachers and students and relationships with peers and other adults inside and outside the school community are but a few of the influences that come into play when teaching and learning occur.[3]

Keep in mind the different levels of interaction and interdependence in these complex social systems. At one level is the mutual dependence of students and teachers in classroom interactions over content and skills during lessons in the black box. Next is the school level, where groups of students interact with adults who have reciprocal ties between themselves across many age-graded elementary and secondary classrooms. Parents and governmental agency adults also bring in concerns and resources that influence schoolwide relationships and routines. Then there is the district level, where decision makers use policy talk and take action in connecting those outside the organization and those inside who are expected to carry out decisions—the administrators and teachers who implement the policy. At the district level, community, state, and national economic, political, and social factors impinge on the community (e.g., immigration, economic recession, mayoral control of schools) and ripple through schools and classrooms.

This multitiered view of a complex system aimed at human improvement suggests the intricacies of overlapping and interacting levels comprising K–12 schooling. At each level, change and continuity are in dynamic, even tense, equilibrium—almost like running as fast as possible just to stay in the same place.[4]

What happens to teaching and learning in the black box of the classroom, then, when policy makers talk about reform and design changes, adopt policies intended to turn around classroom lessons, and then direct administrators and teachers to put those policies into practice?

Earlier chapters recounted how reformers created structures to get teachers to use new technologies, put new science content and skills into lessons, and—through establishing standards, testing, and accountability—produce gains in student achievement. Even when new funding structures such as reducing class size in lower elementary school grades and creating charter schools were put into place, classroom practices continued much as they had before. So structures that sought to reshape how teachers teach and students learn led to classrooms where teachers created hybrids of old and new teaching practice. Again and again, teachers adapted to these structural reforms by using mixes of traditional and nontraditional practices to fit the contours of their classrooms. Teachers did, indeed, make some changes; just not the fundamental—second-order—shifts in practice that reformers sought. Why?

Common Explanations for Change and Continuity in Classroom Practice

From policy makers, researchers, practitioners, journalists, and informed observers, including parents, those with and without stakes in the reform game, I have distilled frequently given explanations for why classroom practices, even when counting modest changes teachers made in routine tasks and activities, has remained largely stable. The list is hardly exhaustive or inclusive. It does, however, cover the major explanations I have seen in the literature on school reform.

What keeps teaching largely stable are teaching traditions dating back centuries that are reinforced by each generation of new teachers, supported by popular social beliefs, and fortified by the age-graded school structure.

Historical traditions of teacher-centered instruction to transfer knowledge, skills, and values have dominated teaching for centuries. Those who enter the teaching profession copy favorite teachers and adopt their instructional habits. These familiar forms of teaching persisted not only through habit but also because teachers believed they were both efficient and effective.[5] Moreover, since the nature of teaching is conservative—i.e., transmitting existing knowledge, skills, and values to the young—the occupation has attracted people who believe that such practices are both socially responsible and had worked for them when they were students and thus should be kept.

During the industrialization and urbanization of the United States in the nineteenth and twentieth centuries, the age-graded school ended the dominance of the one-room rural schoolhouse and continues to reign as the main way to organize schools. Its structure and lines of authority have limited teacher autonomy. Age-graded schools separate teachers into self-contained classrooms, carve curriculum into grade-level chunks for delivery to students, and require annual assessments of students to determine which ones get promoted or retained. District office and principal authority curb teachers' autonomy outside of class but much less so inside their classrooms.

Once teachers close their doors, the structure of self-contained and separate classrooms does allow a constrained autonomy. Teachers decide on which lessons (or parts thereof) they continue to teach and which ones they change. They decide to use old technologies and try out new ones. They experiment with new materials while using ones that worked in earlier lessons. They engage students in familiar activities and switch to ones that promise better learning. Blended practices emerge in different classrooms as teachers try out mixes of old and new. This age-graded structure, then, permits limited autonomy for both stability and change to coexist in the same classroom, but at the same time the organizational structure isolates and insulates teachers from one another, hampering collaboration across grades and departments.

Historic traditions of teaching renewed each generation by those who absorbed those habits as students and now teach in age-graded classrooms are further fortified by popular beliefs held by large proportions of taxpayers and voters. Most Americans believe that a "real school" is where teachers teach in age-graded, self-contained classrooms (e.g., first-graders learn to read; eighth- and ninth-graders take algebra) and where children and youth do what they are told. That is how students learn. Such beliefs sustain traditional forms of teaching, grant a limited amount of autonomy to teachers, and keep a complex system of many interacting parts working day in and day out.

Thus, traditions in ways of teaching, the people who enter teaching, the age-graded school structure, and pervasive social beliefs about what "real" teaching and "real" schools combine to explain continuity in classroom practice periodically seasoned by teacher-crafted changes.[6]

What has kept (and keeps) classroom practice largely stable has been teacher resistance to reform.

Teacher resistance comes in many colors. Many teachers, for example, actively prize what they do daily in classrooms and believe, for example, that teacher-centered instruction is more effective than student-centered instruction and judge efforts to use a new technology or curriculum to transform one to the other as uninformed. They resist such initiatives.

And then there are teachers who have heard the rhetoric of reform many times, participated in similar reforms, or seen them adopted and pushed into classrooms with little effect on learning. Many of these teachers resist new ideas and programs by being minimally compliant and making small changes or do as little as possible short of insubordination for well-justified reasons.

So one reason many reform initiatives fail is that teachers are reluctant to adopt changes that challenge their beliefs in teacher-centered instruction or that, in time, will be withdrawn. One often-forgotten example of top-down reform accompanied by lush rhetoric will do. Consider the hullabaloo over getting rid of social promotion in New York City in the early 1980s. For many years, reformers had criticized teachers and principals moving students to the next grade when they lacked the requisite knowledge and skills; social promotion had become a highly charged symbol of low academic standards. The then-chancellor, Frank Macchiarola, instituted a Promotional Gates program in which "gateway" tests in reading and math were administered to third- and seventh-grade students. If students didn't pass, they would have to repeat the grade. After a few years, so many students failed the test and were retained in one grade that they eventually dropped out of school. When data confirmed that outcome, the Promotional Gates program disappeared. A decade later, another chancellor, Rudy Crew, attacked social promotion by holding back thirty-five thousand students, requiring them to take special summer classes to advance to the next grade. Of that number, nearly twenty-five thousand had failed the annual tests, but almost a fifth of those failures occurred because of mistakes made by district officials. The chancellor quickly ended the program. Implementing untested ideas systemwide once can be chalked up to policy maker error. However, putting those same untested ideas into practice after failing the first time is dumb. Many teachers protested, but most watched, listened, and complied as policy makers stumbled.

Second, teacher resistance occurs because significantly changing classroom routines demands far too much time, energy, and skills—especially so given onerous workplace conditions they already face: large classes, tightly packed schedules, scrambling for instructional materials, and lack of support staff.

Third, most educational policy makers do not actively seek teacher cooperation in designing, adopting, and implementing decisions aimed at reshaping classroom practices—other than token representation on advisory committees or ad hoc consultation. So many teachers feel excluded from decisions that affect their classrooms and scoff at or ignore their supervisors when they hear the rosy promises that the next best reform will achieve.

Active or passive teacher resistance, then, tilts classroom practice far more toward continuity than change.[7]

Fundamental errors in policy maker thinking and actions in designing and converting policies into classroom practice keep teaching stable.

Policy makers seeking educational reform make two fundamental thinking errors. First, they believe that redesigning, dumping, or replacing key structures—governance, organization, and curriculum—will dramatically change teacher instruction and student learning. Second, they believe that public schools and classrooms are complicated, not complex, systems.

As a result, many policy makers see schooling as a collection of complicated structures that can be broken down into discrete segments and reengineered through algorithms and flowcharts to perfection—like piloting a Boeing 737—rather than as a complex, dynamic, and very messy multilevel system like air traffic control, with controllers adapting constantly to varying weather conditions, aircraft downtime, and daily peak arrivals and departures.[8]

Many policy makers treat school system structures like mechanisms with gears and cogs. They issue directives seeking school and classroom reforms and talk as if administrators and practitioners will carry out the orders put forth in the memos, flowcharts, and policy manuals. Too many loose connections, unmapped but interdependent relationships, unpredictable events, and ambiguous directives combine into a weblike, complex system that confounds what policy makers seek, what administrators request, and what teachers end up doing. Reengineering school organizations to fundamentally change classroom patterns and make them closer to the "flight of a bullet" remains a fantasy.[9]

What worsens the fundamental error of seeing schooling as a complicated set of structures in need of overhaul rather than a tangled maze of structures, events, and relationships is that reform-driven policy makers often want teachers to put contradictory goals into classroom practice.

Since the late 1980s, to cite one instance, the standards, testing, and accountability movement has pressed for exacting and intellectually challenging content and skills to be learned by all students. With the Common Core standards on the horizon, the fulfillment of this three-decade vision of a rigorous, intellectually engaging curriculum available to every U.S. student is on the cusp of being put into practice. Yet even in the best of situations, where well-prepared teachers and ample resources are present, those worthy curriculum and instructional aims conflict with one another.[10]

Consider that teachers, researchers, and policy makers have disagreed—and continue to do so—as to which strategies are best for engaging all students intellectually. Child-centered or subject-centered curriculum? Teacher-centered or student-centered pedagogies? How best to teach reading, math, social studies, foreign language, and science?

Moreover, insuring that every student has access to challenging ideas is no guarantee that every student will become intellectually engaged with ideas, because there is a multilayered curriculum in schools where teachers vary in what they decide to teach. Recall the science curriculum elaborated in chapter 2 where the taught curriculum differs from the intended or official one, which in turn differs from the learned and tested curricula. Also, students vary in motivations, aptitudes, and background. Access to knowledge, then, does not guarantee engagement. That curricular and student variation nearly guarantee that, even with the best of teacher efforts under the best of working conditions, substantial numbers of children and youth will be interested in other things than those ideas prescribed by a demanding curriculum.[11]

Compounding that fundamental error is that policy makers have only a dim idea of what teachers are thinking, much less doing everyday in their classrooms. While nearly all school board members have been students and sat a few feet away from teachers for over a dozen years, few have taught in public school classrooms. The same can be said for most federal- and state-level policy makers. Generally, district superintendents have been teachers early in their careers but there is a growing tendency to hire non-educator superintendents in big cities (e.g., lawyer Joel Klein in New York; former Colorado governor Roy Romer in Los Angeles; ex-U.S. Army generals Julius Becton in Washington, D.C., and John Stanford in Seattle).[12] Such administrators' lack of firsthand knowledge of daily work conditions underscores the simple fact that teachers and policy makers live in separate worlds where experiences, values, and incentives differ dramatically.

David Labaree summed up those differences crisply:

Teachers focus on what is particular within their own classrooms; reformers focus on what is universal across many classrooms. Teachers operate in a setting dominated by personal relations; reformers operate in a setting dominated by abstract political and social aims. Teachers draw on clinical experience; reformers draw on social scientific theory. Teachers embrace the ambiguity of classroom process and practice; reformers pursue the clarity of tables and graphs. Teachers put a premium on professional adaptability; reformers put a premium on uniformity of practices and outcomes.[13]

In being unable to see the world from teachers' perspectives, policy makers intent on transforming how teachers teach and students learn have a serious credibility problem in mobilizing teachers to support their reform agenda. And without teacher support for reform-driven policies, few significant changes will occur in daily lessons.

Class Warfare, a recent book by lawyer and writer Steven Brill illustrates this point.[14] Brill interviewed current members of the reform-driven policy elite. He reported that these influential elected officials, donors, hedge fund managers, CEOs, and high-tech entrepreneurs saw the structure of collective bargaining—whereby teacher unions and the school board negotiate contracts—as causing poor academic performance in urban schools. They believe that without union contracts, first-rate teachers who could be evaluated and paid on the basis of their performance would raise student test scores. Stellar teachers would make "no excuses" and get students to achieve, while ineffective teachers would be fired.

Enamored of Ivy league graduates in Teach for America, New Leaders for New Schools, and hedge fund founders, Brill writes over eighty chapters portraying union officials as villainous and making heroes of ex-chancellors Joel Klein of New York City and Michelle Rhee of Washington, D.C.; the founders of KIPP schools; and a Teach for America graduate who worked in a Harlem charter school. These heroes promote more charter schools, work to curb teacher union influence, recruit new teachers and principals from hitherto untapped pools of candidates, and embrace performance-based evaluation and compensation.

Brill illustrates the complexity of reforming schools and the separate worlds that teachers and reform-driven policy makers inhabit in his final chapter. Over four hundred pages into the book, after painting teacher unions as wearing black hats and KIPP leaders and Teach for America novices wearing white ones, he pivots 180 degrees. In that chapter, he reveals to readers that Jessica Reid, that gallant Teach for America graduate who in earlier chapters said "to do this right, you have to be on all the time" and went on to serve as an assistant principal in a charter school—resigned, explaining, "This wasn't a sustainable life, in terms of my health and my marriage."[15]

In another telling episode, a founder of KIPP admits to Brill that the model of recruiting supertalented teachers who worked in those charter schools twelve-plus hours a day week after week could never supply enough teachers to reform urban schools across the nation.[16] Finally, capping this stunning turnabout, Brill recommends one of the "villains"—Randi Weingarten, the head of the American Federation of Teachers—as the next chancellor of the largest school district in the nation.[17]

Forget the structural reforms that Brill recommended throughout the book. Forget the "no excuses" mantra that reform-driven policy makers and their entourages he interviewed repeated and praised. Brill seems to have had an epiphany.

Since we cannot rely on superheroes to staff and run schools, no reform agenda can ever move beyond headlines in media and scattered success stories in schools without the support of mainstream teachers and union leaders. Even after Brill's "who's who" of policy makers, CEOs, and philanthropists pursued a reform agenda in urban districts, his enthusiasm leaked out of his "no excuses" balloon and he came to see that without most teachers working with policy makers, little of real worth happens in schools and classrooms.

There is another significant error that policy makers commit as a result of inhabiting a different world from teachers. They and their elite cadre confuse teacher quality with teaching quality. They believe that personal traits of teachers—smart, determined, energetic, caring, intellectually curious—produce student learning rather than the classroom and school settings. Both are intertwined and crucial, of course, but policy makers and their influential camp followers have accentuated personal traits far more than the organizational and social context in which teachers work. So if students score low on tests, then who the teachers are, their personal traits, credentials, and attitudes come under close scrutiny, rather than the age-graded school, neighborhood demography, workplace conditions, and resources that support teaching. The person overshadows the place.[18]

And for obvious reasons. Reform-enthused policy makers can have some measure of influence over who is in the schools, but they have much less influence on changing neighborhood demographics or poverty. But in attributing far more weight to individual teacher traits rather than seriously working to alter the situation in which teachers teach, policy makers end up having a cramped view of teach*ing* quality. They ignore that quality teaching is complex because it includes both *good* and *successful* teaching, a distinction often missing from policy makers' vocabulary. Both good and successful teaching are necessary to reach the threshold of quality instruction and make student learning possible. To lead us through the thicket of complexity, I lean on Gary Fenstermacher and Virginia Richardson's analysis of quality teaching.[19] These researchers help us parse *quality teaching* into distinctions between *good* and *successful* teaching and learning while revealing serious conceptual errors that policy makers have made and continue to make.

Good teaching is about the how and what of classroom practice. For example, the task of getting a child to understand the theory of evolution, or the Declaration of Independence, or prime numbers in ways fitting students' ages and consistent with best practices in the field. *Successful teaching*, however, is about what the child learns; for example, getting the same child who was taught these subjects to write three paragraphs filled with relevant details and present-day examples that demonstrate understanding of the theory of evolution or the Declaration of Independence, or to use Eratosthenes' Sieve.

Good and successful teaching, then, are not the same nor does one necessarily lead to the other. How can that be?

Fenstermacher and Richardson point out that *learning*, like teaching, can also be distinguished as good or successful. The above examples of student proficiency on the theory of evolution, the Declaration of Independence, and prime numbers demonstrate *successful learning*. *Good learning*, however, requires other factors: the student is willing to learn and puts forth effort; the student's family, peers, and community support learning; the student has the place, time, and resources to learn; and, finally, the student has *good teaching*.

In short, good teaching is one of four necessary components of good learning. "No excuses" policy makers make the mistake of squishing together *good teaching* and *successful learning*. In doing so, they erase three critical factors that are equally important in getting students to learn: the student's own effort, support of family and peers, and the opportunity to learn in school. Current hoopla over paying teachers for their performance based on student test scores is an expression of this conflation, and the ultimate deception of parents, voters, and students that good teaching naturally leads to successful learning.

Not only does this policy maker error about the quality of classroom instruction confuse the personal traits of the teacher with teaching, it also nurtures a heroic view of school improvement where superstars such as Geoffrey Canada, Jaime Escalante, and Erin Gruwell (who were the subjects of the films *Waiting for Superman, Stand and Deliver,* and *Freedom Writers,* respectively), labor day in and day out to get their students to ace AP calculus tests and become accomplished writers and achieve in Harlem schools. No profession—doctors, lawyers, military officers, or nuclear physicists—can depend on superstars, as Steven Brill found out with Jessica Reid, to get their work done every day. Nor should all teachers have to be heroic. Policy makers attributing quality far more to individual traits in teachers than to the context in which they teach leads to confusing good teaching with successful learning, resulting in even further collateral damage to the profession by setting up the expectation that only heroes need apply.[20]

By stripping away from good learning essential factors of students' motivation, social context, and the opportunities they have to learn in school, policy makers inadvertently twist the links between teaching and learning into a simpleminded formula that miseducates the public they serve. They encourage a generation of idealistic newcomers to become classroom heroes who end up deserting schools wholesale within a few years because they find out that good teaching does not lead automatically to successful learning.

Which of These Explanations Best Accounts for Continuity and Change in Classroom Practice?

I have considered various explanations for why teaching practice remains stable even as teachers adopt different changes in their classrooms. Constancy and change are properties of complex systems. Those explanations that take into consideration both stability and change, recognize the political and institutional dynamics inherent to complex organizations, especially ones that seek to improve human beings, I find most consistent with the half-century of experiences I have had in schools and evidence that I and other researchers have gathered.[21]

Schools have always been complex systems with traditions of teaching that have persisted over time. New teachers seeking to help children and youth found out about teaching when they were students watching their teachers as they proceeded through the grades. Those age-graded structures imposed both freedom and restraint on teachers. Even with these situational constraints, teachers and students generally accepted the received structures. Moreover, educators, students, and parents remain constant in their beliefs and persist in patterns in behavior in the face of the uncertainties and unpredictability that accompany complex systems.

Examples include those new teachers in a district startled by receiving letters that they will be let go in June because the governor reduced the state budget in the middle of the school year. Or a principal who receives an unexpected ultimatum from parents who want a particular second-grade teacher for their children—and unless the principal complies, they will visit the superintendent.

Teachers have expertise in subject matter, knowledge of children and youth, and pedagogical skills, but such knowledge and skills are insufficient to overcome the uncertainties inherent to teaching content to students from different backgrounds, interests, and motivations in places where unpredictable events and interactions occur frequently. Increasing that uncertainty and unpredictability in complex school systems is that teaching is a helping profession, like social work, psychotherapy, and medicine, among others. Add the predicament common to the helping professions that teachers are utterly dependent on their students for learning to occur. Teachers can engage in *good* teaching, but without student cooperation and active involvement, support from parents, and sufficient resources in the workplace, *good* learning may not translate into *successful* learning.

These complex systems, in combination with the predicaments of the helping professions, help to account for both constancy and change in classroom practice. And that is the crucial point: teachers do not robotically teach as they were taught or instinctively abhor making changes. On the contrary, they frequently make changes in their classroom content, activities, and use of technologies. In creating hybrids of practice, teachers maintain the uneasy equilibrium of stability and change that exists in classrooms and schools.

The concept of *dynamic conservatism* involving both continuity and change to maintain a tenuous balance in classrooms and schools comes into play here. Institutions often fight to remain the same. Professionals in complex institutions frequently respond to major reforms by adopting those parts of the changes that will maintain stability. Consider, for example, administrators adding new courses on critical thinking to meet reformers' demand for twenty-first-century skills. Or teachers urging students to bring their laptops to class to do Internet searches, take notes, and work in teams to make PowerPoint presentations. These teachers have made changes in how they teach while maintaining a familiar flow of lessons. They have "hugged the middle" between traditional and nontraditional ways of teaching.[22]

Those reformers dead set on redesigning classrooms and schools, however, scorn hybrid teaching practices; transformation is necessary. Institutional stability is dysfunctional, they argue. It keeps worthy fundamental changes at arm's length.[23]

What creates hurdles for teachers and administrators is when policy makers intent on improving schools err in viewing schools as complicated rather than complex systems. Too many decision makers lack understanding of dynamic conservatism. Or they *do* understand it and choose to ignore it because they see these systems as ineffective, even pathologically unworkable, and in need of reengineering. In adopting reforms that will jolt the system sufficiently to substantially alter teaching and learning, policy makers have mistakenly grafted practices borrowed from other organizations onto schools (e.g., zero-based budgeting in the 1970s; management by objectives and restructuring in the 1980s; pay-for-performance and loosening credential requirements in the 1990s and since). No surprise, then, that policy makers treating complex systems as complicated ones in adopting and implementing school reforms have triggered both active and passive teacher resistance.

In defining institutional and political concepts in terms of complex and complicated systems and explaining dynamic conservatism and the predicaments common to helping professions, I have woven together a tapestry that helps me to explain why classroom practices over time have changed in many respects but still have largely remained stable and familiar to each generation of teachers, students, and parents. For me, this tapestry of an explanation clarifies why there has been much change in schools and classrooms but so little reform of the fundamental structures—age-graded schools, school governance, staffing, societal inequalities—that sustain continuity in teaching practices.

I have one reservation about this explanation, however. In pointing out the differences between complex and complicated systems, I may have given too little attention to the major influence that reform-driven policy makers and entrepreneurial business and civic elites have had in steering the past two decades of school improvement.

For over three decades, civic and business leaders and philanthropists have led a movement intent on converting schools into places where students will be prepared to compete with other nations' students in knowledge and skills to enter jobs in a global economy. This dominant coalition, however, has competed with other reformers from the political center and left who have criticized this goal for ignoring civic engagement, social injustices, and the well-being of children and youth, as well as focusing far too much on standardized test scores.

Charges and countercharges have been hurled between reformers. "No excuses" reformers point out that good schools and teachers can overcome poverty. They scorn the half-measures of teachers using laptops unimaginatively in classrooms. They point out that, with sufficient charter schools and less union resistance to performance-based evaluation, their reform efforts would yield a great return on investment. Other critics label these policy elites *corporate reformers* who seek the privatization of public schools.

Blaming Corporate Reformers—an Oversimplication

Those using the epithet *corporate reformers* argue that the current dominant reform agenda seeks to turn schools into market-driven organizations where consumer choice reigns and teaching and learning are commodities to be packaged and delivered.

Veteran teacher and writer Stanley Karp has this to say about such reformers:

[T]he testing regime . . . is the main engine of corporate reform to extend the narrow standardization of curricula and scripted classroom practice that we've seen under No Child Left Behind and drill down even further into the fabric of schooling to transform the teaching profession and create a less experienced, less secure, less stable and less expensive professional staff . . .

A larger corporate reform goal, in addition to changing the way schools and classrooms function, is reflected in the attacks on collective bargaining and teacher unions and the permanent crisis of school funding across the country. These policies undermine public education and facilitate its replacement by a market-based system that would do for schooling what the market has done for health care, housing, and employment: produce fabulous profits and opportunities for a few and unequal outcomes and access for the many . . . [24]

Educational historian, blogger, and critic Diane Ravitch expresses a similar opinion:

The corporate reformers have done a good job of persuading the media that our public schools are failing because they are overrun by bad teachers, and these bad teachers have lifetime tenure because of their powerful unions.[25]

Critics also see antipathy toward unions and an uncritical embrace of online instruction, often sold and delivered by for-profit companies, as more evidence of corporate reform.[26]

I have tried to avoid such terms because, in my opinion, they imply certainty about reformers' motives, smell of conspiratorial decision making, and ignore the unvarnished embrace of markets and business practices that has swept across all U.S. institutions, including schools, in the past quarter-century. I am allergic to such implications, smells, and neglect of what runs through the entire society. My allergy derives from the following points:

• While the current generation of civic and business leaders, donors, and elected federal officials—policy elites—believe in the crucial importance of schooling spurring economic growth and believe in market forces advancing equal opportunity and democracy, such similarities in beliefs do not a conspiracy make.
• Policy elites have varied, not uniform, motives (e.g., create competitive markets between schools, increase equal opportunity for poor and minority children and youth, expand parental choice, enlarge

individual liberty). These varied and contradictory values make it difficult to sustain cabals, much less take united action.

- Policy elites drawn from overlapping but distinct spheres of influence (e.g., CEOs, donors, elected officials, think tank pundits, etc.) vary in their aims and strategies. They are seldom organized enough to maintain secrecy, control the flow of information, and follow through with decisions. But they can and do move in the same direction that suggests concerted effort even if at times they trip and fall.[27]

- Policy elites are pragmatic decision makers. While ideologies vary in strength among elites, more often than not, policies evolve out of practical decisions often made under political and economic conditions that require action to advance an overall agenda (e.g., abandon small schools as a reform strategy and embrace pay-for-performance plans).

How do I know this? Much comes from direct but limited experience with policy elites and research on educational decision making. It is no secret, for example, that since the collapse of the Soviet Union, market-based ideas have swept across U.S. institutions. Ideas, language, and practices drawn from the for-profit sector have seeped into military operations, governmental agencies, hospitals, prisons, and churches. Outsourcing and privatization have spread. Unrelenting focus on outcomes, the bottom line, has become a staple in public institutions. School leaders are hardly alone in importing business practices, seeing education as a commodity, and adopting the vocabulary of markets.[28]

I raise these points to make clear that I avoid such phrases as *corporate reformers* because they suggest far more coherence and joint action than occurs in the real world of politics and policy making. I do understand how many educators under unceasing attacks for decades can see profit-driven conspiracies to destroy public schools in the words and actions of well-heeled donors, federal officials, and entrepreneurs who attack unions; champion charter schools and vouchers; and urge that student test scores be used to sort out effective from ineffective teachers.

But my experience and research have uncovered no conspiracies to privatize public schools or deliberately bash teachers. What I see among educators and policy elites are differences in political beliefs, values, and language over the direction public schools should take in an ever-changing global economy, one in which both business and government have always been involved in making decisions. Convergent interests can fuel a reform movement but such a coming together of varied groups hardly constitutes a conspiracy or becomes an unstoppable force.

Consider vouchers. Since political conservatives first embraced government-paid vouchers for parents to use in choosing schools in the 1970s, each time they put vouchers (by the way, they were initially proposed by political liberals!) on state and local ballots, voters turned the measures down. Even with a 2002 U.S. Supreme Court decision allowing vouchers to be used for religious schools, there is little public support for them. There are, then, limits to what even convergent interests can achieve in directing school reform.[29]

Positive Outcomes of Three Decades of Economic-Driven School Reforms

Whether readers agree or disagree with characterizing policy elites as *corporate reformers*, in forging my explanation for the stability and change that occurs in the black box of the classroom, I have highlighted the errors of reform-driven policy makers and entrepreneurial business and civic elites for supporting initiatives that have, in my judgment, been unhelpful in schools and misled the public. Yet though I have criticized these policy makers, I must also point out positive outcomes these reform-minded, diverse policy elites have achieved over the past three decades.

1. Hastening the shift from defining school effectiveness as the level of resources that go into schooling children and youth to exclusive concentration on outcomes.

Since the late-nineteenth century, policy makers judged school quality and effectiveness by how much money was spent per student, the credentials teachers possessed, the condition of facilities, and instructional resources given to teachers and students—or what economists call *inputs*. There was a basic trust in how teachers taught and administrators ran schools. Those judgments of quality and trust in educators have changed dramatically in the past half-century.

The use of student test scores to assess school effectiveness and student learning began in the mid-1960s, when the Elementary and Secondary Education Act of 1965 mandated that standardized test scores be used to evaluate the success of Title I programs targeting low-income schools. By the end of the 1970s, urban school reformers had begun to compare and contrast those high-scoring urban elementary schools enrolling poor and minority children with schools in neighborhoods with similar enrollments that were low performers. Ronald Edmonds and others noted the factors that were associated with high-performing schools, and throughout the 1980s, Effective Schools programs spread slowly across urban districts.[30]

With the publication of *Nation at Risk* in 1983 and frequent media attention on U.S. students' ranking on international tests, active reform coalitions lobbied federal, state, and local officials to overhaul and restructure failing U.S. schools. Presidents George H.W. Bush and Bill Clinton initiated programs throughout the 1990s that used test scores and other outcome measures such as dropout rates, percentages of students graduating high school, and numbers of graduates attending college to determine program effectiveness. Many states required tests and public reporting of student outcomes in attendance, dropouts, and high school graduates. With the passage of NCLB in 2001, the federal government mandated states to use test scores and other outcomes to determine whether schools were succeeding or failing. Those that were failing had to be improved or closed.

By 2013, the entire vocabulary of effective schooling had shifted nearly 180 degrees from *inputs* to *outputs*. If an input like per-pupil expenditure is used, more often than not, it highlights discrepancies between high-expenditure districts with mostly low-income students scoring poorly on tests than similar districts spending fewer dollars but harvesting higher test scores. How much money is spent on schools—the criterion of effective schools used for nearly a century—has been replaced by ranking schools on the basis of test scores. The once-upon-a-time trust in teachers and administrators has shifted radically to nearly total reliance on measurement.

Although I consider diminished public trust in teachers over the past few decades as a significant loss for U.S. schools in recent decades, I do consider the increased focus on student outcomes as a positive outcome since it directed public attention to those in-school factors that can be solidly linked to changes in student performance, albeit on the constricted measure of test scores. How schools are governed and organized, what knowledge and skills students are expected to learn, whether teachers work alone or collaborate, how teachers teach and students learn—all become factors that can be (and should be) connected to student outcomes including other measures beyond standardized test scores. But responsibility for student outcomes should not be loaded onto teachers' shoulders alone. Yet it has been, through policy maker rhetoric coupling poor schools to poor teaching rather than considering out-of-school factors.

So the past half-century has accelerated intense attention on what teachers do, how they are evaluated, and student outcomes, a movement that now has coalesced into an—and here is my criticism—exclusive concentration on test scores supplemented occasionally by other student outcomes.[31]

2. Tapping nontraditional pools for new teachers and administrators.

With the growth of teacher education in colleges and universities throughout the twentieth century, a single path emerged to becoming a teacher certified to teach elementary and secondary school and becoming a principal and superintendent. To become a teacher, one needed a bachelor's degree with a major in a subject area that included state-required courses and a minimum amount of time in schools working as an apprentice teacher. Principals and superintendents were subject to similar state requirements for administrative credentials acquired from universities.

With the surge of school reform in the 1960s, teacher education institutions came under attack for monopolizing the market. Entrepreneurial educators seeking ways of improving urban schools and backed by federal and philanthropic funding looked to other sources for teachers. Returned Peace Corps volunteers, midcareer military personnel, and women returning to the workplace became sources of new teachers. Most already had bachelor's degrees, so alternative paths to attaining certification beyond taking courses in a university-based credential emerged throughout the 1970s. District-based credential programs, ad hoc one-year university programs, and similar efforts supplied a small but steady stream of recruits for urban and suburban schools.[32]

As reform-driven coalitions sought to overhaul U.S. schools in the 1980s and 1990s, teacher education programs came under increasing attack. More alternative paths to becoming a teacher, building on earlier programs, emerged, including Teach for America, The New Teacher

Project, and similar ventures; new paths for principals and superintendents were also emerging. These alternative paths for recruiting, training, and placing novices in hard-to-fill posts in urban schools have significantly challenged the worth of conventional university-based teacher education programs and traditional pathways for new teachers and administrators to enter schools.[33]

3. Increasing parental choice of public schools—charters, magnets, and portfolios of options.

Parents could choose among alternative schools in the 1960s. In Arlington, Virginia, where I served as superintendent in the 1970s and early 1980s, elementary and secondary schools, ranging from nontraditional to traditional, were available, and still exist. Many other districts offered similar choices. What the current expansion of parental choice has done is expand choice into areas hitherto unexplored.[34] It has expanded professional and popular views of successful schools.

For example, whatever one thinks of KIPP schools, there is little doubt that they have provided alternative visions and proof that minority and poor children can succeed—much as an earlier generation of Effective Schools did in the 1980s and 1990s. The same can be said of charter school networks such as Aspire, Green Dot, and Leadership Public Schools, as well as blended learning schools, whose mixes of online and regular classroom teaching appeal to parents. New kinds of schooling have become possible that stretch far beyond alternatives of the 1960s and 1970s.

While that expanded parental choice has yet to satisfy pent-up demands for more high-achieving schools in many cities and while the aim of creating competitive pressure on urban districts to copy such models has yet to lead to altered teaching practices or duplication of such schools within districts, it is clear in 2013 that new structures for parent choice have broadcast different visions of what can be achieved with low-income and minority students and opened up opportunities that simply did not exist earlier.

There have been costs, however. The idea of public charters and alternatives broadening the supply of schools to meet increasing demands from parents and the notion of customizing schools to appeal to certain groups of parents have led to schools being advertised in ways similar to other commodities in a market-driven society—as products that can be purchased, used, and then tossed aside. Brand-name schools as consumer products to be bought by individual parents mock the very point of tax-supported public schools—a public good, benefiting society. Moreover, in some districts where charters are a substantial portion of the public schools, neighborhood schools have died a slow death.[35]

In examining both the positive outcomes and the costs involved, I would still judge the worth of reformers' achievements over the past three decades an overall plus. *Overall plus* means that there are many negatives still to be addressed. Negatives appear in the possibility that the accelerated shift in defining quality from inputs to outputs has gone too far and too fast. Negatives appear in decreased trust in teachers and administrators and using student test scores to determine individual teacher effectiveness even when validity and reliability of such value-added measures are suspect. Negatives appear in the unceasing hype surrounding charter schools as the panacea for turning around low-performing urban students, even as many such schools fail for fiscal and academic reasons. Negatives appear in the constant rhetoric of business and civic leaders, eager to transform U.S. schools with fewer dollars, pointing out that it is not how much school boards have to spend but *how* it is spent that matters. These negatives are substantial and not to be swept aside as trivial. They argue for policy makers, researchers, and voters striking a better balance between inputs, processes, and outcomes in assessing public schools.

What Should Be Done?

In pointing out positive and negative ideas and outcomes I see emerging from three decades of policy elites pushing for U.S. public schools to grow smarter students—better human capital—to sustain a strong economy, there are, inescapably, persistent policy disadvantages to this direction. These include reliance on particular structures (e.g., age-graded schools, state and district inequities in funding, standards-based curriculum and testing, technology) to transform teaching and learning and, most detrimental, policy makers' values and incentives wedded to insufficient knowledge about what happens in schools and classrooms contributing to substantial errors in their thinking and actions. What, then, can be done in a complex system of interdependence and interrelationships subject to unpredictable events and uncertain outcomes to exploit the positives without worsening the negatives?

Because public schooling is a complex institution and teaching is a helping profession aimed at human improvement, sticky predicaments and unpredictable outcomes are inevitable. Treating public schools and classrooms as complicated places that can be redesigned by shrewd policy makers and entrepreneurs through top-down decisions and new structures may have some merit at first. Yet such a view is, at worst, a significant error and, at best, insufficient to overhaul teaching practices in the black box of the classroom.

Current civic and business leaders among the reigning policy elites—biennial and quadrennial elections mean that they and their appointed entourages move in and out of state capitals and Washington, D.C.—vary in their motives, short- and long-term interests, and stamina. Likewise, they have a weak capacity to work closely together for long periods of time. What that means to me is that there is much room for insurgent school reformers—teachers, administrators, academics, parents, engaged citizens, and policy makers—to chart different directions for school improvement, challenging the three-decade-long campaign to make schools an arm of a knowledge-based economy and teachers its mechanics.

Charting a different direction will not be easy when U.S. presidents from both political parties for the past quarter-century have promoted more and better schooling as essential for building a strong economy. Public opinion polls and a steady drumbeat of warnings from civic and business leaders, donors, and pundits about the economic and political dangers facing the United States in coming decades have further fortified mainstream ideas that the only course for U.S. schools, especially in racially and ethnically segregated cities, is to have high test scores that rival other nations' and for every student to attend college and get a job in the knowledge economy. Nonetheless, there are voices that counter that conventional thinking.

Progressives of all stripes interested in decreasing economic inequalities and increasing social justice, nurturing the whole child, and promoting schools containing networks of family and community services—disparate as these factions are—have come together on different occasions to oppose this reform agenda. The Save Our Schools movement, for example, sponsored a march in Washington in 2011 for those opposed to the contemporary school reform agenda, especially the dominance of standardized testing. Groups of parents (e.g., United Opt Out) have enlisted principals, teachers, and parents who petition state and local school boards to stop testing and protest standardized tests by keeping their children home when state tests are given. Whether these groups and others like them, offering alternative visions of reform and mobilizing to influence district, state, and national decision makers, will succeed politically to override the current standards-based testing and accountability policies, I cannot say. But these and other opposing voices will persist.[36]

As important as political mobilizing is to modify the current reform rhetoric and policy direction, another venue for change has been, and will continue to be, teachers working collectively across grade levels, departments, and schools to improve their content knowledge and teaching skills. For many years, teachers, administrators, researchers, and a sprinkling of policy makers have concentrated on both traditional and innovative professional development and learning communities to build teachers' capacities in knowledge of subject and teaching skills to improve instruction in schools and districts. Such school-based efforts converge on the teacher simply because within the complex system of schooling, the teacher-student relationship is fundamental to student learning and that relationship is forged in the classroom.[37]

Let me be clear about what I mean by *improve instruction* through professional development and learning communities. Throughout this book, I have described frequent efforts of reform-driven academics and policy makers to shift the dominant teacher-centered pedagogy (e.g., knowledge and skills-driven, bound to texts, homework, teacher telling, etc.) to a more student-centered one (e.g., big ideas tied to multidiscipline curricula, focus on student involvement and decision making in learning). For many top-down reformers, *improve* means shifting from teacher-centered to student-centered instruction, the assumption being that such pedagogies will get students to manage their learning better than when directed wholly by teachers and textbooks, and thus achieve goals of independent thinking and lifelong learning.

For the most part, these top-down efforts, in the form of new and renovated structures of funding, charter schools, technologies, and testing regimes have failed to substantially change teaching practices. Individually and collectively, teachers have, of course, made changes by creating hybrids of teacher- and student-centered instruction. But for practitioners working in the complex environment of the classroom—where students bring different motivations, varied interests, and a range of aptitudes and abilities—no one way of teaching would ever suffice. A broad repertoire of teaching activities and tasks has a better chance of working than any doctrinaire pedagogy.

Professional development and learning communities are, of course, structures. They do differ, however, in design and adaptability from those structures and programs that policy makers have copied from the private sector (e.g., mayoral control, Total Quality Management, competency-based standards, management by objectives, accountability and testing). These borrowed structures have been inadequate in coping with interdependent, unpredictable complex systems, especially in changing substantially what occurs in the black box of classrooms. But structures designed and aimed at working with individuals and groups of teachers in schools through professional development—sometimes awful, sometimes inspirational, and sometimes practical—have existed for decades.

What promises to increase the worth of districtwide professional development, especially if based within schools and involving teachers in the planning, are those efforts concentrating on prevailing beliefs among teachers about teaching and learning, current norms in the school community, and classroom practices. When teachers work together to examine student work and analyze classroom lessons, they figure out collectively what works and what doesn't work, and they build a culture of learning across grade levels in elementary schools and within departments in secondary schools. They build and share *pedagogical capital*—a scarce resource because isolation is endemic to age-graded schools. That pedagogical capital blends ambitious lessons and traditional ones of teacher- and student-centered practices, rather than a single one-best-way of teaching. Such hybrids working within adaptable structures of professional development and site-based learning communities are tailored for complex, weblike systems like schools.[38]

When teachers, administrators, and parents collaborate within schools and districts, they create and sustain climates that support good *and* successful teaching drawn from different pedagogies. Such collaboration comes far closer to achieving good student learning than big-ticket structural reforms such as funding, authorizing charter schools, mayoral control of schools, accountability and testing, and new curricula. Whether such sustained collaboration and creation of these communities in schools can significantly change routine practices and produce gains in student achievement has yet to emerge clearly. Still, even without clear evidence that such communities of practice are successful by current metrics, supporting teachers to figure out together what works best with their students—rather than having error-prone policy makers direct their efforts to improve practice—remains worthwhile. It would far more effectively allow them to build their capacities while forging strong relationships with students—the soil from which learning springs.[39]

Examples of school-based efforts of teachers would help. In elementary and secondary schools, learning communities illustrate how teachers come together voluntarily to determine how and what their students are learning. They analyze common problems that arise in lessons and teaching district curriculum standards; they observe one another and see how colleagues use blends of old and new practices; they build trust, cooperate, and focus on instructional improvement. They try out activities and lessons a peer used. They create a culture of learning.

The work of Fred Newmann, Rick DuFour, Milbrey McLaughlin and Joan Talbert, Judith Little, Anthony Bryk, and many others profiles elementary grade-level teams and secondary academic departments sprouting slowly into school-based learning communities. In these profiled schools—from "Hancock" Elementary School in Chicago to Boones Mill elementary school in rural Virginia, from Aragon High School's social science department in San Mateo, California, to Lakeside Southwest (Washington) High School's science department—teachers forged teams over time that trusted one another as they worked together on instructional improvement.[40]

At Aragon High School, for example, Christine Foster reported about the work of social studies teachers:

> [T]eachers in the social studies . . . department . . . share an office, which becomes a central gathering place. During lunch each day, anywhere from 15 to 25 teachers show up and swap ideas about lesson plans, tests and classroom management. [T]eachers . . . are so close that a group of 20, including spouses, took a ski trip. "That's a missing

ingredient for a lot of teachers. It makes you want to go to school, and not just for students," [says department head Lee Swenson.][41]

In such communities, teachers agree to disagree. They trade techniques and lessons. Their beliefs shift. Teaching practices change. Teacher isolation and insulation from one another—the effects of age-graded school structures—bit by bit disappear. And some of these learning communities had sufficient continuity in teacher and principal leadership to have lasted for decades.

Occasionally, depending on the quality of principal leadership, elementary grade-level teams and secondary academic departments grew into school-based communities—even before the phrase *professional learning communities* was invented. Examples come from the alternative schools of the 1970s, the Effective Schools movement in the 1980s, and the Coalition of Essential Schools in the 1990s. For example, Deborah Meier founded Central Park East Secondary School in New York City's Harlem in 1974 and then a network of small secondary schools, staying until 1995; Ray Anderson became principal of H-B Woodlawn in Arlington, Virginia, in 1978 and remained until 2004; Ann Cook and Herb Mack established Urban Academy in New York City in 1986 and continue directing the school. Stability in teacher and principal leadership is a necessary condition for school-based learning communities to survive and thrive.[42]

In some instances, school systems have cultivated both professional development across their districts and school-based learning communities focused on instructional improvement. In Pittsburgh, Pennsylvania, in the early 1980s, for example, superintendent Richard Wallace closed a high school with low test scores and declining enrollment and reopened it as a magnet school for students and training center for the district's high school teachers. Between 1983 and 1989, the teacher center brought in nearly one thousand teachers from eleven other district high schools to spend eight weeks learning the Madeline Hunter approach to lessons, content knowledge in their discipline, and ways to improve their teaching through seminars, observations of master teachers, and conferences. After eight weeks, teachers returned to their high school assignments. Evaluations posted high teacher satisfaction with the experience, difficulties in adjusting to their classrooms after they returned, and gains in student test scores.[43]

Between the late-1980s and mid-1990s, New York City Community District 2, under the leadership of Superintendent Anthony Alvarado, stressed continuous instructional improvement across forty-eight elementary and middle schools. Through a variety of mechanisms such as a Professional Development Laboratory, Intervisitations and Peer Networks, and an Instructional Consulting Service, principals worked closely with teachers on instructional improvement because "good ideas come from talented people working together" and "collegiality, caring, and respect" make a difference in what occurs in classrooms. Targeted instructional improvement led to focused literacy programs in over a dozen low-performing schools. In those schools, teachers taught lessons that were a "more intensive, more structured, and more teacher-centered version of the district's broader literacy program." And the district's academic achievement rose annually moving up into the ranks of higher-performing community districts.[44]

Also consider how the largely minority and poor Sanger Unified School District in California's Central Valley, with nearly eleven thousand students in nineteen schools, approached instructional improvement through professional development. In 2004, the district itself and seven schools were designated as failing under NCLB and placed into Program Improvement, a state effort to turn around failing schools. Within five years, all seven schools had recovered sufficiently to leave Program Improvement and four of those schools became California Distinguished Schools. In addition, by 2009, twelve of the thirteen elementary schools exceeded the target score of 800 that the state set for the Academic Performance Index. This is an extraordinary accomplishment for a high-poverty, largely minority district facing all of the complexity that such systems encounter daily.[45]

How did they do it? Opinions differ, of course, on which factors made the difference but researchers and informed observers do agree on the following:

• Continuing superintendent leadership over the long haul; Marc Johnson has been superintendent since 2002, and Rich Smith has been his deputy since 2004.
• Steadfast focus on instructional improvement through direct instruction to meet state curriculum standards and improve performance on state tests

- Establishing systematic and intensive districtwide professional development and school-based teacher learning communities aimed at improved classroom practices in daily lessons

Evaluators described the strategy:

They adopted the [Rick] DuFour's model of teacher professional learning communities (PLCs) as the vehicle for teachers to work collaboratively to improve student achievement and develop a sense of collective responsibility. They chose a model of direct instruction, Explicit Direct Instruction (EDI), with structures designed to help low-performing and language-minority students work on grade-level standards with frequent checking for understanding. To support students struggling at grade level, district leaders designed their own version of Response to Intervention (RTI), creating both in-class intervention and a range of intervention classes to meet the specific needs of students at risk of falling behind. To provide added help to English learners, the district expanded its emphasis on English language development (ELD).[46]

Johnson's vision and inspiration, Smith's practical implementation of the vision in getting teachers to collaborate and create schools and classrooms where teaching and learning were prized, and the above multifaceted program help explain the successful turnaround of the failing Sanger district.

Teacher collaboration and districts providing support for their efforts to build teachers' capacities to teach were central to what happened in Sanger, Community District 2, and Pittsburgh. And so it was for grade-level and departmental learning communities and schoolwide groups of teachers working together, with administrative support, in adapting to the DNA of complex systems to achieve instructional effectiveness and student academic improvement.

Will such a ground-level strategy of building structures that enable teachers and administrators to work together in creating cultures of learning in classrooms, schools, and districts lead to good and successful teaching and then successful student learning? I hope so—but in all honesty, I do not know.

What I do know is that inside the black box of classrooms is a complex world where interdependent social and intellectual relationships fashioned between teachers and students over what content and skills are to be learned and how they are learned is influenced by many factors inside and outside the classroom. I know that attention must be paid to that complexity.

I know that no single way of teaching works best with all students— note that in her Harlem elementary and secondary schools, Deborah Meier used project-based learning and applied the teaching and learning principles guiding the Coalition of Essential Schools. Superintendent Richard Wallace had the Schenley High School Teacher Center in Pittsburgh focused on teacher-centered lessons; Sanger Unified School District's teachers used direct instruction in elementary schools; and New York City's Community District 2 concentrated on teacher-centered, prescriptive lessons for low-performing students while using other approaches in higher-performing schools.

I know that the world of classrooms is marked by continuity and many small changes—seldom ones that fundamentally turn around the dynamic of that complex world. In that world, the basic teacher-student relationship, one that is shaped by both persistent continuity and incremental changes, one that is constantly negotiated and renegotiated, determines the degree to which good and successful teaching occur.

I know that structures such as the age-graded school do influence in expected and unexpected ways what happens in classrooms. But other structures that policy makers believe will reshape what teachers do— such as district and school governance; new curricular standards; organizing schools into K–8, 7–12; or other configurations; or going from big to small schools—have had few effects on classroom practices and, consequently, students' academic outcomes. In short, new structures and changes in existing ones may be necessary to get teachers to consider changes in routines, but those new and renovated structures are insufficient to change significantly what happens daily in classrooms and then produce student learning.

Finally, I know that the complexity of the classroom is mirrored in interdependent relationships and unpredictable events that occur in schools and across the district. People and resources interact. Incremental changes happen. Yet continuity in both relationships and practices persists. Dynamic conservatism, that characteristic of complex systems, helps to unravel the puzzle of the black box, explaining why much classroom change occurs but so little fundamental reform in practice.

In the introduction, I compared school reform to a hurricane. In ending this book, I want to mix this hurricane metaphor with that of the black box I have used in the title and throughout the book. Yes, it is a mixed metaphor and has its obvious dangers, but here goes:

On that quiet ocean floor, where life is largely undisturbed by the surface roar of the hurricane, sits the black box of the classroom. Top-down policies creating new structures enter the black box; teachers adapt to those structures, sometimes changing old practices, sometimes not. Whether those changed and habitual practices lead to students learning remains unmapped. Within that black box, then, is another complex world filled with patterns of change and stability in interdependent relationships blended with unanticipated events and unpredictable responses. Not only do reformers have to parse the hurricane metaphor but also they need to know clearly what happens inside the black box if they want to move beyond passionate rhetoric to improve teaching and learning in U.S. classrooms.

Notes

Introduction

1. I use the phrase *policy elites* interchangeably with *top policy makers, civic and business leader coalitions,* and *reformers.* I use these terms to refer to loose networks of corporate leaders, public officials (including top educational policy makers), foundation executives, academics, and wealthy entrepreneurs who circulate ideas consistent with their views of problems and solutions, champion particular reforms, use both public and private funds to run projects, and strongly influence decision making. Not unlike policy elites in business and civic affairs who are involved in growing a stronger economy, improving health care, protecting national security, strengthening foreign policy, and safeguarding the environment, policy entrepreneurs and reformers have ready access to media, are capable of framing problems, and set a public agenda for discussion. Or as one member in good standing wrote: "In public policy, it matters less who has the best arguments and more who gets heard—and by whom" (Ralph Reed, cited in Dana Milbank, *Homo Politicus: The Strange and Barbaric Tribes of the Beltway* [New York: Doubleday, 2008], 68). Political party labels do not define these elites, although there are clearly Republican and Democratic members who wear their affiliation on their sleeve and, when administrations change, move in and out of office. I do not use the phrase *policy elites* to suggest conspiratorial groups secretly meeting and designing action plans. Nor do I bash elites. I suggest only that these overlapping networks of like-minded individuals share values and tastes and seek school improvements aligned with those values and tastes. As *influentials,* they convene frequently in different forums, speak the same policy talk, and are connected closely to sources of public and private influence in governments, media, businesses, academia, and foundations. They help to create a climate of opinion that hovers around no more than a few hundred national policy leaders and smaller numbers at state and local levels. Familiar with the ways of the media, these policy elites extend and shape that climate of opinion by closely working with journalists who report what they say, write, think, and do. Few members of these loosely connected policy elites, however, have had direct or sustained experience with school principals or teachers, much less engaged in the teaching of children. Yet their recommended policies, their "common sense" about what the nation, state, district, and teachers should do, touch the daily lives of both educators and children. See John Kingdon, *Agendas, Alternatives, and Public Policies* (Boston: Little, Brown, 1984); James Fallows, *Breaking the News* (New York: Random House, 1996); William Safire, "Elite Establishment Egghead Eupatrids," *New York Times Magazine,* May 18, 1997. For a survey of experts as to who are the "influentials" currently shaping school reform policy, see Christopher Swanson and Janelle Barlage, "Influence: A Study of the Factors

Shaping Educational Policy," (Washington, DC: Editorial Projects in Education Research Center, December 2006). For rich descriptions of a medley of reform-minded high-tech entrepreneurs, donors, public officials, and recent additions into policy elites, see Steven Brill, *Class Warfare* (New York: Simon and Schuster, 2011) and Patrick McGuinn, "Fight Club," *Education Next*, 12, no. 3 (2012), http://educationnext.org/fight-club/.

2. The past four U.S. presidents, as well as federal legislators, state governors and legislatures, CEOs, and business groups have communicated this message of school reform for more than three decades. From the *Nation at Risk* report (1983) to President Barack Obama's 2011 State of the Union message, the linkage between education and a healthy economy has been directly and forcefully stated. In his 2011 State of the Union address, President Obama said:

> Maintaining our leadership in research and technology is crucial to America's success. But if we want to win the future—if we want innovation to produce jobs in America and not overseas—then we also have to win the race to educate our kids.

> Think about it. Over the next ten years, nearly half of all new jobs will require education that goes beyond a high school education. And yet, as many as a quarter of our students aren't even finishing high school. The quality of our math and science education lags behind many other nations. America has fallen to ninth in the proportion of young people with a college degree. And so the question is whether all of us—as citizens and as parents—are willing to do what's necessary to give every child a chance to succeed. (From: http://www.huffingtonpost.com/2011/01/25/obama-state-of-the-union-_1_n_813478.html.)

> Amplified consistently by media and rock-star journalists, the essential point is that the low performance of U.S. students on international tests is a blinking red light signaling that nation's economic health and international competitiveness are in danger. Nowhere is this crucial point made more evident than in the bipartisan endorsed NCLB legislation (2002). See Patrick McGuinn, *No Child Left Behind and the Transformation of Federal Education Policy, 1965–2005* (Lawrence, KS: University Press of Kansas, 2006); and Thomas Friedman, *The World Is Flat* (New York: Farrar, Strauss, and Giroux, 2005).

3. Norton Grubb and Marvin Lazerson, *The Education Gospel: The Economic Power of Schooling* (Cambridge, MA: Harvard University Press, 2004); Larry Cuban, *The Blackboard and the Bottom Line: Why Schools Can't Be Businesses* (Cambridge, MA: Harvard University Press, 2005); Harvey Kantor and David Tyack, eds., *Work, Youth, and Schooling* (Stanford, CA: Stanford University Press, 1982).

4. Critics of the contemporary school reform agenda of test-based accountability, evaluating and paying teachers on the basis of test scores, more charter schools, and Common Core standards point to the stakeholders in the civic, philanthropic, and business led coalition (e.g., the Walton, Gates, and Broad foundations; hedge fund managers; mayors) that have linked education and the economy since the 1980s. They argue that the reform agenda seeks to turn schools into market-driven

organizations where consumer choice reigns. Critics call such policies *neoliberal* and *corporate school reform*. These terms are not meant as compliments.

5. Some researchers have plowed this ground well, and I have learned from them as well as from my experiences as a teacher and superintendent. In particular, Richard Elmore and his colleagues have looked explicitly at the linkage between school structures and classroom practice in three elementary schools. See Richard Elmore, Penelope Peterson, and Sarah McCarthey, *Restructuring in the Classroom: Teaching, Learning, and School Organization* (San Francisco: Jossey-Bass, 1996). Jesse Goodman looked at Individually Guided Education and other initiatives and the values that drive past and current generations of reformers who call for restructuring; see Jesse Goodman, "Change Without Difference: School Restructuring in Historical Perspective," *Harvard Educational Review* 65. no. 1, (1995): 1–30. Fred Newmann, who launched school restructuring projects in the late 1980s and early 1990s, often pointed out that "new structures may be necessary but they are insufficient . . ." Moreover, even fundamental structural changes in schools could result in "highly traditional or progressive forms of instruction . . . In short, organizational structure provides no particular educational content"; see Fred Newmann, "Beyond Common Sense in Educational Restructuring: The Issues of Content and Linkage," *Educational Researcher* 22. no. 2 (1993): 4–13.

6. Larry Cuban, "Constancy and Change in Schools," in *Contributing to Educational Change: Perspectives on Research and Practice*, ed. Phillip W. Jackson (Berkeley, CA: McCutchan, 1988), 85–105.

7. The terms *first order* and *second order* are drawn from Paul Watzlawick, John Weakland, and Richard Fisch, *Principles of Problem Formation and Problem Resolution* (New York: Norton, 1974), 10–11; Larry Cuban, *The Managerial Imperative: The Practice of Leadership in Schools* (Albany, NY: State University of New York Press, 1988), 228–232. For an example of "real reform," see: "Real School Reform, Now," *New York Observer*, January 17, 2012, http://www.observer.com/2012/01/real-school-reform-now/.

   a. For an example of the use of the words *revolution* and *transformation* to mean fundamental change, in a TED talk, Sir Ken Robinson, former Director of Arts In Schools Project in England and University of Warwick professor, now an international adviser on education, said: "Every education system in the world is being reformed at the moment and it's not enough. Reform is no use anymore, because that's simply improving a broken model. What we need — and the word's been used many times during the course of the past few days — is not evolution, but a revolution in education. This has to be transformed into something else"; see http://dotsub.com/view/c2084af6-a6b8-4b5c-abd8-11946f8c624c/viewTranscript/eng.

8. David Tyack and I, in writing *Tinkering Toward Utopia* (Cambridge, MA: Harvard University Press, 1995) used *tinkering* in a positive way, especially in regard to teachers being involved in those changes.

9. Donald Schön, *Beyond the Stable State* (New York: W.W. Norton, 1973).

10. There are instances, however, when thoughtful policy makers, reformers, and

practitioners plan strategically to make a series of first-order changes that accumulate, over time, into a fundamental change (e.g., desegregation in the South in the period 1955–1970, or the small-high-school movement of 1980s–2010).

a. I want to thank Leonard Waks for his critical deconstruction of *fundamental* and *incremental* changes. His parsing of these terms and criticism of my use of *incremental* I found helpful, as was his distinguishing between *organizational*—which I focus on—and *institutional*, or the larger field to which educational organizations belong, a concept I have not included in the past or here. I doubt whether he will be satisfied with how I have reworked the concept but I do want to thank him, nonetheless, for getting me to think further about planned change in schools. See Leonard Waks, "The Concept of Fundamental Educational Change," *Educational Theory* 57, no. 3 (2007): 277–295.

11. Carl Kaestle, *Pillars of the Republic: Common Schools and American Society, 1780–1860* (New York: Hill and Wang, 1983), 30–61; Jonathan Zimmerman, *Whose America? Culture Wars in the Public Schools* (Cambridge, MA: Harvard University Press, 2002), 132–185.

12. Philip Jackson, *The Practice of Teaching* (New York: Teachers College Press, 1986), 98–114.

13. Judi Harris, "Our Agenda for Technology Integration: It's Time to Choose," *Contemporary Issues in Technology and Teacher Education* 5, no. 2 (2005), http://www .citejournal.org/vol5/iss2/editorial/article1.cfm.

14. Arthur Zilversmit, *Changing Schools: Progressive Education Theory and Practice, 1930–1960* (Chicago: University of Chicago Press, 1993); Larry Cuban, *How Teachers Taught* (New York: Teachers College Press, 1993).

15. For centuries, different labels have been attached to what I call *teacher-centered* and *student-centered* instruction. John Dewey labeled the former *traditional* and the latter *progressive*. Philip Jackson delineated both as traditions of teaching stretching back centuries. He called the former *mimetic* and the latter *transformative*. He preferred *conservative* rather than *liberal*, allowing for much overlap between the two traditions but without the political baggage accompanying the terms. See Jackson, *The Practice of Teaching*, 98–145.

16. Dorothy Shipps, *School Reform, Corporate Style: Chicago, 1880–2000* (Lawrence, KS: University Press of Kansas, 2006); Jack Schneider, *Excellence for All: How a New Breed of Reformers Is Transforming America's Public Schools* (Nashville, TN: Vanderbilt University Press, 2011); Frederick Hess, *Revolution at the Margins: The Impact of Competition on Urban School Systems* (Washington, DC: Brookings Institution Press, 2002); Joanne Barkan, "Got Dough? How Billionaires Rule Our Schools," *Dissent*, 2001, http://dissentmagazine.org/article/?article=3781; McGuinn, *No Child Left Behind*.

17. John Goodlad, *A Place Called School* (New York: McGraw-Hill, 1984); David Cohen and Heather Hill, *Learning Policy* (New Haven, CT: Yale University Press, 2001); Larry Cuban, *Hugging the Middle: How Teachers Teach in an Era of Testing and Accountability* (New York: Teachers College Press, 2009).

18. Laura S. Hamilton et al., "Accountability and Teaching Practices: School-level

Actions and Teacher Responses," in *Strong States, Weak Schools: The Benefits and Dilemmas of Centralized Accountability (Research in the Sociology of Education*, vol. 16), ed. Bruce Fuller et al. (Bingley, UK: Jai Press, 2008), 31–66; Cuban, *Hugging the Middle*; Christopher Lubienski, "Innovations in Education Markets: Theory and Evidence on the Impact of Competition and Choice in Charter Schools," *American Educational Research Journal* 40, no. 2 (2003): 395–443.

19. Nonetheless, the policy talk continues to promote the transformational power of new technologies in schools. In announcing a new national technology plan, U.S. secretary of education Arne Duncan said: "We have the opportunity to completely reform our nation's schools. We're not talking about tinkering around the edges here. We're talking about a fundamental re-thinking of how our schools function and placing a focus on teaching and learning like never before." Arne Duncan, "Using Technology to Transform Schools," remarks by Secretary Arne Duncan at the Association of American Publishers Annual Meeting, March 3, 2010.

20. I need to stress the obvious. Change occurs all the time in schools. Teachers alter classroom activities; schools launch new programs; districts mandate new procedures. And stability is ever-present. Teachers have daily routines; schools have schedules; districts have standard operating procedures that employees follow weekly. In short, stability is a defining trait of organizational structures. And so is change. To maintain stability, changes must occur. Stability and change are the yin and yang of classrooms, schools, and districts. The interdependency keeps organizations in equilibrium. No classroom, school, or district is frozen in amber; they are constantly changing. Teaching hybrids of student-centered and teacher-centered pedagogies evolve over time. Hybrid schools that blend online learning with regular teacher-led class of twenty-five students arise; districts develop portfolios of school options from which parents choose. The phrase *dynamic conservatism*, which Donald Schön coined in reference to organizations that "fight to remain the same," captures the frequent changes that strengthen continuity in practice. See Donald Schön, *Beyond the Stable State* (New York: Norton, 1973), 32.

21. I use the phrase as Paul Black and Dylan William did in "Inside the Black Box: Raising Standards Through Classroom Assessment," *Phi Delta Kappan* (October 1998): 139–148.

22. Hugh Mehan, *Learning Lessons* (Cambridge, MA: Harvard University Press, 1979); Zina Steinberg and Courtney Cazden, "Children as Teachers—As Peers and Ourselves," *Theory into Practice* 18, no. 3 (1979): 258–266. Moreover, videotaped lessons have been made in German, Japanese, and U.S. classrooms in the 1990s. See, for example, James Stigler, *The TIMSS Videotape Classroom Study*, NCES 99-074 (Washington, DC: National Center for Education Statistics, 1999).

23. See http://www.gatesfoundation.org/united-states/Pages/measures-of-effective-teaching-fact-sheet.aspx.

24. Mary Kennedy, "Attribution Error and the Quest for Teacher Quality," *Educational Researcher* 39, no. 8 (2010): 591–598.

25. Yun Xiang et. al., *Do High Flyers Maintain Their Altitude? Performance Trends of Top Students* (Washington, DC: Thomas Fordham Institute, September 2011).

26. Jaekyung Lee, "Low Marks for 'High Flyers' Report," http://nepc.colorado.edu/ thinktank/review-high-flyers. Quote is on p. 11.
27. Tyack and Cuban, *Tinkering Toward Utopia*.
28. Seymour Sarason, *The Culture of the School and the Problem of Change* (Boston: Allyn and Bacon, 1982).
29. I am indebted to the work of Milbrey McLaughlin, who over the years has plotted the geography of policy implementation in schools and planted clear markers for researchers like myself to follow that terrain. See, for example, "Implementation as Mutual Adaptation: Change in Classroom Organization," *Teachers College Record* 77, no. 3 (1976): 339–351; and "Listening and Learning from the Field: Tales of Policy Implementation and Situated Practice," in *The Roots of Educational Change*, ed. Anne Lieberman (Amsterdam: Springer, 2005), 58–72.
30. See *Larry Cuban on School Reform and Classroom Practice* (blog), http://larrycuban .wordpress.com/2009/09/09/chains-or-spagetti-metaphors-of-implementation/, and http://larrycuban.wordpress.com/2009/09/12/from-policy-to-classroom-practice-pushing-spaghetti/.
31. For amusing mixes of metaphors see: "Grammar Tip of the Day," http://gtotd .blogspot.com/2007/07/do-not-mix-metaphors.html.

Chapter 1

1. The history of Las Montanas and the changes that have occurred since 1976 can be found in Beverly Carter, *The Limits of Control: Case Studies of High School Science Teachers Responses to State Curriculum Reform, 1981–1987* (unpublished doctoral dissertation, Stanford University, 1990), 85–86, 94–96, and 106–107; "Western Association of Schools and Colleges Self-Study, 1993–1994," *Focus on Learning*, Western Association of Schools and Colleges, Self-Study Report, 1996–1997.
2. Much of the following content, test score results and data on computer access and use at Las Montanas in the 1990s comes from Larry Cuban, Heather Kirkpatrick, and Craig Peck, "High Access and Low Use of Technologies in High School Classrooms," *American Educational Research Journal* 38, no. 4 (2001): 813–834; and "High-Tech Schools, Low-Tech Learning," in Larry Cuban, *Oversold and Underused: Computers in the Classroom* (Cambridge, MA.: Harvard University Press, 2001), 68–98.
3. History of principals is drawn from interviews with teachers and administrators and two accreditation reports (1993 and 1996). Figures for enrollment in interdisciplinary programs come from Las Montanas' application for the Bay Area School Reform Collaborative (BASRC) grant (property of author), p. 33.
4. Interview with one of the two remaining teachers. Quote is taken from application to BASRC, p. 30.
5. BASRC Report, February 1, 1999; Digital High School Grant application, March 1999 Information based on interview with tech coordinator.
6. Heather Kirkpatrick and Craig Peck were the graduate students who I hired as research assistants on the project. Kirkpatrick is now Vice President of Education

at Aspire Public Schools, a charter management organization, and Peck, who served as principal of a New York City small high school, is now assistant professor in educational leadership at the University of North Carolina, Greensboro.

7. Over a seven-month period, we interviewed a dozen teachers and an equal number of students in the school. We surveyed nearly 90 percent of the faculty and one-third of the student body. We shadowed six students. The librarian provided us with sign-up sheets in the LMC. Finally, we analyzed accreditation reports, proposals for launching school-wide reforms and technology initiatives, and newspaper articles. We also examined student newspaper articles and school yearbooks.

8. All names of individuals and the school are pseudonyms. I have adapted this vignette of Alison Piro from when it first appeared in Cuban, *Oversold and Underused*, 68–71.

9. For the 2008–2010 study of the high school, Craig Peck and I submitted a proposal to the foundation that had funded the original grant in 1998. We wanted to examine the impact of 1:1 computing on a school that had stationary labs in 1998 and in what ways, if any, student and teacher use of computers for instruction had changed from the earlier study. The proposal was turned down. We revised the proposal and it was turned down a second time. Without funding Craig could not do the study—he was in North Carolina—so I decided to do the study without funding since I lived in northern California and the school had granted us access to study the 1:1 computing. Craig volunteered for one week to help me observe classes, interview teachers, and distribute a student survey in October 2009.

10. The chronology of principal tenure and events at Las Montanas between 1998 and 2010 comes from interviews with Carolyn Claus, Carl Hooper, three teachers who had been at the school for that decade, and school documents in the author's possession.

11. Thomas Timar and Kris Chyu, "State Strategies to Improve Low-Performing Schools: California's High Priority Schools Grant Program," *Teachers College Record* 112, no. 7 (2010): 1897–1936.

12. Interviews with Carolyn Claus, December 2008, January and May 2009, April 2010.

13. Interviews with technology coordinator Carl Hooper, October 2008, March 2009, May 2010.

14. Interview with David Bastedo, September 2011.

15. For the 2008–2010 study, I interviewed 22 of 33 academic subject teachers, surveyed 830 students of nearly 1,100 in the school (with the assistance of Craig Peck), shadowed 5 students, and used LMC sign-up sheets (2008–2009 and 2009–2010) for mobile labs and space in the LMC.

16. An interactive whiteboard is a large display screen connected to a computer and projector. With access to the Internet, IWBs run software that permit both students and teacher—using a stylus or pen, even a finger—to make presentations, capture notes from tablet computers and previous lessons, see videos, and scores of other applications, including "clickers," that permit a class of students to respond to teacher and textbook questions.

17. Note that teachers with ninth- to eleventh- graders in their classes may have had

their students use laptops in classroom lessons and would not have been captured by the LMC data.

18. Dan O'Connell, "An Inquiry-Based Approach to Teaching Photosynthesis and Cellular Respiration," *American Biology Teacher* 70, no. 6 (2008): 350–356.

19. Kerpoof is a software program that students can use to create artwork and animation; see http://www.kerpoof.com/teach.

20. Two Apple applications that had been loaded onto all laptops distributed to students.

21. I do not include myself among those critics. In *How Teachers Taught* (New York: Teachers College Press, 1993), I looked at teaching historically in urban, suburban, and rural schools between the 1890s and the 1980s and concluded that the dominant form of instruction was teacher-centered blended with some student-centered practices. Even after periodic and sustained reform efforts to move teacher-centered to student-centered instruction (both kinds of teaching are defined in that study), teacher-centered hybrids remained the default form of instruction. Over a decade later, in the midst of state and federal school reform legislation—NCLB—I looked at teaching practices in three urban districts, again collecting classroom reports and observing teachers. There I found that most teachers had created hybrids of teacher-centered and student-centered practices. In effect they "hugged the middle" on a continuum of teaching. See *Hugging the Middle: How Teachers Teach in an Era of Testing and Accountability* (New York: Teachers College Press, 2009). In both studies, I did not state a preference for one or the other kind of teaching practice.

22. In neither the 1998–1999 nor 2008–2010 study at Las Montanas did I spend time in the technology subject classrooms (e.g., multimedia computers, computer programming, computer graphics, etc.). All of these rooms were equipped with desktop computers and the most recent software for students to use. These courses were electives.

23. I have mentioned that turnover in faculty between 1998–1999 and 2010 was 99 percent. However, the faculties of Las Montanas at both points of time came from similar educational, racial, ethnic, and socioeconomic backgrounds. Perhaps, one might say, the teachers at Las Montanas in 2010 were a younger generation very familiar with technology and drawn to the school because of it being a technology magnet in the district. In interviewing twenty-two of the thirty-plus academic subject teachers at the high school in 2008–2010, I asked them their reasons for joining the faculty. Of the twenty-two interviewees, only three said they came to Las Montanas because it was a technology magnet or had heard of the 1:1 computing program.

24. The issue of change as perceived by individual teachers and by a researcher poses a dilemma for the researcher. At Las Montanas, for example, It was clear to me—and data I collected from student surveys, the media center sign out sheets for mobile carts, and extensive classroom observations confirm this point—that frequency and pervasiveness of technology use (e.g., PowerPoint lectures, interactive whiteboards, clickers, students taking notes, doing digital worksheets, and viewing video segments) had increased substantially since 1998–1999, albeit unevenly across academic subjects.

Moreover, most of the academic subject teachers I surveyed and interviewed told me that they had, indeed, made changes in how they prepared lessons and used electronic devices for administrative and instructional tasks. They told me that they have become more efficient in record keeping, assigning grades and homework, and teaching lessons. Additionally, they saw that their students responded well to these changes in their teaching.

Now here is where the dilemma pinches me. In my observations of lessons, I saw that teachers had, indeed, made changes in practices. They prepared lessons differently (e.g., some teachers found video snippets for the lesson that students watched). During many lessons, students used computers for assignments, projects, note taking, Internet searches, etc. These were activities that I had seen far less in Las Montanas classrooms a decade earlier. Yet to me, sitting in the back of the room, all of those changes added up to an enhancement of teacher-centered lessons, not a move toward student-centered instruction—what policy makers wanted, vendors promised, and techno-enthusiasts sought. (See, for example, Seymour Papert, *The Children's Machine: Rethinking School in the Age of the Computer* (New York: Basic Books, Inc, 1993); Michael Hannafin and Susan Land, "The Foundations and Assumptions of Technology-Enhanced Student-centered Learning Environments," *Instructional Science* 25 (1997): 167–202.

One way out of this dilemma is to explore what each party means by *change* and then determine who judges the worth of the change. *Change* clearly meant one thing to teachers and another to researchers like me. Teachers had, indeed, made a cascade of *incremental* changes in their daily lessons. Researchers such as me, however, trying to keep in mind what policy makers intended to happen after purchasing and deploying computers, looked for *fundamental* changes in teaching. In my case, getting teachers to shift from traditional to nontraditional instruction in seating arrangements, lesson activities, teacher-talk, use of projects, etc. Las Montanas teachers saw substantial *incremental* "changes," while I saw little *fundamental* "change." So whose judgment about change matters most? "Should researchers consider changes in teachers' work from the perspective of new policies like the framework? Or should they be considered from the teachers' vantage point?" (David K. Cohen, "A Revolution in One Classroom: The Case of Mrs. Oublier," *Educational Evaluation and Policy Analysis*, 12, no. 1 [1990], 312).

Researchers publish their studies and teachers seldom tell their side of the story—although teacher-bloggers are now airing their views far more than a decade ago. Teachers' perceptions of change have to be respected and voiced because they have indeed altered their practices incrementally and as any practitioner (lawyers, doctors, accountants) will tell you, that is very hard to do.

The truth is that the Las Montanas teachers who declared that they had changed had clearly expanded their repertoire of practices. They blended the old with the new. They had created hybrids of innovative and traditional practices in lessons they taught. I must honor teachers' incremental changes in their creating hybrids of old and new practices while, at the same time, acknowledge few shifts in fundamental patterns of teaching that designers of innovations had intended. That would be a way of reconciling this dilemma in writing about Las Montanas.

25. "Las Montanas" High School, *Focus on Learning*, a self-study submitted to Western Association of Schools and Colleges, March 21–24, 2010, pp. 71–143.

26. Ibid.
27. Student Accountability Report Card, "Las Montanas" High School, Grades 9–12 for 2009–2010, pp. 12–13.
28. Ibid.
29. Ibid.

Chapter 2

1. Charles Silberman, *Crisis in the Classroom: The Remaking of American Education* (New York: Random House, 1970), 293–294.
2. Ken King, Lee Shumow, and Stephanie Lietz, "Science Education in an Urban Elementary School: Case Studies of Teacher Beliefs and Classroom Practices," *Science Education* 85, no. 2 (2001): 89–110.
3. For a wide-ranging, sophisticated, and insightful analysis of the concept of curriculum, different perspectives on curriculum historically, and the different layers that I describe, see Philip Jackson, "Conceptions of Curriculum and Curriculum Specialists," *Handbook of Research on Curriculum*, ed. Philip W. Jackson (New York: Macmillan, 1992), 3–40; also see Elliot Eisner, "Curriculum Ideologies," in *Handbook of Research on Curriculum*, 302–326; Charles Bidwell and Robert Dreeben, "School Organization and Curriculum," in *Handbook of Research on Curriculum*, 345–362.
4. California State Board of Education, *Science Framework for California Public Schools: Kindergarten Through Grade Twelve* (Sacramento CA: State Department of Education, 2004). As the preface states, the framework is "California's blueprint for our science curriculum, instruction, professional preparation and development, and instructional materials" (p. v).
5. Ibid., 2.
6. See California Department of Education, "Preface," *Science Framework for California Public Schools*, http://www.cde.ca.gov/ta/tg/sr/sciencepreface.asp.
7. Mary Kennedy, *Inside Teaching: How Classroom Life Can Undermine Reform* (Cambridge, MA: Harvard University Press, 2005); Andrew Porter, "A Curriculum Out of Balance: The Case of Elementary School Mathematics," *Educational Researcher*, 1989, 18(5), 9–15; Donald Freeman and Andrew Porter, "Do Textbooks Dictate the Content of Mathematics Instruction in Elementary Schools," *American Educational Research Journal*, 1989, 26(3), 403–421; Laura Hamilton et al., "Studying Large-Scale Reforms of Instructional Practice," *Educational Evaluation and Policy Analysis* 25, no. 1 (2003): 1–29; James Spillane and John Zeuli, "Reform and Teaching: Exploring Patterns of Practice in the Context of National and State Mathematics Reform, *Educational Evaluation and Policy Analysis* 21, no. 1(1999): 1–27; Linda Cronin-Jones, "Science Teacher Beliefs and Their Influence on Curriculum Implementation," *Journal of Research in Science Teaching* 28, no. 3 (1991); 235–250; Larry Cuban, "The Hidden Variable; How Organizations Influence Teacher Responses to Secondary Science Curriculum Reform," *Theory into Practice* 34, no. 1 (1995): 4–11; Laura Hamilton "Studying Large-scale Reforms of Instructional Practice."

8. John Dewey, *Experience and Education* (New York: Macmillan, 1938), 48; Philip Jackson, *Life in Classrooms* (New York: Holt, Rinehart, and Winston, 1968), 33–34.

9. Jonathan Osborne, "Engaging Young People with Science: Thoughts About Future Direction of Science Education," in *Proceedings of the Linnaeus Tercentenary Symposium*, ed. Cedric Linder, Leif Ostman, and Per-Olof Wickman (Uppsala University, Sweden, May 2007), 105–112; Terry Lyons, "Different Countries, Same Science Classes: Students' Experiences of School Science in Their Own Words," *International Journal of Science Education* 28, no. 6 (2006): 591–613.

10. I use the metaphor of metal links in a policy chain to compare a new curricular framework that travels from federal and state policy makers to schools and classrooms. Classroom teachers as the last link at the end of the chain convey military images of privates saluting sergeants who then salute lieutenants with duties getting snappily discharged. In the command-and-control authority structure, fulfilling one's obligation is more important than having autonomy. There are other images that can be used rather than links in a chain. Consider the children's game of telephone and pushing spaghetti. The telephone game suggests miscommunications that end up in hilarious misinterpretations of what was intended by the original policy. Pushing strands of wet spaghetti suggests futility in getting a policy ever to be put into practice in classrooms. Autonomy trumps obligation in this metaphor. All have been used from time to time.

   a. I offer another comparison that, I believe, best explains the variation in lessons in the layer I call the *taught curriculum* that exists after a new curricular structure is put into place. Consider police officers who decide whether or not to give a traffic citation, social workers who determine what kind of help a client needs and where to find that help, emergency room nurses who decide which sick and injured need immediate attention and which ones can wait as "street-level bureaucrats." Include teachers who determine whether to stick with the lesson plan or diverge when an unexpected event occurs or students are less responsive. All of these professionals work within large rule-driven organizations but daily make on-the-spot decisions as they interact with the public. Each of these professionals is obligated to follow organizational rules yet has discretion to make decisions. In effect, they reconcile the dilemma of obligation and autonomy by interpreting, amending, or ignoring decisions—such as new science curricula—delivered to them by superiors. See Michael Lipsky, *Street-level Bureaucracy: Dilemmas of the Individual in Public Services* (Cambridge, MA: MIT Press, 1980).

11. John Dewey, "Science as Subject-Matter and as Method," *Science* 31 (1910): 122.

12. Joseph Rice, *The Public-School System of the United States* (1893; rep. New York: Arno Press, 1969), 60.

13. Ibid., 242.

14. David Tyack, *The One Best System* (Cambridge, MA: Harvard University Press, 1974), 183. The quote comes from Arthur Powell, Eleanor Farrar, and David Cohen, *The Shopping Mall High School* (Boston: Houghton Mifflin, 1985), 240.

15. Herbert Kliebard, *The Struggle for the American Curriculum, 1893–1958* (Boston: Routledge & Kegan Paul, 1986), 9–12.

16. George DeBoer, *A History of Ideas in Science Education* (New York: Teachers College Press, 1991), 49–50; also see Theodore Sizer, *Secondary Schools at the Turn of the Century* (New Haven, CT): Yale University Press, 1964). Many districts established manual training schools, later called vocational or technical schools for students who did not want to attend the classical high school and wanted to prepare for commercial and industrial jobs upon graduation. See Marvin Lazerson and Norton Grubb, *American Education and Vocationalism* (New York: Teachers College Press, 1974), 1–56.

17. An excellent synthesis of the progressive movement in education can be found in David Labaree, *Someone Has to Fail* (Cambridge, MA: Harvard University Press, 2010), 83–105; For a description of the various groups of progressive reformers in the early twentieth century, see David Tyack and Elisabeth Hansot, *Managers of Virtue* (New York: Basic Books, 1982), 105–114; for an intellectual history of the progressive movement, see Lawrence Cremin, *The Transformation of the School* (New York: Vintage Press, 1961).

18. Henry Perkinson, *The Imperfect Panacea: American Faith in Education*, 4th edition (New York: McGraw-Hill, 1995); Labaree, *Someone Has to Fail*, 163–194.

19. DeBoer, *A History of Ideas in Science Education*, 67–84; also see Lawrence Cremin, "The Revolution in American Secondary Education, 1893–1918," *Teachers College Record* 56 (1954–1955): 293–308; Kliebard, *The Struggle for the American Curriculum, 1893–1958*, 113–115. The CRSE report has been severely criticized by historians and reformers since the 1960s especially for its support of different curricula for students and the creation of the comprehensive high school. For a defense of the CRSE report and a sharp attack upon its critics, see William Wraga, "A Progressive Legacy Squandered: The Cardinal Principles Report Reconsidered," *History of Education Quarterly* 41, no. 4 (2001): 494–519.

20. Labaree, *Someone Has to Fail*, 99–101.

21. Cited in ibid., 71.

22. From Elliot Downing's chapter on biology in *A Program for Teaching Science* (National Society for the Study of Education, 1932), cited in ibid., 97.

23. David Donahue, "Serving Students, Science, or Society? The Secondary School Physics Curriculum in the United States, 1930–65," *History of Education Quarterly* 33, no. 3 (1993): 327.

24. DeBoer, *A History of Ideas in Science Education*, 80–82, 96. One supporter of the traditional concept-driven chemistry course who disliked focusing on the household relevance of chemistry said in 1915: "It seems to me little short of robbery to waste [a student's] course with chickenfeed of the fruit-spot, ink-spot, grease-spot, garbage-can type—a proceeding which leaves him, at the end, ignorant of chemistry but the fortunate possessor of a few bits of household information" (ibid., 81).

25. Diane Ravitch, *Left Back: A Century of Failed School Reform* (New York: Simon & Schuster, 2000), 198.

26. For a study of Muncie, Indiana, including the high school, see Robert and Helen Lynd, *Middletown* (New York: Harcourt, Brace, 1959), 192–193. They describe twelve different courses of study that were available to students.

27. Craig Kridel and Robert Bullough, Jr., *Stories of the Eight-Year Study: Reexamining Secondary Education in America* (Albany, NY: State University of New York Press, 2007), 155–156. This student-written report from the campus high school at Ohio State represented the height of progressive educators' dream of student-centered teaching where teachers and students planned together what content would be studied, students chose the problems to be researched. The teacher acted as a guide and helper for students as they gathered information, sifted it, and made sense of what they found. Then students worked together to report on the problem to the entire class. Keep in mind, however, that there was much variation among progressive classes in the thirty schools that were part of the Eight-Year Study. See, for example, Larry Cuban, *How Teachers Taught* (New York: Teachers College Press, 1993), 83–91.

28. Cuban, *How Teachers Taught*, 83–91.

29. See Ravitch, *Left Back*; Larry Cuban, *How Teachers Taught*; Arthur Zilversmit, *Progressive Education Theory and Practice, 1930–1960* (Chicago: University of Chicago Press, 1993); Labaree, *Someone Has to Fail*, 134–162.

30. Popular criticisms of public schools in the early 1950s were Arthur Bestor, *Educational Wastelands* (Champaign-Urbana, IL: University of Illinois Press, 1953); Albert Lynd, *Quackery in the Public Schools* (Boston: Little, Brown, 1953).

31. Peter Hlebowitsh and William Wraga, "The Reemergence of the National Science Foundation in American Education," *Science Education* 73, no. 4 (1989): 405–418.

32. Wayne Welch, "Twenty Years of Science Curriculum Development: A Look Back," *Review of Research in Education* 7 (197): 282–306.

33. James Patterson, *Grand Expectations: The United States, 1945–1974* (New York: Oxford University Press, 1996), 165–205.

34. Much of the following history I draw from secondary sources on the history of science curricula. I used: Welch, "Twenty Years of Science Curriculum Development"; DeBoer, *A History of Ideas in Science Education*; Paul Hurd, *Biological Education in American Secondary Schools, 1890–1960* (Boulder, CO: Biological Sciences Curriculum Study, 1961); J. Myron Atkin and Paul Black, *Inside Science Education Reform: A History of Curricular and Policy Change* (New York: Teachers College Press, 2003); Kliebard, *The Struggle for the American Curriculum, 1893–1958*; Rodger Bybee, "Science Curriculum Reform in the United States," 1995, http://www.nationalacademies.org/rise/backg3a.htm.

35. The quote is cited in Welch, "Twenty Years of Science Curriculum Development," 84. For a description of the Woods Hole conference and the launching of science curriculum reform, see Jerome Bruner, *The Process of Education* (Cambridge, MA: Harvard University Press, 1962).

36. Welch, "Twenty Years of Science Curriculum Development."

37. Ibid.

38. Ibid.

39. "Teacher-proof" curriculum materials are packages given to teachers where the purposes of the curriculum, the materials, tests, and lessons are thoroughly integrated to minimize the influence of teachers' adding and subtracting content.

These packages contain manuals with directions for using all of the technological aids in the package, scripts for particular lessons, quizzes to give students, and scores of other materials that teachers are expected to use but not alter. On a continuum of teacher involvement in curriculum, "teacher-proof" anchors the pole of minimal to no involvement; see http://investigations.terc.edu/library/bookpapers/role_of_curriculum.cfm.

40. DeBoer, *A History of Ideas in Science Education*, 166–167.

41. Ibid. For influence of new texts on traditional ones, see Susan Quick, "Secondary Impacts of the Curriculum Reform Movement: A Longitudinal Study of the Incorporation of Innovations of the Curriculum Reform Movement into Commercially Developed Curriculum Programs," (unpublished doctoral dissertation, Stanford University, 1978).

42. Stanley Helgeson et al., *The Status of Pre-College Science, Mathematics, and Social Science Education, 1955–1975*, vol. 1: *Science* (Washington, DC: National Science Foundation, 1978); Robert Stake and Jack Easley, eds., *Case Studies in Science Education*, vol. 1 (Champaign-Urbana, IL: University of Illinois Center for Instructional Research and Curriculum Evaluation, 1978).

43. Helgeson, *The Status of Pre-College Science, Mathematics, and Social Science Education, 1955–1975*, 31–32, 34.

44. Stake and Easley, *Case Studies in Science Education*, 91.

45. Ibid.

46. Ibid., Booklet 3, 3–90.

47. Welch, "Twenty Years of Science Curriculum Development," 303.

48. Ibid. A British researcher studying the Nuffield Project in science drew a similar conclusion. See J.J. Wellington, "What's Supposed to Happen, Sir? Some Problems with Discovery Learning," *School Science Review*, 1981, 63, 167–173.

49. Ronald Anderson, "Reforming Science Teaching: What Research Says About Inquiry," *Journal of Science Teacher Education* 13, no. 1 (2002): 1–12.

50. James Shymansky, William Kyle, and Jennifer Alport, "The Effects of New Science Curricula on Student Performance," *Journal of Research in Science Teaching* 20, no. 5 (1983): 387–404; Ted Bredderman, "Effects of Activity-Based Elementary Science on Student Outcomes: A Quantitative Analysis," *Review of Educational Research* 53. no. 4 (1983): 499–518; Anderson, "Reforming Science Teaching."

51. Angelo Collins, "National Science Education Standards: Looking Backward and Forward," *Elementary School Journal* 97, no. 4 (1997): 299–313.

52. Jonathan Osborne, "Towards a Science Education for All: The Role of Ideas, Evidence and Argument," http://research.acer.edu.au/research_conference_2006/9.

53. Ibid., 300. The issue of scientific literacy—however defined—goes back to the progressives in the early decades of the twentieth century who called for connecting science to the real world and introducing teaching practices that involved students actively in defining problems, developing alternative solutions, evaluating those solutions and deciding what to do. While the seeds of "science literacy" can be found then, the phrase came into general use in the 1950s. However, then and since, it has had multiple meanings so the ambiguity over its purposes and

explicit meaning have become even more contested with pressures for putting more and more graduates into the math, engineering, and science pipeline leading to the workplace. See Jonathan Osborne, "Science Education for the 21st Century," *Eurasia Journal of Mathematics, Science, and Technology* 3, no. 3 (2007): 173–184; George DeBoer, "Scientific Literacy: Another Look at its Historical and Contemporary Meanings and Its Relationship to Science Education Reform," *Journal of Research in Science Education* 37, no. 6 (2000): 582–601.

54. Joan Paisley et al., "Looking Inside the Classroom: Science Teaching in the U.S.," *Science Education* 13, no. 1 (2004): 1–12.

55. National Center for Education Statistics, "What Happens in Classrooms? Instructional Practices in Elementary and Secondary Schools, 1994–1995," NCES 1999-348 (Washington, DC: U.S. Department of Education, 1999), 16, 19. A sample of nearly four thousand public and private school teachers constitute the data for this report. The limitations of this survey and teacher reports are included. See pp. 4–5.

56. Collins, "National Science Education Standards," 303–306. Collins was a key member of the staff that drafted and produced the final version of the standards. An insider's view of this process comes from a member of the committee that gave direction to developing the standards. See Myron Atkin's account in J. Myron Atkin and Paul Black, *Inside Science Education Reform* (New York: Teachers College Press, 2003), 152–154. Atkin made clear to me after reading a draft of this chapter that teacher education and professional development were considered key instruments of building teacher capacities in science knowledge and skills. For an analysis of inquiry as a way of teaching science, see Ronald Anderson, "Reforming Science Teaching: What Research Says About Inquiry," *Journal of Science Teacher Education* 13, no. 1 (2002): 1–12.

57. National Research Council, *National Science Education Standards* (Washington, DC: National Academy Press, 1996), 25.

58. See Richard Duschl, "Assessment of Inquiry," in *Everyday Assessment in the Science Classroom*, ed. Myron Atkin and Janet Coffey (Arlington, VA: NSTA Press, 2003), 41–60. For teaching science language to urban minorities, see Bryan Brown and Eliza Spang, "Double Talk: Synthesizing Everyday and Science Language in the Classroom," *Science Education* 92, no. 4 (2008): 708–732.

59. National Center of Educational Statistics, *Digest of Educational Statistics, 2008* (Washington, DC: U.S. Department of Education, 2008), p. 203, Table 138. The 2012 results for eighth-graders in life, earth, and space sciences show slight improvement over results for 2009 and a narrowing of the achievement gap between minorities and whites. Percentage of students scoring in the Advanced category stayed the same. In what appeared to me as a huge leap in logic, the Commissioner of the National Center of Education Statistics noted that students whose teachers reported "never" or "hardly ever" used "hands-on" science activities in class (two percent) had the lowest scores. Over 90 percent of teachers reported using such activities from daily to a few times a month implying that such activities caused higher scores when such a comparison is only a correlation; see http://nces.ed.gov/whatsnew/commissioner/remarks2012/05_10_2012.asp.

60. National Center for Educational Statistics, *Condition of Education, 2009*, Special Supplement, "U.S. Performance Across International Assessments of Student Achievement," NCES 2009-083 (Washington, DC: U.S. Department of Education, 2009); Tom Loveless, "How Well Are American Students Learning?" (Washington, DC: Brown Center on Education Policy, Brookings Institution, 2010), 7.
61. Educational Testing Service, Policy Information Report, *Exploring What Works in Science Instruction: A Look at the Eighth Grade Science Classroom* (Princeton, NJ: Educational Testing Service, 2009), 3.
62. Ibid., 9.
63. President Barack Obama on the "Importance of Education Reform," http://www.whitehouse.gov/photos-and-video/video/importance-education-reform#transcript. Ten years earlier, President George W. Bush said:

    Both parties have been talking about education reform for quite a while. It's time to come together get it done so that we can truthfully say in America, "No child will be left behind—not one single child . . . "

    We share a moment of exceptional promise—a new administration, a newly sworn-in Congress, and we have a chance to think anew and act anew.

    All of us are impatient with the old lines of division. All of us want a different attitude here in the nation's capital. All in this room, as well as across the country, know things must change.

    We must confront the scandal of illiteracy in America, seen most clearly in high-poverty schools, where nearly 70 percent of fourth graders are unable to read at a basic level. We must address the low standing of America test scores amongst industrialized nations in math and science, the very subjects most likely to affect our future competitiveness. We must focus the spending of federal tax dollars on things that work. Too often we have spent without regard for results, without judging success or failure from year to year.
    http://georgewbush-whitehouse.archives.gov/news/releases/2001/01/20010123-2.html.
64. Website for Common Core standards sponsored by the National Governors Association and the Council of Chief State School Officers is at: http://www.corestandards.org/.
65. National Research Council, *A Framework for K–12 Science Education: Practices, Crosscutting Concepts, and Core Ideas* (Washington, DC: National Academy Press, 2011).
66. Ibid.
67. In 1991, the National Science Teachers Association asked the National Research Council to develop standards for science education. According to the publication of *Inquiry*, "Between 1991 and 1995, groups of teachers, scientists, administrators, teacher educators, and others organized by the NRC produced several drafts of the *Standards* and submitted those drafts to extensive review by others in these same roles." While teachers were clearly involved in the creation of science standards that were published in 1996, still this was not a bottom up effort where teachers across the nation or even critical masses of science teachers championed

standards for teaching science. See *Inquiry and The National Science Education Standards: A Guide for Teaching and Learning* (Washington, DC: National Academy Press, 2000), preface.

Chapter 3

1. National Commission on Excellence in Education, *A Nation at Risk* (Washington, DC: U.S. Department of Education, 1983); Jack Schneider, *Excellence for All: How a New Breed of Reformers Is Transforming America's Public Schools* (Nashville, TN: Vanderbilt University Press, 2011), 11–40.

2. Kent McGuire, "Business Involvement in Education in the 1990s," *Politics of Education Association Yearbook, 1989*, 107–117; Tim Mazzoni, "State Policy-Making and School Reform: Influences and Influentials," *Journal of Education Policy* 9, no. 5 (1994): 53–73. James Fallows, "How America Can Rise Again," *The Atlantic*, January/February 2010, http://www.theatlantic.com/magazine/archive/2010/01/how-america-can-rise-again/7839/.

3. Sherman Dorn, *Accountability Frankenstein: Understanding and Taming the Monster* (Charlotte, NC: IAP Press, 2007), 9–10.

4. "Quality Counts," *Education Week*, January 11, 1999; "Quality Counts," *Education Week*, January 13, 2000; Margaret Goertz and Mark Duffy, *Policy Briefs: Assessment and Accountability Across 50 States* (Philadelphia: Consortium for Policy Research in Education, 2001).

5. Larry Cuban, *The Blackboard and the Bottom Line: Why Schools Can't Be Businesses* (Cambridge, MA: Harvard University Press, 2005), 15–38.

6. For examination of the assumptions embedded in the standards-based reform aimed at teachers, see Hilary Loeb, Michael Knapp, and Ana Elfers, "Teachers' Responses to Standards-Based Reform: Probing Reform Assumptions in Washington State," *Education Policy Analysis Archives* 16, no. 8 (2008), http://epaa.asu.edu/epaa/v16n8/; Kathryn McDermott, "'Expanding the Moral Community' or 'Blaming the Victim'? The Politics of State Education Accountability Policy," *American Educational Research Journal* 44, no. 1 (2007): 77–111; Marshall Smith and Jennifer O'Day, "Systemic School Reform," in *The Politics of Curriculum and Testing: Politics of Education Association Yearbook 1990*, ed. Betty Malen and Susan Fuhrman (New York: Falmer Press, 1991), 233–267. For an analysis of excellence and equity as the twin purposes of recent reforms, see Jack Schneider, *Excellence for All: How a New Breed of Reformers Is Transforming America's Public Schools* (Nashville, TN: Vanderbilt University Press, 2011).

7. For an analysis of the making of NCLB in the U.S. Congress and the compromises that produced the final legislation, see Patrick McGuinn, *No Child Left Behind and the Transformation of Federal Education Policy, 1965–2005* (Lawrence, KS: University Press of Kansas, 2006), 165–195.

8. The adjectives *coercive, mean, nice,* and *hardnosed* come from Frederick Hess, *Tough Love for Schools: Essays on Competition, Accountability, and Excellence* (Washington, DC: AEI Press at American Enterprise Institute, 2006), 77–78; See the varied responses from

an array of policy makers, researchers, administrators, and educators at: http://www.edweek.org/ew/articles/2012/01/05/15nclb_perspectives.h31.html?tkn=X-LTFjLB9deqCd53KQJhZBIJaXX2wAJ2bZ816&cmp=clp-edweek#jennings.

9. Steven Brill's *Class Warfare* (New York: Simon and Schuster, 2011) captures in vivid detail the members of the policy elites who have been in the corporate and entrepreneurial vanguard of promoting charter schools, testing and accountability, pay-for-performance plans, and related reforms. Interviewing over two hundred of these leaders, he populates his book with heroes and villains—mostly teacher union leaders. Readers wanting an inside look at "no excuses" reformers, Brill is an apt tour guide.

10. Brian Stecher, "Consequences of Large-Scale High-stakes Testing on School and Classroom Practice," in *Making Sense of Test-Based Accountability in Education*, ed. Laura Hamilton et al. (Santa Monica, CA: RAND, 2002), 79–100; James Spillane, Leigh Parise, and Jennifer Sherer, "Organizational Routines as Coupling Mechanisms: Policy, School Administration, and the Technical Core," *American Educational Research Journal* 48, no. 3 (2011): 586–619; Lorrie Shepard and Mary Smith, "Effects of Kindergarten Retention: A Qualitative Study of Teacher's Beliefs and Practices," *American Educational Research Journal* 25 (1987): 307–333; Richard Allington, "Reading Lessons and Federal Policy Making," *Elementary School Journal* 107, no. 1 (2006): 3–15.

11. Brian Stecher et al. *Pain and Gain: Implementing No Child Left Behind in Three States 2004–2006* (Santa Monica, CA: RAND, 2008); for districts increasing time for instruction in English language arts and math and decreasing time spent on science, social studies, and other subjects in elementary schools, see Jennifer McMurrer, "Instructional Time in Elementary Schools: A Closer Look at Changes for Specific Subjects," (Washington, DC: Center on Educational Policy, 2008); for a case study of one Annapolis, Maryland, school coping with low test scores and the effects of NCLB in 2005–2006, see Linda Perlstein, *Tested: One American School Struggles To Make the Grade* (New York: Henry Holt, 2007).

12. Quoted in Elizabeth Graue and Erica Johnson, "Reclaiming Assessment Through Accountability That Is 'Just Right,'" *Teachers College Record* 113, no. 8 (2011), http://www.tcrecord.org, ID Number: 16175.

13. Ibid.

14. Stecher, "Consequences of Large-Scale High-stakes Testing on School and Classroom Practice," 90–91. Laura Hamilton, "Testing What Has been Taught," *American Educator* 34, no. 4 (Winter 2010–2011): 47–51; in many districts across the nation, Knowledge is Power Program (KIPP) has demonstrated what can occur with low-income minority students in elementary and middle schools; Jay Mathews, *Work Hard, Be Nice: How Two Inspired Teachers Created the Most Promising Schools in America* (Chapel Hill, NC: Algonquin Books, 2009); a critical look at KIPP can be found in Brian Lack, "No Excuses: A Critiques of the Knowledge Is Power Program (KIPP) Within Charter Schools in the USA," *Journal for Critical Education Policy Studies* 7, no. 2 (2009): 127–153.

15. Larry Cuban, *Hugging the Middle: How Teachers Teach in an Era of Testing and Accountability* (New York: Teachers College Press, 2009), 20, 31.

16. Brian Stecher et al. *Pain and Gain*, xv–xvi.
17. McMurrer, "Instructional Time in Elementary Schools."
18. First Things First is described in Janet Quint, "Meeting Five Critical Challenges of High School Reform: Lessons from Research on Three Reform Models" (New York: MDRC, May 2006).
19. Larry Cuban, *As Good as It Gets: What School Reform Brought to Austin* (Cambridge, MA: Harvard University Press, 2010), 94–96. Reagan High School escaped being closed in 2008 and in the following two years. Turnover in principals continued since then and district officials adopted another national model of improvement; see: http://www.reaganraiders.org/.
20. Perlstein, *Tested.*
21. Ibid., 22–23.
22. Ibid., 87.
23. Ibid., 246.
24. Ibid., 272.
25. See Larry Cuban, *How Teachers Taught* (New York: Teachers College Press, 1993); and Cuban, *Hugging the Middle.*
26. Donald Campbell, "Assessing the Impact of Planned Social Change," Occasional Paper #8 (Hanover, NH: Public Affairs Center, Dartmouth College, December 1976), 49.
27. Ibid., 52.
28. Sandeep Jauhar, MD, "The Pitfalls of Linking of Doctor's Pay to Performance," *New York Times*, September 8, 2008, http://www.nytimes.com/2008/09/09/health/09essa.html; see also Richard Rothstein, *Grading Education: Getting Accountability Right* (Washington, DC: Economic Policy Institute and Teachers College Press, 2008), 79–85.
29. Jane Hannaway and Laura Hamilton, *Accountability Policies: Implications for School and Classroom Practices* (Washington, DC: Urban Institute, 2008); Eva Baker et al., *Problems with the Use of Student Test Scores to Evaluate Teachers*, Briefing Paper #278 (Washington, DC: Economic Policy Institute, 2010); Dan Koretz, *Measuring Up: What Educational Testing Really Tells Us* (Cambridge, MA: Harvard University Press, 2008).
30. Laura Hamilton and Brian Stecher, "Improving Test-Based Accountability," in Hamilton et al., *Making Sense of Test-Based Accountability in Education*, 122 ; Arne Duncan, "Escaping the Constraints of 'No Child Left Behind,'" *Washington Post*, http://www.nytimes.com/2008/09/09/health/09essa.html.
31. Bruce Fuller et al., "Gauging Growth: How To Judge No Child Left Behind?" *Educational Researcher* 36, no. 5 (2007): 268–278.
32. Michael Hout and Stuart Elliott, eds., *Incentives and Test-Based Accountability in Education* (Washington, DC: National Academy of Sciences, 2011); Eric Hanushek, "Grinding the Anti-Test Ax," *Education Next* 12, no. 2 (2012), http://educationnext.org/grinding-the-antitesting-ax/; Mark Schneider, in "The Accountability Plateau" (December 2011, The Fordham Institute) claimed that math NAEP test scores across the nation at the fourth and eighth grades rose substantially between

2000 and 2005—the result of what he calls *consequential accountability* but read-ing scores flattened out at those grades (pp. 15–16); Helen Ladd, "Holding Schools Accountable Revisited," 2007 Spencer Foundation Lecture in Education Policy and Management, presented to the Association for Public Policy Analysis and Management, Washington, DC, November 2007; Lisa Guisbond, "NCLB's Lost Decade of Educational Progress: What Can We Learn from This Policy Failure?" *FairTest*, January 2012, http://fairtest.org/NCLB-lost-decade-report-home.

33. Steven Glazerman and Liz Potamites, "False Performance Gains: A Critique of Successive Cohort Indicators," Working Paper, Mathematica: Policy Research, December 2011, 13.

34. Sherman Dorn, *Accountability Frankenstein*, 127. Dorn points out the methodolog-ical baggage that accompanies the concept of accountability when it is quantified (see pp. 126–129).

35. Alyson Klein, "Critics of NCLB Ask Congress to Overhaul It," *Education Week*, February 23, 2007, pp. 1, 26; Linda Darling-Hammond, "Evaluating No Child Left Behind, *The Nation*, May 21, 2007; Sam Dillon, "For a Key Education Law, Reauthorization Stalls," *New York Times*, November 6, 2007.

36. Twenty-four states had been granted waivers from key NCLB mandates by June 2012. Another thirteen states applied for waivers and have not yet been approved. Alyson Klein, "Five More States Get NCLB Waivers," *Education Week* blogs, June 29, 2012, http://blogs.edweek.org/edweek/campaign-k-12/2012/06/five_more_states_get_nclb_waiv.html.

37. Hess, *Tough Love for Schools*, 78.

38. In "The Connection Between Research and Practice," (*Educational Researcher* 26, no. 7 [1997]:4–12), Mary Kennedy points out four hypotheses to explain the gap between the production of educational research and practitioners' use of those find-ings. One of the four—the education system itself is inherently unable to respond consistently and rationally to research studies—finds support in the wake of NCLB's impact on schools and teaching practices.

Part Two

1. I focus on both primary care and specialty physicians. Specialists practice surgery, psychiatry, obstetrics, cardiology, radiology, oncology, and scores of other sub-spe-cialties. Included in primary care are family medicine, internal medicine, pedi-atrics, and other doctors who are the first contact for patients with non-emergency medical problems. These physicians diagnose and treat common illnesses and med-ical conditions. They collect patient information from the presented symptoms, the person's medical history, a physical examination, and basic medical tests like blood work and X-rays. They then make a diagnosis and plan with patient what next steps to take in treatments including referral to specialists. Primary care doctors also coun-sel and educate patients on preventing illnesses and encouraging healthy behaviors. They coordinate a patient's care when specialists are involved. Like specialists, they provide services in their offices, emergency rooms, hospitals, and nursing homes.

My rationale is that both kinds of physicians are similar to K–12 teachers who, using their expertise, get to know students, develop relationships with them, and figure out how best to teach knowledge and skills and help students learn. I include specialist teachers like special education, reading, math, etc. In the literature on the practices of physicians, a number of medical researchers have labeled what doctors do in their practice a *black box*. Kurt Stange, MD, for example, and his colleagues say: "Because of the lack of direct data on the patient-physician encounter and the limited number of research studies that assess community practice settings, policymakers view many aspects of family practice and specialist decision-making as obscured within a black box. The comparison to teaching practices in classrooms has been similarly labeled. See Kurt Stange, MD, et. al., "Illuminating the 'Black Box': A Description of 4454 Patient Visits to 138 Family Physicians," *Journal of Family Practice* 46 (1998): 377–389. Also see: James Tulsky, MD, et. al., "Opening the Black Box: How Do Physicians Communicate About Advance Directives?" *Annals of Internal Medicine* 129, no. 6 (1998): 441–449; Lawrence Weed and Lincoln Weed, "Opening the Black Box of Clinical Judgment: An Overview," *British Medical Journal* 319 (1999): 1279.

2. Kenneth Ludmerer MD and Michael Johns MD, "Reforming Graduate Medical Education," *JAMA* 294, no. 9 (2005): 1083–1087; Linda Darling-Hammond, et. al., "The Design of Teacher Education Programs," in *Preparing Teachers for a Changing World*, ed. Linda Darling-Hammond and John Bransford (San Francisco: Jossey-Bass, 2005), 390–441.

3. Ann Boulis and Jerry Jacobs, *The Changing Face of Medicine: Women Doctors and the Evolution of Health Care in America* (Ithaca, NY: Cornell University Press, 2008).

4. David Sackett et. al., "Evidence-Based Medicine: What It Is and What It Isn't," BMJ, 1996, http://www.bmj.com/content/312/7023/71?view=long&pmid=8555924; Mary Kennedy, "The Connection between Research and Practice," *Educational Researcher* 26, no. 4 (1997): 4–12.

5. Tom Van Riper, "America's Most Admired Professions," *Forbes.Com*, July 28, 2006, http://www.forbes.com/2006/07/28/leadership-careers-jobs-cx_tvr_0728admired.html.

6. The dilemmas that professionals face in the helping professions are well known among the inhabitants of each occupation. The work of David K. Cohen has brought together these cross-professional quandaries in *Teaching and Its Predicaments* (Cambridge, MA: Harvard University Press, 2011). He examines teachers, psychotherapists, social workers, pastors, and organizational developers who "work directly on other humans in efforts to better their minds, lives, work, and organizations" (p. 4). Although he initially excludes medical doctors from human improvement, he does allow that occupations change over time and that doctors may be included: "Physicians conventionally defined their work in terms of patients' physical health and many still do, but increasingly they see that physical health can depend on how well patients understand their problems and how firmly they commit to the solutions; hence physicians work more and more on understanding and mutual commitment" (p. 19). He is correct in that the thinking about medical practice has

moved from physician-centered to patient-centered where doctors routinely include patients' questions, concerns, and views in diagnosing and treating illnesses. See, for example, Christine Laine, MD, and Frank Davidoff, MD, "Patient-Centered Medicine; A Professional Evolution," *JAMA* 275, no. 2 (1996): 152–155.

7. Overall health outcomes such as infant mortality, child survival beyond age five, life expectancy, etc. are frequently used indicators of a nation's well being. So are related metrics that capture the incidence of drinking alcohol, smoking, sexually transmitted diseases, etc. The connections between these outcomes and preventive, chronic, and acute medical care available to Americans is the same linkage I have made between efforts of policymakers to change classroom teaching so as to produce higher student achievement. See Barbara Starfield, MD, "Is U.S. Health Really the Best in the World?" *JAMA* 284, no. 4 (2000): 483–485; Mark Schuster, Elizabeth McGlynn, and Robert Brook, "How Good Is the Quality of Health Care in the United States?" *Milbank Quarterly* 83, no. 4 (2005): 843–895.

Chapter 4

1. Christine Laine and Frank Davidoff, "Patient-Centered Medicine," *JAMA* 275, no. 2 (1996): 152.

2. Ronald Epstein, MD, et al. "Communicating Evidence for Participatory Decision Making," *JAMA* 291, no. 19 (1996): 2359–2366; Simon Whitney, MD, et al., "A Typology of Shared Decision Making, Informed Consent, and Simple Consent," *Annals of Internal Medicine* 140, (2003): 54–59.

3. Paul Starr, *The Social Transformation of American Medicine* (New York: Basic Books, 1983), chapter 3. Also see Eliot Freidson, *Profession of Medicine* (Chicago: University of Chicago Press, 1988), 71–84.

4. David Rothman, *Beginnings Count: The Technological Imperative in American Health Care* (New York: Oxford University Press, 1997), 9–10; Freidson, *Profession of Medicine,* 23–46.

5. The term *American Creed* comes from a Swedish sociologist's two-volume study of the U.S. in the 1930s. It is a distillation of beliefs and values representing what Americans hold sacred in their country such as equal opportunity, fair treatment of all people, and justice. See Gunnar Myrdal, *An American Dilemma: The Negro Problem and Modern Democracy* (New York: Harper & Bros, 1944).

6. Robert Berenson, MD, and Eugene Rich, MD, "U.S. Approaches to Physician Payment: The Deconstruction of Primary Care," *Journal of General Internal Medicine* 25, no. 6 (2010): 613–618. That figure is lower when specialty doctors are considered and the spread of health maintenance organizations (HMOs) particularly under "managed care" since the 1990s. See Rothman, *Beginnings Count,* 157–158.

7. Atul Gawande, "The Cost Conundrum," *New Yorker,* June 1, 2009, 36–44.

8. Jerome Groopman, "What's the Trouble? How Doctors Think," *New Yorker,* January 29, 2007, 36–41.

9. John Wennberg, Elliot Fisher, and Jonathan Skinner, "Geography and the Debate over Medicare Reform," *Health Affairs,* 2002, http://content.healthaffairs.org/content/

early/2002/02/13/hlthaff.w2.96.citation. David Leonhardt, "Making Health Care Better," *New York Times*, November 8, 2009.

10. Michael Dill and Edward Salsberg, *The Complexities of Physician Supply and Demand—Projections Through 2025* (Washington, DC: Center for Workforce Studies, American Association of Medical Colleges, November 2008), 17; U.S. Department of Health and Human Services, Agency for Healthcare Research and Quality, "Primary Care Workforce Facts and Stats, No. 1: The Number of Practicing Primary Care Physicians in the United States," October 2011, http://www.ahrq.gov/research/pcwork1.htm; Elmer Abbo, MD, et al., "The Increasing Number of Clinical Items Addressed During the Time of Adult Primary Care Visits," *Journal of General Internal Medicine* 23, no. 12 (2008): 2058–2065; Jeffrey Farber, MD, Albert Siu, MD, and Patricia Bloom, "How Much Time Do Physicians Spend Providing Care Outside of Office Visits," *Annals of Internal Medicine* 147 (2007): 693–698. In Faber, Siu, and Bloom's study, nearly eight additional hours a week were reported in non-reimbursable activities carried out by sixteen physicians in a largely geriatric practice; Richard Baron,MD "What's Keeping Us So Busy in Primary Care? A Snapshot from One Practice," *New England Journal of Medicine* 362 (2010): 1632–1636.

11. Committee on Quality of Health Care in America, Institute of Medicine, *Crossing the Quality Chasm: A New Health System for the 21st Century* (Washington, DC: National Academy Press, 2001), 17–18.

12. Ibid., 41–42.

13. Stanley Reiser, *Medicine and the Reign of Technology* (New York: Cambridge University Press, 1978). To be clear, when I refer to *medical technology*, I mean the equipment, devices, drugs, procedures, and processes used to deliver diagnoses and treatments to patients.

14. Toby Gosden et al., "Impact of Payment Method on Behaviour of Primary Care Physicians: A Systematic Review," *Journal of Health Services Research and Policy* 6, no. 1 (2001): 44–55; Alan L. Hillman, MD, MBA, Mark V. Pauly, PhD, and Joseph J. Kerstein, MBA, "How Do Financial Incentives Affect Physicians' Clinical Decisions and the Financial Performance of Health Maintenance Organizations?" *New England Journal of Medicine* 321 (1989): 86–92, http://www.nejm.org/toc/nejm/321/2/; Gawande, "The Cost Conundrum." My close friend, Joel Merenstein (an MD in family medicine) once told me that the most powerful technology he and other doctors use is their pens and prescription pads.

15. Brenda Sirovich, MD, "Too Little? Too Much? Primary Care Physicians' Views on U.S. Health Care," *Archives of Internal Medicine* 171, no. 17 (2011): 1582–1587. Roni Rabin, "Doctor Panels Recommend Fewer Tests for Patients," *New York Times*, April 4, 2012. Howard Brody, MD, had written a commentary urging doctors to take the high moral ground when it comes to escalating costs and not ask for diagnostic tests when the evidence clearly does not call for them and stop prescribing drugs or treatments when clinical trials demonstrate no effects even when patients ask for them. See "Medicine's Ethical Responsibility for Health Care Reform—The Top Five List," *New England Journal of Medicine* 362 (2010): 283–285.

16. The thought experiment comes from Gawande, "The Cost Conundrum."

17. Joel Merenstein suggested this in reading a draft of this chapter. For shrinking number of primary care physicians, see Thomas Bodenheimer, MD, "Primary Care—Will It Survive?" *New England Journal of Medicine* 355 (2006): 861–864.

18. Nicholas Bakalar, "No Extra Benefits Are Seen in Stents for Coronary Artery Disease," *New York Times*, February 28, 2012.

19. Rothman, *Beginnings Count*, 10–11.

20. K. Ashish, MD, et al. "Use of Electronic Health Records in U.S. Hospitals," *New England Journal of Medicine* 360 (2009): 1628–1638; Emily Walker, "EHR Adoption Way Up in Hospitals," *MedPage Today*, February 17, 2012, http://www .medpagetoday.com/PracticeManagement/InformationTechnology/31245; "Physicians Using Electronic Health Technology, Express Positive Views," press release, U.S. Department of Health and Human Services, July 17, 2012, http://www.hhs .gov/news/press/2012pres/07/20120717a.html.

   A half-century ago, the Akron Children's Hospital and IBM installed an experimental digital electronic record system. The hospital administrator said in 1962: "If we can mechanize much of this routine clerical work, our doctors and nurses will be able to spend more of their time using their professional training to give more direct and attentive care to patients." No one knows what happened to the experiment but the hospital is again undertaking a conversion to EHR. See Steve Lohr, "The 'Miracle' of Digital Health Records Fifty Years Ago," *New York Times*, February 17, 2012, http://bits.blogs.nytimes.com/2012/02/17/ the-miracle-of-digital-health-records-50-years-ago/?emc=eta1.

21. Robert Wood Johnson Foundation, "Reform in Action: Does Use of EHRs Help Improve Quality?" 2011, http://www.rwjf.org/files/research/72480af4qehr201106.pdf.

22. Emma Schwartz, "Can Cleveland Clinic Be a Model for Digital Medicine?" *Huffington Post*, May 25, 2011, http://www.huffingtonpost.com/2009/12/02/can-cleveland-clinic-be-a_n_376842.html; Steve Lohr, "Digital Records May Not Cut Health Costs, One Study Cautions," *New York Times,* March 5, 2012.

23. Danny McCormick et al. "Giving Office-Based Physicians Electronic Access to Patients' Prior Imaging and Lab Results Did Not Deter Ordering of Tests," *Health Affairs* 31, no. 13 (2012): 488–496.

24. Ibid.

25. Steve Lohr, "Digital Records May Not Cut Health Costs, Study Cautions."

26. Quote comes from Steve Lohr, "Electronic Health Records, A Study and Perspective," *New York Times*, March 6, 2012, http://bits.blogs.nytimes.com/2012/03/06/ electronic-health-records-a-study-and-perspective/.

27. While studies of physicians engaged in practice include surveys, interviews, self-reports of individual clinical practices, and researchers' direct observations, such investigations have been uncommon. There are, of course, firsthand accounts of specialty work from Mark Kramer, *Invasive Procedures* (New York: Penguin Books, 1979); Jerome Groopman, *How Doctors Think* (New York: Mariner Books, 2007); Atul Gawande, *Better: A Surgeon's Notes on Performance* (New York: Picador, 2007); Abraham Verghese, *My Own Country: A Doctor's Story of a Town and Its People in*

the Age of AIDS (New York: Simon & Schuster, 1994). For doctors writing of their experiences, see: Rita Charon, "Narrative Medicine: Form, Function, and Ethics," *Annals of Internal Medicine* 34, no. 1 (2001): 83–87. For similar studies and first-hand reports of primary care physicians, see Kurt Stange, MD, et al., "Illuminating the 'Black Box,'" *Journal of Family Practice* 46 (1998): 377–389; Jeffrey Borkan, MD, "Examining American Family Medicine in the New World Order: A Study of Five Practices," *Journal of Family Practice* 48, no. 8 (1999): 620–627; Benjamin Crabtree et al., "Understanding Practice from the Ground Up," *Journal of Family Practice* 50, no. 10 (2001): 881–887; Kimberley Yarnell, MD, "Primary Care: Is There Enough Time for Prevention? *American Journal of Public Health* 93, no. 4 (2003): 635–641; Jeffrey Farber, MD, et al., "How Much Time Do Physicians Spend Providing Care Outside of Office Visits?" *Annals of Internal Medicine* 147, no. 10 (2007): 693–699; Baron, "What's Keeping Us So Busy in Primary Care?" For nine groups of doctors making recommendations on diagnostic tests, see Rabin, "Doctor Panels Recommend Fewer Tests for Patients."

28. Laura Tollen, "Physician Organization in Relation to Quality and Efficiency of Care: A Synthesis of Recent Literature," Report 89 (New York: Commonwealth Fund, April 2008); David Newman, "Accountable Care Organizations and the Medicare Shared Savings Program," November 4, 2010, Congressional Research Service, Report R41474, www.crs.gov; Gawande, "The Cost Conundrum." The word *iPatient* comes from Abraham Verghese, "Treat the Patient, Not the CT Scan," *New York Times*, February 26, 2011.

29. Elliott S. Fisher, Douglas O. Staiger, Julie P. W. Bynum, and Daniel J. Gottlieb, "Creating Accountable Care Organizations: The Extended Hospital Medical Staff," *Health Affairs* 26, no. 1 (2007): 44–57.

30. Bruce, Japsen, "Small-Picture Approach Flips Medical Economics," *New York Times*, March 13, 2012.

31. Sara Michael, "The Future of Health Care," *Physicians Practice* 20, no. 6 (2010), http://www.physicianspractice.com/display/article/1462168/1589685; "A Doctor's Vision of the Future of Medicine," *Daily Beast*, June 26, 2009, http://www.thedaily beast.com/newsweek/2009/06/26/a-doctor-s-vision-of-the-future-of-medicine.html; Adam Liptak, "Supreme Court Upholds Health Care Law, 5-4, in Victory for Obama," *New York Times*, June 29, 2012.

32. Verghese, "Treat the Patient, Not the CT Scan."

33. Alan Hillman, MD, et al., "How Do Financial Incentives Affect Physicians' Clinical Decisions and the Financial Performance of Health Maintenance Organizations," *New England Journal of Medicine* 321, no. 2 (1989): 86–92; Arnold Epstein, MD et al., "Paying Physicians for High Quality Care," *New England Journal of Medicine* 350 (2004): 406–410; Michael Baumann and Ed Dellert, "Performance Measures and Pay for Performance," *Chest* 129, no. 1 (2006): 188–191.

34. Jerry Cromwell et al., eds., *Pay for Performance in Health Care: Methods and Approaches* (Research Triangle Park, NC: RTI Press, 2011).

35. Hector Rodriguez et al., "The Effect of Performance-Based Financial Incentives on Improving Patient Care Experiences A Statewide Evaluation," *Journal of General*

Internal Medicine 24, no. 12 (December 2009): 1281–1288; Meredith Rosenthal et al., "Climbing Up the Pay-For-Performance Learning Curve: Where Are the Early Adopters Now?" *Health Affairs* 26, no. 6 (November 2007): 1674–1682; Jerome Groopman and Pamela Hartzband, "Why 'Quality' Care Is Dangerous," *Wall Street Journal*, April 8, 2009; Peter Lindenauer, MD, et al., "Public Reporting and Pay for Performance in Hospital Quality Improvement," *New England Journal of Medicine* 356 (2007): 486–496; Mark Chassin, MD, et al. "Accountability Measures—Using Measurement to Promote Quality Improvement," *New England Journal of Medicine* 363 (2010): 683–688.

36. Groopman and Hartzband, "Why 'Quality' Care Is Dangerous."
37. Pauline Chen, "A Report Card for Doctors," *New York Times*, June 16, 2011, http://well.blogs.nytimes.com/2011/06/16/a-report-card-for-doctors/.
38. Danielle Ofri, MD, "Quality Measures and the Individual Physician," *New England Journal of Medicine* 363 (2010): 606–607.
39. Ibid.
40. For an insightful view of this struggle over the decades and currently, see David Leonhardt, "Making Health Care Better," *New York Times*, November 8, 2009.
41. Freidson, *Profession of Medicine*, 391.
42. Donald Campbell, "Assessing the Impact of Planned Social Change," Occasional Paper #8, Public Affairs Center, Dartmouth College, December 1976, 49–54.
43. Sandeep Jauhar, MD, "The Pitfalls of Linking Doctors' Pay To Performance," *New York Times*, September 8, 2008.
44. Rachel Werner, MD, et al., "The Unintended Consequences of Coronary Artery Bypass Graft Report Cards," *Circulation* 111 (2005): 1257–1263.
45. Clemens Hong, MD, et al., "Relationship Between Patient Panel Characteristics and Primary Care Physician Clinical Performance Rankings," *JAMA* 304, no. 10 (2010): 1107–1113.
46. Barbara Starfield, MD, "Is U.S. Health Really the Best in the World?" *JAMA* 284, no. 4 (2000): 483–485; Mark Schuster, Elizabeth McGlynn, and Robert Brook, "How Good Is the Quality of Health Care in the United States?" *Milbank Quarterly* 83, no. 4 (2005): 843–895.

Chapter 5

1. *Education Week*, "School Finance," June 20, 2011, http://www.edweek.org/ew/issues/school-finance/.
2. Maurice Dyson, "The Death of Robin Hood? Proposals for Overhauling Public School Finance," *Georgetown Journal on Poverty Law and Policy* 9, no. 1 (2004): 1–52; Alexandra Greif, "Politics, Practicalities, and Priorities: New Jersey's Experience Implementing the Abbott V Mandate," *Yale Law and Policy Review* 22, no. 2 (2004): 615–657.
3. Barbara Nye, Larry Hedges, and Spyros Kostantopoulos, "The Long-Term Effects of Small Classes: A Five-Year Follow-Up of the Tennessee Class Size Experiment," *Educational Evaluation and Policy Analysis* 21, no. 2 (1999): 127–142. As far as I

could tell, researchers looking at the Tennessee schools have not linked different ways of teaching to achievement results.

4. George Bohrnstedt and Brian Stecher, eds., *What We Have Learned About Class Size Reduction in California* (Santa Monica, CA: RAND Corporation, 2002), 15.

5. Ibid., 22.

6. John Hattie, "The Paradox of Reducing Class Size and Improving Learning Outcomes," *International Journal of Educational Research* 43 (2005): 387–425. For changes in classroom practices, see 403–410.

7. The National Alliance for Public Charter Schools, "Dashboard," 2011, http://dashboard.publiccharters.org/dashboard/schools/year/2011.

8. Katrina Bulkley and Jennifer Fisler, *A Review of the Research on Charter Schools* (Philadelphia: Consortium for Policy Research, University of Pennsylvania, Graduate School of Education, June 2002) 1–2.

9. Katherine Barghaus and Erling Boe, "From Policy to Practice: Implementation of the Legislative Objectives of Charter Schools," *American Journal of Education* 118 (2011): 57–85.

10. Christopher Lubienski, "Innovations in Education Markets: Theory and Evidence on the Impact of Competition and Choice in Charter Schools," *American Educational Research Journal* 40, no. 2 (2003): 395–443.

11. Ellen Goldring and Xiu Cravens, "Teachers' Academic Focus On Learning In Charter And Non-Charter Schools," presentation at National Conference on Charter School Research, Vanderbilt University, September 28, 2006, p. 9.

12. See http://www.kipp.org/faq.

13. Jay Mathews, *Work Hard, Be Nice: How Two Inspired Teachers Created the Most Promising Schools in America* (Chapel Hill, NC: Algonquin Books, 2009).

14. Leadership Public School teachers had designed readers for various courses including this geometry class; these teacher-designed lessons contained the sequence of parts I described and accompanying worksheets with questions.

15. Teachers at LPS designed Exit Ticket. Using recycled iPods and cell phones, students could point and click on answers on a screen. Because they were iPods, students used other functions beyond the "clicker" one. Teachers wrote the apps for the devices, including iPads, to use for instantaneous feedback from students.

16. Larry Cuban, *Hugging the Middle: How Teachers Teach in an Era of Testing and Accountability* (New York: Teachers College Press, 2009).

17. Fred M. Newmann et al., "Instructional Program Coherence: What It Is and Why It Should Guide School Improvement Policy," *Educational Evaluation and Policy Analysis*, 23, no. 4 (2001): 297–321.

18. Mathews, *Work Hard, Be Nice*; David Whitman, "An Appeal to Authority: The New Paternalism in Urban Schools," *Education Next*, 4, no. 8 (2008), http://education-next.org/an-appeal-to-authority/; Paul Tough, "What It Takes to Make a Student," *New York Times*, November 26, 2006, http://www.nytimes.com/2006/11/26/magazine/26tough.html?pagewanted=all.

19. CREDO, "Multiple Choice: Charter School Performance in 16 States," (Stanford, CA: Center for Research on Education Outcomes, Stanford University, June

2009); Philip Gleason et al., "The Evaluation of Charter School Impacts," Final Report (Washington, DC: U.S. Department of Education, Institutes of Education Sciences, 2010); Martin Carnoy et al., "Worth the Price? Weighing the Evidence on Charter School Achievement," *Education Finance and Policy* 1, no. 1 (2006): 151–161.

20. Clarke Canfield, "iPads Take Place Next to Crayons in Kindergarten," *USA Today*, April 13, 2011 at, http://www.usatoday.com/tech/news/2011-04-13-ipads-kindergarten.htm; Justin Reich, Richard Murnane, and John Willet, "The State of Wiki Usage in U.S. K–12 Schools," *Educational Researcher* 41, no. 3 (2012): 7–15.

21. For typical examples, see: Damian Bebell and Laura O'Dwyer, "Educational Outcomes and Research from 1:1 Educational Settings," *Journal of Technology, Learning, and Assessment* 9, no. 1 (2012): 1–15; John Fensterwald, "Mixed Results Using iPads," *Thoughts on Public Education*, April 18, 2012, http://toped.svefoundation.org/2012/04/18/mixed-results-using-ipads-for-algebra/.

22. The *novelty effect*, sometimes referred to as the *halo effect* or even the *placebo* effect has been mentioned early on in the literature on educational technology. See Richard Clark and Brenda Sugrue, "Research and Instructional Media, 1978–1988," in *Educational Media Technology Yearbook 1988*, ed. Donald P. Ely (Englewood, CO: Libraries Unlimited, 1988), 19–36.

23. While there are too many studies to cite here, sorting out those that are sponsored by vendors (e.g., Intel Corporation, "The Positive Impact of 'eLearning'" (San Jose: Intel Corporation White Paper on Education, 2009) and advocates of technology in schools (e.g., John Schacter, "The Impact of Education Technology on Student Achievement" [Santa Monica, CA: Milken Exchange on Education and Technology, 1999]) from rigorously done studies, including meta-analyses, completed by independent scholars is essential. Of the latter group, here is a sampling: U.S. Department of Education, Institute of Educational Sciences, "Effectiveness of Reading and Mathematics Software Products: Findings from the First Student Cohort," Report to Congress, March 2007; Mark Warschauer and Tina Matuchniak, "New Technology and Digital Worlds: Analyzing Evidence of Equity in Access, Use, and Outcomes," *Review of Research in Education*, 34, no. 1 (2010): 179–225; Deborah Lowther et al., "Does Technology Integration 'Work' When Key Barriers are Removed?" paper presented at American Educational Research Association Conference, New York City, 2008; Damian Bebell and Laura O'Dwyer, Educational Outcomes and Research from 1:1 Computing Settings," *Journal of Technology, Learning, and Assessmen* 9, no. 1 (2010): 5–14.

24. Clayton Christensen, Curtis Johnson, and Michael Horn, *Disrupting Class: How Disrupting Innovation Will Change the Way the World Learns* (New York: McGraw-Hill, 2008); Terry Moe and John Chubb, *Liberated Learning; Technology, Politics, and the Future of American Education* (New York: John Wiley, 2009).

25. Joel Klein, "The Promise of Education Technology (It's Not Just About Lighter Backpacks)," *Huffington Post*, February 3, 2012, http://www.huffingtonpost.com/joel-i-klein/digital-textbooks-education-technology_b_1253009.html.

26. Barbara Means et al., *Evaluation of Evidence-Based Practices in Online Learning: A Meta-Analysis and Review of Online Learning Studies* (Washington, DC: U.S.

Department of Education Office of Planning, Evaluation, and Policy Development Policy and Program Studies Service, 2009); 2010 Annual Letter from Bill Gates: Online Learning, http://www.gatesfoundation.org/annual-letter/2010/Pages/education-learning-online.aspx; Tamara Battaglino et al., "The Costs of Online Learning" (Working paper Series from Thomas B. Fordham Institute, January 2012); For a rebuttal to this working paper and its methodology for calculating costs, see Bruce Baker, "Misunderstanding and Misrepresenting 'Costs' and 'Economics' of Online Learning," January 16, 2012, http://nepc.colorado.edu/blog/misunderstanding-misrepresenting-costs.

27. Stephanie Saul, "Profits and Questions at Online Charter Schools," *New York Times*, December 13, 2011.

28. John Fensterwald, "Learning Labs 101," Scholastic, http://www.scholastic.com/browse/article.jsp?id=3757077.

29. Larry Cuban, "'I Saw the Future and It Works': A Visit to a Hybrid School," February 13, 2012, http://larrycuban.wordpress.com/2012/02/13/i-saw-the-future-and-it-works-a-visit-to-a-hybrid-school/. University of Chicago psychologist Benjamin Bloom and others created the taxonomy of cognitive domains in the mid-1950s. It has been used often in K–12 classrooms as a basis for teaching different forms of thinking; see Lorin Anderson et al., *A Taxonomy of Learning, Teaching, and Assessing: A Revision of Bloom's Educational Objectives* (Boston: Allyn and Bacon, 2000).

30. Rocketship sponsored studies of its charter schools in San Jose and announced large gains in student achievement; see http://rsed.org/index.php?page=academic-performance.

31. Richard Clark, "Reconsidering Research on Learning from Media," *Review of Educational Research* 53 (1983): 445–459; Barbara Means and Kerry Olson, *Technology and Education Reform* (Darby, PA: Diane Publishing Co., 1997), 23–26.

32. Christensen, Johnson, and Horn, *Disrupting Class*; Heather Wolpert-Gawron, "Blended Learning: Combining Face-to-Face and Online Education," *Edutopia*, http://www.edutopia.org/blog/blended-online-learning-heather-wolpert-gawron; Means et al., *Evaluation of Evidence-Based Practices in Online Learning*.

33. Michael Feuer, Lisa Towne, and Richard Shavelson, "Scientific Culture and Educational Research," *Educational Researcher* 31, no. 8 (2002): 4–14; for a direct comparison between EBM and EBE see John Willinsky, "Extending the Prospects of Evidence-Based Education," *Insight* 1, no. 1 (2001): 23–41. Also, there is now a journal for evidence-based education called *Better* and an article by Steven Fleischman, "Before Choosing, Ask Three Questions," *Better* 3 (2012): 6–7. For the Cochrane Collaborative, see http://www.cochrane.org/; for Campbell Collaborative, see http://www.campbellcollaboration.org/; for What Works Clearinghouse, see http://ies.ed.gov/ncee/wwc/.

34. Philip Jackson, *Life in Classrooms* (New York: Holt, Rinehart, and Winston, 1968), 166–167.

35. Quoted in Elliot Eisner, "Educational Objectives: Help or Hindrance?" *School Review* 75 (1967): 551–552.

36. Ibid.

37. N.L. Gage, *The Scientific Basis for the Art of Teaching* (New York: Teachers College Press, 1978).

38. Walter Doyle, "Paradigms for Research on Teacher Effectiveness," *Review of Research in Education* 5 (1977): 163–198; N.L. Gage and Margaret Needels, "Process-Product Research on Teaching: A Review of Criticisms," *Elementary School Journal* 89, no. 3 (1989): 253–300; Cuban, *Hugging the Middle.*

39. Sarah Garland, "Federal Teacher Evaluation Requirement Has Wide Impact," *The Hechinger Report*, April 15, 2012, http://hechingerreport.org/content/federal-teacher-evaluation-requirement-has-wide-impact_8360/.

40. Bill and Melinda Gates Foundation, "Working with Teachers to Develop Fair and Reliable Measures of Effective Teaching: The MET Project," *The MetLife Survey of The American Teacher: Teachers, Parents, and the Economy, 2011* (March 2012), 6–7; also see teacher opinions on the worth of standardized test scores as compared with other sources of data on students. Yet it is student test scores on these tests that federal and state decision makers use to evaluate and pay teachers. See Scholastic, Inc. and the Bill and Melinda Gates Foundation, *Primary Sources: 2012: America's Teachers on the Teaching Profession*, 27–29.

41. Daniel Weisberg et al., *The Widget Effect* (Washington, DC: The New Teacher Project, 2009).

42. There is a crucial distinction between *good* and *successful* teaching and an equally important one between *successful* teaching and *successful* learning that avid reformers ignore. See Gary Fenstermacher and Virginia Richardson, "On Making Determinations of Quality in Teaching," *Teachers College Record* 107 (2005): 186–213.

43. Louis Freedberg, "Pioneered in California, Publishing Teachers' 'Effectiveness' Rankings Draws More Criticism," *Ed Source*, March 28, 2012, http://www.edsource.org/extra/2012/pioneered-in-california-publishing-teacher-effectiveness-rankings-draws-more-criticism/6732.

44. William Sanders and Sandra Horn, "The Tennessee Value-Added Assessment System (TVAAS): Mixed Model Methodology in Educational Assessment," *Journal of Personnel Evaluation in Education* 8, no. 3 (1994): 299–311; Daniel McCaffrey et al., "Models for Value-Added Modeling of Teacher Effects," *Journal of Educational Behavioral Statistics* 29, no. 1 (2004): 67–101.

45. Sarah Butrymowicz and Sarah Garland, "How New York City's Value-Added Model Compares to What Other Districts, States Are Doing," March 1, 2012, http://hechingerreport.org/content/how-new-york-citys-value-added-model-compares-to-what-other-districts-states-are-doing_7757/.

46. Greg Toppo, "Survey Finds Teachers Don't Trust Annual State Skills Test," *USA Today*, March 16, 2012, http://www.usatoday.com/news/education/story/2012-03-15/survey-teacher-pay-linked-to-test-scores/53554210/1; Shelli Kurth, "What's Fair in Measuring Teacher Performance," *Voice of San Diego*, http://www.voiceofsandiego.org/opinion/article_f005119e-84ca-11e1-a8c4-001a4bcf887a.html.

47. Linda Darling-Hammond and colleagues summarize the negatives of VAM in "Evaluating Teacher Evaluation," *Education Week*, February 12, 2012, http://www.edweek.org/ew/articles/2012/03/01/kappan_hammond.html. For another view

that argues, on balance, that VAM is worthwhile in evaluating teachers, see Steven Glazerman et al., *Evaluating Teachers: The Important Role of Value-Added* (Washington, DC: Brookings Institution, November 17, 2010), http://www.brookings.edu/reports/2010/1117_evaluating_teachers.aspx. For stability in teacher ratings over time see, Dan Goldhaber and Michael Hansen, "Is It Just a Bad Class? Assessing the Stability of Measured Teacher Performance," CEDR Working Paper #2010-3 (Seattle, WA: Center for Education Data & Research, University of Washington, 2010). On issues of reliability and validity in value-added measures, see Matthew Di Carlo posts April 12 and 20, 2012 at: http://shankerblog.org/?p=5621; and http://nepc.colorado.edu/blog/value-added-versus-observations-part-two-validity.

48. Susan Headden, *Inside IMPACT: D.C.'s Model Teacher Evaluation System*, (Washington, DC: Education Sector, 2011).

49. The IMPACT program can be found at: http://www.dc.gov/DCPS/impact. Two external reports evaluating IMPACT are: Headden, *Inside IMPACT* and Barbara Martinez, *IMPACT in Washington, D.C.: Lessons from the First Years*, October, 2011 (Washington, DC: Democrats for Education Reform); Bill Turque, "Michelle Rhee's D.C. Schools' Legacy in Sharper Focus One Year Later," *Washington Post*, October 15, 2011. For 2012–2013, Chancellor Kaya Henderson announced changes to IMPACT: only 35 percent of teacher ratings will come from students' scores on a D.C. test, with other measures being used, and the number of classroom observations will be reduced. See Lisa Gartner, "D.C. To Weaken Link Between Test Scores, Teacher Ratings," *Washington Examiner*, August 12, 2012, http://washington examiner.com/d.c.-to-weaken-link-between-test-scores-teacher-ratings/article/2503893 #.UIVgUBjlG3c.

50. Headden, *Inside IMPACT*, 5.

51. Dana Goldstein, "Making Sense of Michelle Rhee's Legacy and Teacher 'Churn and Burn,'" October 19, 2011, http://www.danagoldstein.net/dana_goldstein/2011/10/making-sense-of-michelle-rhees-legacy-and-teacher-churn-and-burn.html; Turque, "Michelle Rhee's D.C. Legacy Is in Sharper Focus One Year Later."

52. Stephanie Wright, "How To Improve D.C.'s IMPACT Evaluation System," *Washington Post*, September 1, 2011, http://www.washingtonpost.com/blogs/answer-sheet/post/teacher-how-to-improve-dcs-impact-evaluation-system/2011/08/31/gIQARop3sJ_blog.html; Jay Mathews, "Impact Evaluations Drain This D.C. Principal," *Washington Post*, March 27, 2011, http://www.washingtonpost.com/blogs/class-struggle/post/impact-evaluations-drain-this-dc-principal/2011/03/27/AFIr-8VjB_blog.html; Headden, "Inside IMPACT."

53. Bill Turque, "Memphis Tries D.C.-Style Teacher Evaluation," *Washington Post*, March 31, 2012.

54. Bill and Melinda Gates Foundation, "Working with Teachers to Develop Fair and Reliable Measures of Effective Teaching: The MET Project," 2010; Steven Sawchuk, "New Teacher Evaluation Systems Face Obstacles," *Education Week*, December 11, 2009.

55. Sawchuk, "New Teacher Evaluation Systems Face Obstacles"; Julia Koppich and Camille Esch, " Grabbing the Brass Ring: Who Shapes Teacher Policy?" *Educational*

Policy 26, no. 1 (2012): 79–95; to hear Charlotte Danielson describe her framework see: http://www.youtube.com/watch?v=Th1Zrfq1I1s; to view the twenty-two components used in Hillsborough, see http://www.ascd.org/publications/books/106034/chapters/The-Framework-for-Teaching@-An-Overview.aspx. For many years, teacher unions, contrary to current conventional wisdom, have collaborated with district leaders in, for example, New Haven, Connecticut; Denver Colorado; Toledo, Ohio; and Pittsburgh, Pennsylvania to develop programs where teachers worked closely with administrators to establish new ways of evaluating teacher performance. See Steven Sawchuk, "New Attitudes Shaping Labor-District Relations," *Education Week*, November 16, 2011, 2–5.

56. Anthony Cody, "VAM Gets Slammed: Teacher Evaluation Not a Game of Chance," *Education Week*, March 9, 2012, http://blogs.edweek.org/teachers/living–in–dialogue/2012/03/vam_gets_slammed_teacher_evalu.html.

57. Steven Glazerman et al., "Evaluating Teachers: The Important Role of Value-Added," Brookings Institution, November 17, 2010, http://www.brookings.edu/reports/2010/1117_evaluating_teachers.aspx; Douglas Harris, "Would Accountability Based on Teacher Value-Added Be Smart Policy?" presented at conference at University of Madison, Madison, Wisconsin, June 19, 2008; Douglas Harris, *Value-Added Measures in Education: What Every Educator Needs to Know,* (Cambridge, MA: Harvard Education Press, 2011).

58. Helen Ladd, "Dallas School Accountability and Incentive Program," *Economics of Education Review* 18 (1999): 1–16; Thomas Kane and Douglas Staiger, "The Promise and Pitfalls of Using Imprecise School Accountability Measures, " *Journal of Economic Perspectives* 16, no. 4 (2002): 91–114; Carolyn Kelley, Herbert Heneman III, and Anthony Milanowski, "Teacher Motivation and School-based Performance Rewards," *Educational Administration Quarterly* 38, no. 3 (2002): 372–401.

59. Jackson, *Life in Classrooms*, 166.

60. Many observers would be startled by this statement about morbidity and mortality rates unaffected by the structures I identified. Observers would point to the reduced lethality of such diseases as AIDS and different cancers; they would point to the many diseases that now have therapies that can extend life (e.g., kidney dialysis, chemotherapies, and radiation for particular cancers). What such observers overlook are many factors such as economic inequalities, how nations deliver health care, ethnic and racial discrimination, and others that also shape rates of morbidity and mortality. See Barbara Starfield, "Is U.S. Health Really the Best in the World?" *JAMA* 284, no. 4 (2000): 483–485.

61. Donald Schön coined the phrase *dynamic conservatism* to mean that institutions fight to remain the same. Institutions, he argued, resist reform by adopting those changes that will maintain institutional stability. Incremental changes are no longer satisfactory in times of great change. Institutional dysfunction keeps worthy fundamental changes at bay. What is needed are "learning institutions" untethered to their traditional moorings that can deal with conflict and ambiguity and respond quickly to changes in the larger environment.

Schön was writing at a time—late-1960s and early 1970s—when talk and action to reform government, criminal justice, housing, employment, health care, and education dominated social and political movements of the day, and *dynamic conservatism* connoted institutional resistance to worthy reforms. How to overcome these institutions' natural inclination to survive in the face of attacks dominated reformers' thinking at the time. This oxymoron, clearly not a compliment to leaders of such institutions, helped to create some understanding among particular reformers of how hard it was to alter fundamentally traditional institutions.

I do not place a positive or negative value on *dynamic conservatism*. I see the phrase as a helpful way of understanding how medicine and schooling as institutions cope with reforms that seek to overturn long-standing principles and practices. See *Beyond the Stable State: Public and Private Learning in a Changing Society* (New York: Norton, 1973). For a critique of Schön's argument, see Rose Goldsen, "The Technological Fix: Existential version Beyond the Stable State," *Administrative Science Quarterly* 20, no. 3 (1975): 464–468.

Chapter 6

1. Philip Jackson, *Life in Classrooms* (New York: Holt, Rinehart, and Winston, 1968), 166–167.
2. Gökçe Sargut and Rita McGrath, "Learning to Live with Complexity," *Harvard Business Review*, September 1, 2011, 69–76; Brent Davis and Dennis Sumara, "Learning Communities: Understanding the workplace as a Complex System," *New Directions for Adult and Continuing Education*, 2001, 85–96; Jennifer O'Day, "Complexity, Accountability, and School Improvement," *Harvard Educational Review* 72, no. 3 (2002): 293–329.
3. Anne Burns and John Knox, "Classrooms as Complex Systems: A Relational Model," *TESL-EJ* 15, no. 1 (June 2011), http://www.tesl-ej.org/wordpress/issues/volume15/ej57/ej57a1/.
4. Karl Weick, "Education Organizations as Loosely Coupled Systems," *Administrative Science Quarterly* 21, no. 1 (1976): 1–19; John Meyer and Brian Rowan, "Institutionalized Organizations; Formal Structure as Myth and Ceremony," *American Journal of Sociology* 83, no. 2 (1977): 340–363; James March, "Footnotes to Organizational Change," *Administrative Science Quarterly* 26, no. 4 (1981): 563–577.
5. I have described mainstream teacher-centered instruction and variations of student-centered teaching in the Introduction and various chapters in the book. For those readers wanting further elaboration, see Larry Cuban, *How Teachers Taught* (New York: Teachers College Press, 1993) and *Hugging the Middle: How Teachers Teach in an Era of Testing and Accountability* (New York: Teachers College Press, 2009) For an incisive and crisp analysis of teaching traditions stretching back millennia and different labels for these traditions that overlap the ones that I use, see Philip Jackson, The *Practice of Teaching* (New York: Teachers College Press, 1986), 98–145.
6. David Tyack and Larry Cuban, *Tinkering Toward Utopia* (Cambridge, MA: Harvard University Press, 1995); Seymour Sarason, *The Culture of the School and the*

Problem of Change (Boston: Allyn and Bacon, 1982); Dan Lortie, *Schoolteacher* (Chicago: University of Chicago Press, 1975); Mary Metz, "Real School: A Universal Drama amid Disparate Experience," *Politics of Education Yearbook, 1989,* 75–91.

7. Andrew Gitlin and Frank Margonis, "The Political Aspect of Reform: Teacher Resistance as Good Sense," *American Journal of Education* 103, no. 4 (1995): 377–405; Donna Muncey and Patrick McQuillan, *Reform and Resistance in Schools and Classrooms* (New Haven, CT: Yale University Press, 1996); Brad Olsen and Lisa Kirtman,"Teacher as Mediator of School Reform: An Examination of Teacher Practices in 36 California Restructuring Schools," *Teachers College Record* 104, no. 2 (2002): 301–324; Linda Darling-Hammond, "Standards, Accountability, and School Reform," *Teachers College Record* 106, no. 6 (2004): 1047–1085; David Labaree, *Someone Has to Fail* (Cambridge, MA: Harvard University Press, 2010).

8. The example of piloting a large aircraft and air traffic control is often used in distinguishing between complicated and complex systems. See, for example, Sargut and McGrath, "Learning to Live with Complexity."

9. Scholars applied institutional theory to schools in the 1980s and 1990s. They emphasized that the rational model of decision makers making policy and bureaucrats putting those policies into action seldom worked in school organizations because policy was "loosely coupled" to the work that teachers did in their classrooms. Social beliefs, myths, and ceremonies about schooling helped smooth out the disjunctures between policy and practice but teachers had little direct supervision and had sufficient autonomy to embrace or ignore policy directives. Much of the delineation of institutional theory mirrored a later generation of social science scholars using complexity theory to characterize schools and classrooms. See Richard Scott and John Meyer, *Institutional Environments and Organizations* (Thousand Oaks, CA: Sage Publications, 1994); Paul Dimaggio and Walter Powell, "The Iron Cage Revisited: Institutional Isomorphism and Collective Rationality Revisited," *American Sociological Review* 48, no. 2 (1983): 147–160; John Meyer and Brian Rowan, "Institutionalized Organizations: Formal Structure as Myth and Ceremony," *American Journal of Sociology* 83, no. 2 (1977): 340–363; Karl Weick, "Educational Organizations as Loosely-coupled Systems," *Administrative Science Quarterly* 21 (1976): 1–19; Sargut and McGrath, "Learning to Live with Complexity"; Mark Hardman, "Is Complexity Theory Useful in Describing Classroom Learning?" paper presented at European Conference on Educational Research, Helsinki, Finland, August 26, 2010.

10. Forty-five states (2012) have adopted the Common Core standards in math and English. See: http://www.corestandards.org/.

11. Mary Kennedy, *Inside Teaching: How Classroom Life Undermines Reform* (Cambridge, MA: Harvard University Press, 2005), 3–12, 233–235.

12. Tim Quinn, "Preparing Non-Educators for the Superintendency," *School Administrator* 7, no. 64 (2007), http://www.aasa.org/SchoolAdministratorArticle.aspx?id=6636; The Broad Center, "Broad Superintendents Academy Graduates Outperform Their Peers in Raising Student Achievement," news release, August 30, 2010.

13. Labaree, *Someone Has to Fail*, 158.
14. Steven Brill, *Class Warfare* (New York: Simon & Schuster, 2011).
15. Ibid., 20, 424.
16. Ibid., 422.
17. Ibid., 425.
18. Mary Kennedy, "Attribution Error and the Quest for Teacher Quality," *Educational Researcher* 39, no. 8 (2010): 591–598.
19. Gary Fenstermacher and Virginia Richardson, "On Making Determinations of Quality in Teaching," *Teachers College Record* 107 (2005): 186–213.
20. Paul Tough, *Whatever It Takes: Geoffrey Canada's Quest to Change Harlem and America* (New York: Houghton Mifflin Harcourt, 2008); Jay Mathews, *Escalante: The Best Teacher in America* (New York: Henry Holt, 1988); Erin Gruwell and Freedom Writers, *The Freedom Writers Diary* (New York: Broadway publishing, 1999).
21. Brent Davis and Dennis Sumara, "Learning Communities: Understanding the Workplace as a Complex System," *New Directions for Adult and Continuing Education*, 2001, 85–96; Karl Weick, "Education Organizations as Loosely Coupled Systems," *Administrative Science Quarterly* 21, no. 1 (1976): 1–19.
22. Richard Elmore, *Building a New Structure for Leadership* (New York: Albert Shanker Institute, 2000); Donald Schön, *Beyond the Stable State: Public and Private Learning in a Changing Society* (New York: Norton, 1973). See Cuban, *Hugging the Middle*. There are also practical reasons for hybrids of old and new teaching approaches. Those who teach for more than two or three years come to realize that differences among students in their motivations, aptitudes, interests, and backgrounds make multiple ways of teaching, mixes of traditional and innovative practices, sensible because no single teaching method can finesse so many differences among students.
23. John Chubb and Terry Moe, *Politics, Markets, and America's Schools* (Washington, DC: Brookings Institution, 1990); Frederick Hess, *Spinning Wheels: The Politics of Urban School Reform* (Washington, DC: Brookings Institution, 1999).
24. Stan Karp, speech given to Northwest Teachers for Justice, Seattle, Washington, October 1, 2011 at: http://rethinkingschools.org/news/NWTSJKarpOct11.shtml.
25. Diane Ravitch, "A Moment of National Insanity," *Washington Post*, March 1, 2012, http://voices.washingtonpost.com/answer-sheet/diane-ravitch/ravitch-a-moment-of-national-i.html.
26. Lee Fang, "How Online Companies Bought America's Schools," *The Nation*, December 5, 2011 at: http://www.thenation.com/article/164651/how-online-learning-companies-bought-americas-schools?page=full#.
27. For those who insist on seeing conspiracies, one well-funded conservative group, the American Legislative Exchange Council (ALEC) seems to fit the stereotype. ALEC brings together lawmakers, corporate officials, and various interest groups to draft model laws for state legislatures across the nation. They have been successful in getting states to ban collective bargaining and gun laws as well. As Scott Suder, the Wisconsin state co-chairman of ALEC (and Assembly majority leader) told a journalist: "ALEC's basis is free-market, Jeffersonian principles . . . That's my core philosophy: getting government out of the way as much as possible." Among

the different draft laws (on taxes, energy, environment) they distribute to states, a few involve allowing home-schooled and other children to enroll in cyber charter schools and bills to provide up to $13,500 in publicly financed scholarships for children with disabilities to attend private schools or schools outside the district. All of these funds for cyber schools and disabled children come from district school budgets. As one legislator said, ALEC is "taking apart public schools, drip by drip." Yet, even here, because ALEC meetings are not secret and donors such as the wealthy, conservative Koch brothers speak proudly of their funding ALEC, word has spread among opponents upset, even outraged, by the actions of this conservative group; these opponents are fighting back and blunting some of the victories that ALEC had achieved earlier. See Dan Kaufman, "Land of Cheese and Rancor," *New York Times Magazine*, May 27, 2012, 30–33, 46–47.

28. For pervasiveness of market thinking and use of the business model in public institutions, see Michael Sandel, *What Money Can't Buy; The Moral Limits of Markets* (New York: Farrar, Straus, and Giroux, 2012); Mike Konczal, "The Privatization Trap," *Salon*, February 5, 2012, http://www.salon.com/2012/02/05/the_privatization_trap/; also see Janice Cuban's blog on clever marketing tactics to sell products at: http://marketingsparks.wordpress.com/2011/11/14/so-whats-so-wrong-about-product-placement-in-films-the-good-the-brand-and-the-ugly/.

Insofar as personal experiences go, I have learned about policy elites and their variations from direct contact. Once upon a time, I was a dyed-in-the-wool school reformer in the Washington, D.C. schools in the 1960s. I met and worked with national and local policy elites of the day in developing new models for training teachers, creating curriculum for urban youth, and tying together community and schools. What struck me in the years I worked in schools and with these opinion shapers were their intensely held beliefs about reducing social inequalities and doing what was best for children and youth, internal struggles over both the ends and means, and constant tripping over one another in getting things done.

Then I became a district superintendent in the 1970s and early 1980s. As an educational decision maker, I was determined, along with the school board, to improve the district schools. As superintendent in the metropolitan D.C. educational community, I attended many business and social meetings, where I saw political policy elites make decisions. By this time, the elite members I had known years earlier had been replaced by another generation. Again, I was a marginal player but I watched what transpired. Those two experiences in the Washington, D.C., area, left a strong impression on me about how smart, influential, and pragmatic individuals with similar beliefs converge and diverge as issues arise and evaporate.

Now, I am currently on the board of trustees, half of whom are entrepreneurs and high-tech executives in start-up companies, for a four-school charter school network in the San Francisco Bay area. They (I include myself) are clearly dedicated to the mission of getting fifteen hundred low-income minority students into college. My colleagues on the board use their business experience to raise money, monitor budgets, find efficiencies, and expand innovations. Again, I have been struck by the intensity of the beliefs, the mix of motives, and variation among these very smart and committed reformers.

29. James Forman, Jr., "The Rise and Fall of School Vouchers: A Story of Religion, Race, and Politics," *UCLA Law Review* 54 (2007): 547–603.

30. Milbrey McLaughlin, *Evaluation and Reform: The Elementary and Secondary Education Act of 1965, Title 1* (Santa Monica, CA: RAND Corporation, 1974); Stuart Purkey and Marshall Smith, "Effective Schools: A Review," *Elementary School Journal* 83, no. 4 (1983): 426–452; Ronald Edmonds, "Effective Schools for the Urban Poor," *Educational Leadership*, October 1979, 15–24.

31. Linda Darling-Hammond, *Creating a Comprehensive System of Evaluating and Supporting Effective Teaching* (Stanford, CA: Stanford University Center for Opportunity Policy, 2012).

32. David Labaree, *The Trouble with Ed Schools* (New Haven, CT: Yale University Press, 2004); Bethany Rogers, "'Better' People, Better Teaching: The Vision of the National Teacher Corps, 1965–1968," *History of Education Quarterly* 48, no. 3 (2009): 347–372.

33. Wendy Kopp, "Teach for America: Moving Beyond the Debate," *Educational Forum* 58, no. 2 (1994): 187–192; David Labaree, "Teach for America and Teacher Education: Heads They Win, Tails We Lose," *Journal of Teacher Education* 61, no. 1–2 (2010): 48–55.

34. In Arlington, Virginia, teachers founded HB-Woodlawn for students in grades 7–12 in the late 1960s and the Arlington Traditional School that began in 1978. Both are open in 2013; see http://www.apsva.us/domain/10#profiles.

35. Frederick Hess, "Does School Choice Work?" *National Affairs*, 2010, http://www.nationalaffairs.com/publications/detail/does-school-choice-work; Jeffrey Henig, *Rethinking School Choice; Limits of the Market Metaphor* (Princeton, NJ: Princeton University Press, 1994).

36. Deborah Meier, "The Left Wing of the Possible," *Education Week*, May 10, 2012, http://blogs.edweek.org/edweek/Bridging-Differences/; Mark Naison, "Save Our Schools and Vietnam Protests," *LA Progressive*, May 16, 2012, http://www.laprogressive.com/save-our-schools/; Tina Barseghian, "Movement Against Standardized Testing Grows as Parents Opt Out," *Mind/Shift*, http://blogs.kqed.org/mindshift/2012/04/movement-against-standardized-testing-grows-as-parents-opt-out/; "National Resolution on High-Stakes Testing," *FairTest*, April 23, 2012, http://www.fairtest.org/national-resolution-highstakes-testing; Josh Healey, "The Real Education Reformers," *Tikkun* 26, no. 2 (2011): 30–32.

37. Milbrey McLaughlin and Joan Talbert, *Professional Communities and the Work of High School Teaching* (Chicago: University of Chicago Press, 2001); Judith Little and Milbrey McLaughlin, eds., *Teachers' Work* (New York: Teachers College Press, 1993); Anthony Bryk, et. al. *Organizing Schools for Improvement* (Chicago: University of Chicago Press, 2010); John Murray, "Supporting Effective Teaching Learning in American Schools," *Teachers College Record*, April 13, 2012, http://www.tcrecord.org/Content.asp?ContentID=16751; Jacob Mishook and Alethea Frazier-Raynor,

"Beyond Individal Skills: Collective Capacity Building in Nashville," Annenberg Institute for School Reform, http://annenberginstitute.org/commentary/2012/05/beyond-individual-skills-collective-capacity-building-nashville.

38. Milbrey McLaughlin and Joan Talbert, *Building School-Based Teacher Learning Communities* (New York: Teachers College Press, 2006).

39. Vicki Vescio, Dorene Ross, and Alyson Adams, "A Review of Research on the Impact of Professional Learning Communities on Teaching Practices and Student Learning," *Teaching and Teacher Education* 24, no. 1 (2008): 80–91; Diane Wood, "Teachers' Learning Communities: Catalyst for Change or a New Infrastructure for the Status Quo?" *Teachers College Record* 109, no. 3 (2007): 699–739.

40. I have already cited the work of Bryk, McLaughlin and Talbert, and Little. Fred Newmann and his colleagues have written extensively about restructuring schools in the 1980s and 1990s. See Fred Newmann & Associates, *Authentic Achievement: Restructuring Schools for Intellectual Quality* (San Francisco: Jossey-Bass, 1996). "Hancock" Elementary is a pseudonym for a Chicago school. See Anthony Bryk, et al., *Organizing Schools for Improvement: Lessons from Chicago* (Chicago:University of Chicago Press, 2010); Richard DuFour writes about Boones Mill elementary school in: "What Is a Professional Learning Community?" *Educational Leadership* 61, no. 8 (2004): 6–11; for Lakeside Southwest high school's science department, see Douglas Larkin, Scott Seyforth, and Holly Lasky, "Implementing and Sustaining Science Curriculum Reform: A Study of Leadership Among Teachers within a High School Science Department," *Journal of Research in Science Teaching* 46, no. 7 (2009): 813–835; at Aragon high school in San Mateo, California, the social studies department for the past fifty years has had three department heads. I credit Don Hill, who headed the Aragon social studies department for over twenty years since the early-1960s, for creating the norms and climate that fostered social studies teachers to become a "learning community." See Don Hill, "The Strong Department: Building the Department as Learning Community," in *The Subject in Question: Departmental Organization and the High School*, ed. Leslie Siskin and Judith Little (New York: Teachers College Press, 1995), 123–140; Lee Swenson, a teacher in the department since the late-1960s, succeeded Hill when he left for Stanford University and a subsequent career in service learning. Swenson served as department chair for twenty years before retiring. Cristina Trujillo, who apprenticed with Swenson as a student-teacher and then taught in the department, eventually became department head. The continuity in leadership helps to account for the uncommon longevity of this departmental culture. I have listened to and spoken with the above teachers for the past twenty-five years, and team taught a university curriculum and instruction course with Swenson for a decade.

41. Quote from Swenson comes from Christine Foster, "Why Teach?" *Stanford Magazine*, September/October 2001, http://www.stanfordalumni.org/news/magazine/2001/sepoct/features/whyteach.html.

42. The Coalition of Essential Schools, founded by Theodore Sizer in the late-1980s, continues as a network in 2013. See Donna Muncey and Patrick McQuillan, *Reform and Resistance in Schools and Classrooms* (New Haven, CT: Yale University

Press, 1996). For Central Park East elementary schools, see Seymour Fliegel, "Debbie Meier and the Dawn of Central Park East," *City*, Winter 1994, http://www. city-journal.org/article01.php?aid=1414; for H-B Woodlawn, see Dusty Horwin, "Farewell to Hippie High," *Washington Post*, June 13, 2004, http://www .washingtonpost.com/wp-dyn/articles/A26457-2004Jun8.html; for the Urban Academy, see Mary Anne Raywid, "A School That Really Works," *Journal of Negro Education* 63, no. 1 (1994): 93–110. My experience at Glenville High School in Cleveland, Ohio, in the late 1950s and early 1960s included a "learning community" (also see http://larrycuban.wordpress.com/2010/10/06/professional-learning-communities-a-popular-reform-of-little-consequence/).

43. Edward Miech, Bill Nave, Frederick Mosteller, "Large Scale Professional Development for Schoolteachers: Cases from Pittsburgh, New York City, and the National School Reform Faculty," *New Directions for Evaluation*, 2001, 83–100.

44. Richard Elmore and Deanna Burney, *Continuous Improvement in Community District #2, New York City* (Pittsburgh, PA: High Performance Learning Communities Project, Learning Research and Development Center, University of Pittsburgh, 1998). In 2002, Mayor Michael Bloomberg took over district schools and he reorganized the schools, ending community districts.

45. Jane David and Joan Talbert, "Turning Around a High-Poverty School District: Learning from Sanger Unified's Success," an external evaluation for the S. H. Cowell Foundation, November 2010. Also see John Fensterwald, "Lessons from High-peformers," *Thoughts on Public Education*, http://toped.svefoundation. org/2010/10/26/lessons-from-high-performing-districts/.

46. David and Talbert, "Turning Around a High-Poverty School District," 10.

Acknowledgments

In writing this book, I have compiled many debts to friends, colleagues, and family. I greatly appreciated the comments and suggestions from readers of the book prospectus and individual chapters. Thanks go to: Mike Atkin, David Brazer, Bryan Brown, Sondra Cuban, Jane David, David Labaree, Gary Lichtenstein, Joel Merenstein, MD, Danny Merenstein, MD, Jonathan Osbourne, Craig Peck, Jack Schneider, and Selma Wassermann. Craig Peck gets a special thanks for coming out to the Bay area to help me interview teachers and survey students at Las Montanas; as does Sondra Cuban, who read the penultimate draft.

Hovering in the background of this and earlier books I have written has been educational historian David Tyack, my colleague in teaching and writing and friend for over four decades. His example as a scholar and teacher, and as a person of extraordinary humaneness and sensibility, has guided me often in my thinking about the importance of history in making sense of school reforms, the writing that I have done, and the importance of living a decent life.

Like so many other writers, I acknowledge my debt to these friends, colleagues, and family but take full responsibility for the factual accuracy and interpretations offered here.

I have found that no matter how many books I have completed, starting a new one still gives me the jitters. Writing is both satisfying and frustrating, filled with surprises and disappointments. None of my books has come easily to me. As I have gotten older, however, I have discovered that revising and crafting words, sentences, and paragraphs has become as satisfying as creating the questions that drive the book, formulating the arguments, collecting and analyzing evidence, and drawing conclusions. Although I still get a kick out of ensuring an internal consistency between questions, arguments, evidence, and conclusions, what has surprised me is how much pleasure I get from finding just the right word, fashioning vivid phrases that capture accurately an image or idea I want to convey, and rewriting paragraphs a third and fourth time. All of these and more I have experienced in writing this book. So I thank those editors and publishers who have accepted and published my work over these many years.

About the Author

LARRY CUBAN is professor emeritus of education at Stanford University. He has taught courses in the methods of teaching social studies; the history of school reform, curriculum, and instruction; and leadership.

His background in the field of education prior to becoming a professor included fourteen years of teaching high school social studies in big-city schools, directing a teacher education program that prepared returning Peace Corps volunteers to teach in inner-city schools, and serving seven years as a district superintendent.

His most recent books are *As Good As It Gets: What School Reform Brought to Austin* (2010); *Hugging the Middle: How Teachers Teach in an Era of Testing and Accountability* (2009); *Partners in Literacy* (with Sondra Cuban, 2007); *Against the Odds: Insights from One District's Small School Reform* (coauthor, 2010); and *Cutting Through The Hype: The Essential Guide to School Reform* (with Jane David, 2010).

Index